Empirical Finance

Contributions to Economics

www.springeronline.com/series/1262

Sardar M. N. Islam
Sethapong Watanapalachaikul

Empirical Finance

Modelling and Analysis
of Emerging Financial and Stock Markets

With 53 Figures
and 56 Tables

Physica-Verlag

A Springer Company

Series Editors
Werner A. Müller
Martina Bihn

Authors

Dr. Sardar M. N. Islam
Dr. Sethapong Watanapalachaikul
Centre for Strategic Economic Studies
Victoria University
PO Box 14428
Melbourne City MC VIC 8001
Australia
sardar.islam@vu.edu.au
sethapong.watanapalachaikul@vu.edu.au

ISSN 1431-1933
ISBN 3-7908-1551-9 Physica-Verlag Heidelberg New York

Cataloging-in-Publication Data applied for
Library of Congress Control Number: 2004109408

Physica-Verlag is a part of Springer Science+Business Media

springeronline.com

© Physica-Verlag Heidelberg 2005
Printed in Germany

Softcover Design: Erich Kirchner, Heidelberg

SPIN 11014270   88/3130/DK-5 4 3 2 1 0 – Printed on acid-free and non-aging paper

Foreword

This book makes *two key contributions* to empirical finance. First it provides a comprehensive analysis of the Thai stock market. Second it presents an excellent exposition of how modern econometric techniques can be utilised to understand a market.

The increasing globalisation of the world's financial markets has made our understanding of the risk-return relationship in a broader range of markets critical. This is particularly so in emerging markets where market depth and liquidity are major issues. One such emerging market is Thailand. The Thai capital market is of particular interest given that it was the market in which the Asian financial crises commenced. As such an understanding of the Thai capital market via study of the pre and post-crisis periods enables one to shed light on one of the major financial markets events of recent times.

This book provides a quantitative analysis of the Thai capital market using some very useful and recent econometric techniques. The book provides an overview of the Thai stock market in chapter 2. Descriptive statistics and time series models (moving average, exponential smoothing, ARIMA) are presented in chapter 3 followed by market efficiency tests based on autocorrelations in chapter 4. A richer set of models is then considered in chapters 5 through 8. Chapter 5 finds a cointegrating relationship between macroeconomic factors and stock returns. Chapter 6 finds evidence of a speculative bubble pre-crisis but not post-crisis. This is a particularly interesting finding. Chapter 7 finds evidence of calendar anomalies in Thai stock returns. Chapter 8 fits a range of models from the GARCH family to Thai stock market volatility and finds these models do a good job in characterising volatility.

This book should be of special interest to students, researchers, academics, practitioners, and policy makers in the areas of finance, banking, economics and development management.

Professor Robert Brooks
Professor of Financial Econometrics
Dean (Research & Innovation)
RMIT Business
RMIT University, Australia

Abstract, Preface and Acknowledgement

Empirical finance (especially financial studies using financial econometrics) is becoming a very popular academic discipline in finance. An evidence of this fact is Professors Engle and Granger's Nobel prize this year (2003) for their work in financial econometrics. Applying econometric methods to investigate empirical finance (to understand the empirical characteristics of the financial market) and its components such as the stock market is an important area of study in finance not only for academic investigation, but also for policy formulation and investment planning purposes. This book undertakes studies on some common financial econometric methods and issues, some of which have been studied by Professors Engle and Granger, in the context of emerging financial markets of developing countries. This is an essential econometric study of empirical *development finance* for an exploration of the characteristics of the financial market of the emerging stock markets of developing countries.

There are substantial differences in the operation and characteristics of financial markets in developed and developing countries in terms of efficiency, stability, and the effectiveness in promoting economic development. There are different views about the performance and characteristics of the financial markets in both these types of economies. One view stresses the possibility for efficient operation of the market leading to efficient allocation of resources while the others highlights the real life evidence of market failures, market inefficiency, the existence of speculation, bubbles, etc. This study undertakes an empirical study of the characteristics of a developing Asian (Thai) financial market as a case study by applying the methods of financial econometrics to investigate whether and how these characteristics correspond with these views. Emphasis is placed on understanding those special characteristics of the financial system of developing countries which can cause financial market failures, and the existence of market imperfections such as asymmetric information, adverse selection and moral hazard.

The present book is possibly the most comprehensive study of crucial issues affecting the stock market including valuation, predictability, volatility, anomaly and market efficiency. Perhaps, no such study has existed previously, making this book a genuine contribution to the literature.

The stock market plays a major role in a developing economy's financial system. While focusing on Thailand as a case study, this study provides both the researcher in quantitative financial economics and the stock market investor, with an understanding of the financial issues of developing economies in emerging stock markets especially the Asian stock market which have similar characteristics as those of the Thai stock market. The financial issues studied in this book include market efficiency, valuation, predictability, speculative bubbles, anomalies and volatilities, among others.

The findings of this explorative research of the above forms provide information necessary for understanding the state of financial development in a country and formulating policies for corporate finance, choosing between the stock market vs bank based financial development strategies, and financing economic development.

A standard set of all financial econometric methods and models including descriptive statistics and time series econometric methods have been adopted in this study. Many contemporary techniques, approaches and models are used and include simple multivariate regression, run test, ACF model, multi-factor model, exponential smoothing, Holt Winter's model, ARIMA, TSMM, Duration Dependence Test, Weibull Hazard, time-series regression model with dummy variable, and GARCH type models. They are developed in order to examine the financial econometric issues of the Thai stock market. Data for the period of 1975 to 2001 are used to undertake these econometric modeling exercises.

The empirical investigations provide useful information about the behaviour of the Thai financial time series data related to the fair game, white noise, random walk, martingale, stationarity, error correction, cointegration and diffusion processes.

In terms of the operation of the Thai financial system and stock market, this study provides some useful insights. All the characteristics of the Stock Exchange of Thailand analysed in terms of market index prices and returns reveal evidence of inefficiency in the market. Substantial empirical evidence supports the rejection of the hypothesis of the stock price process being white noise in both the short-term and long-term analysis. The notion of existing market inefficiency is supported by the presence of rational bubbles, anomalies and volatility. Anomalies in the stock market (in the form of Monday and the January effects) were evident during the 1992–1996 (the pre-crisis) and 1997–2001 (the post-crisis) periods. The existence of speculative bubbles in the stock market was confirmed by the test models. In addition, volatility in the stock price was high in 1992, 1993, 1997 and 1998 after the Thai financial crisis. High volatility in stock prices and returns was also found in January, February and December. Empirical estimation of stock valuation models reveals that many economic factors are the determinants of the value of Thai stock such as the interest rate, bonds yield, foreign exchange rates, price earning ratio, market capitalization, and the consumer price index.

These characteristics of the emerging stock markets are due to the level of development of the financial systems, institutions and socioeconomic structure in developing countries. Some welfare economics aspects of finance covering these issues are also stated in this study.

The findings of this study provide justification for governments in developing countries adopting financial policies designed to evolve a developed, efficient and social welfare maximising financial market which can ensure efficient allocation of financial resources.

Suggestions for further study in this area and directions for future research are also included.

This study argues for treating *empirical development finance* as a separate discipline in finance since this description can provide information, both analytical and empirical, useful for proper understanding the development process in developing countries.

Since this book is a rigorous research study in finance, it can be used as a reference book by researchers, academics, practitioners, policy markers, and post-graduate students in the area of finance, financial econometrics, financial economics, monetary economics, and development economics. It can also be used as a textbook on empirical finance or finance in the emerging markets or as a reference or as an additional text for a finance subject at the Masters or Doctoral level.

The authors wish to thank M. Kumnick, R. Gupta and M. Clarke for providing research and editorial assistance in preparing this book. This book has benefited from the generosity of N. Billington and P. Sheehan for making the necessary resources available and sharing their knowledge, experience and encouragement in bringing it to completion.

Sardar M. N. Islam and Sethapong Watanapalachaikul
Center for Strategic Economic Studies
Victoria University
Melbourne, Australia
April 2004

Contents

1 Introduction

1.1 Introduction

There has been a rapid growth in empirical studies of the characteristics of the financial system including the stock market (Islam and Oh 2003), an area of study broadly defined as *empirical finance*. Many financial concepts, theories, econometric methods and models have been developed to undertake these exploratory studies for both developed and developing countries for predictive and policy formulation purposes. However, the concepts, principles and models in finance are often derived from, and related to the special economic, institutional, and structural characteristics of developed economies. Therefore, the use of these financial theories and models in explaining the economic realities of nations should also be derived for and applied to developing countries.

Economic theorists, more than any other social scientists, have long been disposed to arrive at general propositions and then postulate them as valid for every time, place and culture. There is a tendency in contemporary economic theory to follow this path to the extreme ... when theories and concepts designed to fit the special conditions of the Western world – and thus containing the implicit assumptions about social reality by which this fitting was accomplished are used in the study of underdeveloped countries, where they do not fit, the consequences are serious. (Myrdal 1981, p. 24)

This argument for using caution in the application of financial concepts, issues and models to developing countries is echoed in studies of the financial system and markets in developing countries by Fry (1995), McKinnon (1973, 1976), Shaw (1973), Stiglitz (1993), and Mishkin (1976), among others. They have argued that the financial markets in developing countries are different from those of developed countries in terms of market characteristics and operations. They are underdeveloped, fragile, unstable, inefficient, fragmented, imperfect and even non-existent in some sectors.

Currently, there are very few comprehensive analyses of the empirical characteristics of financial systems and issues in developing countries using a wide range of financial econometric methods. This book provides a critical study of *empirical finance* with a focus on the application of quantitative financial econometric methods to the investigation of the financial system and stock market of a developing economy and its specific issues such as market efficiency, valuation, predictability, speculative bubbles, anomalies and volatilities. Using the methods of financial econometrics, it undertakes an investigation of the empirical characteristics of the Thai financial system with a focus on the Thai stock market. From the methodological point, this study adopts a *combination of different research methods* including the exploratory, descriptive, analytical and predictive methods.

1.2 Financial System and Issues

The major set of issues of the financial system, which are commonly investigated in the existing literature, include the efficiency of the market, valuation, predictability, volatility, bubbles, and speculative behaviour. Most of the studies on the above issues are based on financial systems of developed economies. A developed financial system is characterised by the efficiency, resilience and stability of its payment, financial and risk management systems and derivatives (Hunt and Terry 2002).

According to Fry (1995), there are four major differences in the financial systems of developed and developing countries. First, financial markets in most developing countries are oligopolistic. Second, although detailed financial regulations exist in all nations, financial regulations are enforced less consistently and less effectively in the developing countries, and may effectively appear quite different in practice. Third, in most developing countries, deposits are converted into tangible assets as inflation hedges, whereas in developed countries' national saving rates may be unaffected by deposit rate saving. Finally, developing countries experience more of the driving forces of financial innovations, reforms and policy recommendations of the IMF and the World Bank than developed countries do.

Since the 1980s, there has been tremendous growth in financial markets on a global scale. The stock market is accepted as an important unit in financial systems and its performance is one of the determinants of the path of a national economy. Financial time-series analysis of the stock market index has therefore become a major area of financial research over the past decades.

The first step in empirical finance research is to identify the characteristics of an ideal financial system conducive to efficient resource allocation, stability of the economy and rapid economic development, which provides socially acceptable financial outcomes. The next step is to test in empirical finance research the underlying empirical characteristics of the financial system of a particular economy by using various quantitative methods including financial econometric methods.

Empirical research of the stock market using time-series analysis began as early as the 1930s with papers by Cowles (1933) and Working (1934). Cowles investigated the predictability of future price changes by market analysts and financial services, while Working focused on the characteristic of random changes in stock prices and commodities.

Kendall (1953) found little evidence that past changes in weekly series could be used in predicting financial prices. This finding underlines the basic concept of the efficient market hypothesis (EMH), where the stock prices should always fully reflect all relevant information and hence, no arbitrage opportunities exist. Therefore, the fundamental value under the expected discounted present value of future cash flow and dividends should always underline the expected value of the stock, i.e. as:

$$v_o = \sum_{n=1}^{\infty} \frac{(CF_n + D_n)}{(1+k)^n} \qquad (1.1)$$

where v_o is the expected value of the stock, CF_n is the cash flow at time n, D_n is the dividend at time n, and k is the expected rate of returns.

According to Kendall (1953), in addition to the EMH, prices cannot be predicted from past changes in a time-series of historical prices. Therefore, successive price changes should be independent. Samuelson (1965a) modeled this property of prices as the random walk:

$$Y_t = Y_{t-1} + \varepsilon_t \qquad (1.2)$$

where Y_t is the price of the stock at time t, and ε_t is the error term.

This proposition reflects the evidence of the efficient market hypothesis. One way the random walk model can be tested is by examining the autocorrelation properties of price changes such as the Autocorrelation and Partial-Autocorrelation Functions. This approach has been developed by Box and Jenkins (1976) as the Autoregressive Integrated Moving Average (ARIMA) model.

Other approaches such as the Capital Asset Pricing Model (CAPM) and the Arbitrage Pricing Theory (APT) are conceptual cornerstones of modern capital market theory and stock valuations. Sharpe and Cooper (1972) and Black, Jensen and Scholes (1972) have provided evidence on the stability of betas and found that the relationship between strategy and return whilst not perfect, is a close one. According to Cuthbertson (1996), APT provides the baseline models of equilibrium asset returns.

There have been extensive studies such as Fama (1965), Cross (1973) and French (1980), which document long-term anomalies in the stock market that seem to contradict the efficient market hypothesis. In the late 1980s, West (1987) also found evidence of rational bubbles in stock prices and returns.

Recently, the study of the stock market has attracted growing attention by academics especially volatility modelling. The study of volatility in the stock market is important for portfolio management in developing countries where the financial system is different from those in developed countries since high volatility could mean greater uncertainty.

1.3 Characteristics of the Emerging Stock Markets in Developing Countries

The characteristics of the emerging stock markets may be classified under three major headings: (1) characteristics specific to the stock market (Binswager 1999); (2) general market related characteristics (Stiglitz 1993); and (3) an underdeveloped financial system (Fry 1995). A considerable number of recent studies have discussed efficiency issues of stock markets in emerging economies. Takagi (2002), Stiglitz (1993) and Allen and Gale (1990) have discussions on market imperfections and failures in developing economies where asymmetric information, moral hazard and adverse selection are likely to be found, especially in the stock market.

According to Binswanger (1999), financial liberalisation and reform caused a relaxation of the aggregate financial constraint in emerging economies, particularly in most developing countries. This relaxation allowed more money to flow into financial markets where it contributed to the emergence of speculative bubbles. But speculative bubbles themselves may be understood as a response to operative real and demand constraints. Consequently, the co-evolution between the real and financial sectors in the economy becomes more complex as speculative bubbles also influence the level of real economic activity. Some of the crucial characteristics of stock markets in developing countries with a high degree of speculation are (see Binswager 1999):

- trading of highly standardized, homogenous, storable products with low transaction costs;
- strong influences of international linkages in the stock market;
- possibility for demand-supply imbalances due to either demand inadequacy of supply shortage;
- frequent trading activities (sequential trading); and
- uncertainty in the direction and size of future price movements, which gives rise to divergent expectations of future price movements among market participants.

Despite strong evidence that the stock market is highly efficient, there have been scores of studies that have documented long-term historical anomalies in the stock market that seem to contradict the efficient market hypothesis. Among these are the studies of Fama (1965), Cross (1973), French (1980), Abraham and Ikenberry (1994), and Al-Loughani and Chappel (2001). Anomalies have been confirmed to exist in international markets and are particularly persuasive. These anomalies, which are not consistent with the existing EMH, concern the relationship between stock returns and variables, such as firm size and earnings-to-price ratios, and seasonal effects, such as the January and turn-of-the-month effects.

There are a number of empirical studies on the Thai stock market. In Sukhamongkhon's dissertation (1994), a model is developed to test the long-run relationship between microeconomic factors on the Stock Exchange of Thailand (SET) by using the Arbitrage Pricing Theory (APT) model. Nuntajindawat (1995) provides the theoretical study and background of market efficiency for the SET, and Kiranand (1999) uses empirical studies to investigate Asian stock markets integration. Some more recent publications on the Thai stock market include the studies of Wongbangpo and Sharma (2002), which investigate the role of select macroeconomic variables among five Asian countries, and Nasseh and Strauss

(2000), which use a cointegration approach to identify the relationship between stock prices and domestic and international macroeconomic activity.

1.4 Financial Econometrics: Methods and Models

To study the characteristics of the financial system and stock market issues, a wide range of financial econometric methods are used (Islam and Oh 2003; Moosa 2003a; Mills 1999; Campbell, Lo and Mackinlay 1997; Cuthbertson 1996). These methods include descriptive statistics such as mean, median, standard deviation, skewness and kurtosis. Other econometric methods include the ordinary least squares method and its extensions, the maximum likelihood method, the unit root test, error correction and cointegration methods, and the linear and non-linear volatility modelling process. Univariate time series econometrics models such as the moving average, exponential smoothing, Holt Winters and autoregressive integrated moving average model, are also used in the study. Applications of these methods provide useful information about the empirical characteristics of the financial system and stock market and the above topics and methods form the subject matter for the discipline of empirical finance. Financial econometric studies of developing countries can be gathered into a separate discipline of empirical development finance such as this book.

1.5 The Thai Financial System and the Emerging Stock Market

The financial sector plays a very crucial role in the Thai economy. Over the past decades, many such as Masuyama et al. (1999) and Lewis (1998) have viewed Thailand's economy as an "economic miracle". Thailand achieved and sustained high rates of economic growth, recording one of the highest average growth rates in the region. During the liberalization and globalization of the financial system, which took place between 1991 and 1993, foreign investors saw Thailand as a lucrative investment destination. The Thai economy responded by removing barriers to the inflow of foreign capital and investment. After the Asian financial and economic crisis in 1996, the Thai economy shifted dramatically from a high growth to a sharp decline in economic activity.

Undoubtedly, the stock market plays a major role in the Thai financial system. Massive investment in Thailand's stock market during 1992–1994 shifted the stock market index up from around 800 points to 1600 points. It is believed that stock market performance underlies the growth of the Thai economy, because its economic characteristics have a profound influence on the allocation of capital resources (Masuyama et al. 1999; Lewis 1998). However, it was the Asian economic crisis that spelt the end of the Thai economic miracle and the announcement of the devaluation of the Thai bath, which followed greatly impacted upon the Thai stock market. By the end of 1997, the stock market index fell to just 370 points.

It is important to have an understanding of the stock market and other financial markets in Thailand to formulate effective economic and financial policies that foster Thailand's economic development. It is also essential to study Thailand's pre- and post-crisis stock market by utilizing quantitative financial econometric approaches that provide an in-depth understanding of the impact of the crisis on various aspects of the Thai stock market such as efficiency, valuation, predictability, speculative bubbles, anomalies and volatility and their possible effect on the economy's slowdown.

1.6 Limitations of Existing Literature and the Motivation

There are several limitations in the existing literature on the empirical studies by using financial econometrics of the emerging stock markets in general, the Thai stock market and the Thai financial system in particular. They can be summarised as follows.

a)   There is no previous econometric study of the stock market that covers a comprehensive set of financial issues of the stock market such as the ones studied in this book in a single volume (although Islam and Oh 2003 covers less comprehensive issues of the analysis of the e-commerce sector). Most of the literature investigates different issues in finance separately (such as valuation, volatility, etc). There is a need for a comprehensive econometric investigation into most of the key issues such as EMH, valuation, forecasting, rational bubbles, anomalies, and volatility.

b)   There is no comprehensive study of the crucial financial issues of the emerging stock market including the Thai stock market. Therefore, there is a need for studies which can provide new analysis, information and insights for emerging stock markets and the Thai stock market in particular.

c)   The methodologies and conclusions of many studies on financial issues such valuation, volatility, bubbles, etc. are controversial and do not promote understanding of these issues. There is a need for making some definite choices about these methodologies and statements about their conclusions regarding these issues.

d)   In the existing literature, the valuation models are based on the concept of market equilibrium and the existence of a perfect market. In an economy like that of Thailand, these conditions do not exist and there is a need for developing an appropriate alternative approach for valuation suitable for analyzing the stock prices and returns in emerging stock markets such as the Thai stock market.

e)   Existing studies use only a small number of variables to estimate the long-run relationship of stock prices or returns which results in ineffective and inaccurate stock valuation and forecasting.

f)   The models in some of the literature are outdated and have been criticized in recent studies for excessive use of regression based analysis in
investigating different financial issues. They have also been criticized for
using discounted cash flow and CAPM methods in stock valuation. There
is a need for adopting available alternatives, possibly more powerful contemporary econometrics and financial models in all relevant issues.

1.7 The Objectives of the Study

1.7.1 Objectives

The major objective of this book is to undertake an econometric study of the complete and comprehensive set of issues of a typical developing economy, especially
the Thai stock market, to acquire a clear understanding of its empirical and behav-
ioural characteristics as a part of the Thai financial system. As with most research
on the stock market, the behaviour of the Thai stock markets at a macro level is
expressed by returns on an index calculated for the period from May 1975 to December 2001. This book will develop a number of quantitative financial economic
and econometric models in order to test market efficiency, stock valuation and return predictability, anomalies and volatility.

To overcome the above limitations of the existing literature, the objectives of
this study are as follows.

1.   To develop a comprehensive set of applications of appropriate financial
econometrics methodology and models to study various issues of the
emerging stock markets and the Thai stock market.
2.   To develop new models and/or use the latest available models and approaches to test various issues and hypotheses about the Thai financial
system and markets to investigate their characteristics.
3.   To state briefly the policy and investment strategy implications of the
findings of this study for the emerging and Thai stock market.

Both time-series univariate modeling and multivariate methods are developed
to accomplish these objectives.

1.7.2 Welfare Economics of Finance: Policies and Institutions

This book will investigate whether resources and information have been allocated
and utilized efficiently (i.e. social welfare maximizing allocation) in emerging
stock markets such as the Thai stock market and to highlight the institutional and
policy implications of these investigations based on the new[3] welfare economies
paradigm (Islam 2001). Therefore, this book is in the discipline of applied welfare

economics of finance. In Chapter 9, some welfare implications of the present study will be stated.

1.8 Contributions of this Research

The contributions of this research are the following.

1. This is possibly the first study of a comprehensive set of financial and financial econometric issues of a stock market.
2. This is the first study to consider the relevancy and appropriateness of using financial econometric fundamentals, concepts, and models in the empirical analysis of a developing economy and emerging stock markets, especially in the Thai financial system.
3. Empirical studies and analyses of the characteristics of the Thai stock market such as market efficiency, rational speculative bubbles, anomalies and volatility, are addressed for the first time in this book.
4. This is probably the first comprehensive research to develop a valuation model, especially for a developing economy, which addresses capital investment decisions and analyses the relationships between the stock price and macro, micro and international economic factors. This model overcomes the limitations of traditional valuation methods.

1.9 Econometric Methodologies and Sources of Data

1.9.1 Econometric Methodologies

In order to analyse empirical characteristics of the stock market, the application of financial econometric methods is essential. From a wide range of financial econometric methods (for surveys of these methods and models, see Islam and Oh 2003; Mills 1999; Cuthbertson 1996), some have been carefully chosen ensuring that they are appropriate to the study of various issues of the Thai stock market. Methods and models include the standard descriptive statistical methods and usual time series econometric techniques such as autocorrelation analysis, integration, moving average, autoregression, ARIMA, cointegration, error correction, and ARCH-type models. These methodology and models have not previously been applied to the emerging stock market, the Thai financial system, or the stock market. The various methodologies adopted in this book to investigate various financial issues are summarised as follow:

1. Descriptive statistics such as mean, median, standard deviation, skewness and kurtosis, and a range of univariate time series methods and models

      including ARIMA, ACF and other smoothing techniques are used to pro-
vide a general understanding of the empirical characteristics of the Thai
stock market.

2. In forecasting techniques, a number of models are developed in order to
   project the next 50-month period stock indexes and returns forecast.
   These models are single exponential smoothing, double exponential
   smoothing, Holt Winter's model, ARIMA, and TSMM whether the stock
   indexes and returns in Thailand possess the properties of martingale,
   white noise, fair game, random walk and stationarity.

3. A nonparametric run test and autocorrelation function model are developed to test the market efficient hypothesis.

4. A new stock valuation model, called the Thai Stock Multi-Factor Model
   (TSMM), is developed to overcome the existing limitations. Prior to the
   use of TSMM, a unit root test is employed to ensure the accuracy of the
   model by using augmented Dickey Fuller, augmented Engle Granger (for
   error correction model) and cointegration methods. Regression methods
   are used also to estimate and test the valuation model.

5. In detecting rational bubbles anomalies, two recent models of duration
   dependent testing, the Duration Dependent Test or Log Logistics
   (McQueen and Thorley 1994) and Weibull Hazard (Mudholkar et al.
   1996) are used.

6. General time-series regression models are used to identify seasonal
   anomalies. The day of the week effect and the January effect have been
   tested.

7. A new approach to identify volatility has been developed by using the
   Autoregressive Heteroscedasticity (ARCH) process. Two linear GARCH
   and three non-linear GARCH models have been used in order to identify
   the volatility of the stock market at a particular time period.

1.9.2 Sources of Data and Computer Programs

Monthly data for closing SET Index levels from the establishment of SET in 1975
until 2001 is used in this study. Daily data has been gathered during 1992 to 2001.
The choice of time period corresponds to the pre- and post-crisis period (duration
of 5 years for each period). These stock price indexes are obtained from Stock Exchange of Thailand CD-ROMs and SET Data Service Department; and the economic factors are gathered from the Bank of Thailand, United Nations (Research
Department), and International Monetary Fund (International Financial Statistics
CD-ROM). A number of statistical software packages such as Microsoft Excel,
MiniTab and Stata have been used in this book.

1.10 Structure of the Book

1.10.1 Chapter Structure

Chapter 2 describes Thailand's financial system and stock market. It provides an introduction, and the motivation for the study. It overviews the financial system in Thailand which consists of five markets: a) the financial market, b) the money and capital market, c) the financial future market, d) the gold and commodities market, and e) the stock market. Later in the chapter, the Thai economic situation is also reviewed to give a broad understanding of the position Thailand took prior to and after the crisis.

Chapter 3 provides summary empirical analyses of the Stock Exchange of Thailand by adopting some descriptive statistics. It starts with the basic concept of returns and descriptive statistics of the SET Index prices from the establishment of the market until December 2001. Later in the chapter, linear and non-linear forecasting techniques are applied to investigate the movements of stock price. These techniques are moving average, single exponential smoothing, double exponential smoothing, Holt Winter's model, and ARIMA.

Chapter 4 reviews the concept of the efficient market hypothesis where stock prices should always fully reflect the information available and price changes should be independent. The non-parametric run test and autocorrelation function model are used to identify the autocorrelation of the stock price.

Chapter 5 introduces a new valuation model called Thai Stock Multi-Factor Model (TSMM). This model overcomes the limitations of existing models such as the DCF, CAPM and APT. This model allows other macroeconomic factors in each market, previously discussed in Chapter 2, to have some influence on the stock price and hence reflects the long-run relationships between the stock price and these factors.

Chapter 6 uses the latest models to detect the rational speculative bubbles of the Thai stock market. McQueen and Thoreley's (1994) Duration Dependence Test and Mudholkar et al.'s (1996) Weibull Hazard Test are applied to identify the presence of bubbles. The chapter describes why these models are considered superior to the traditional unit-root test.

Chapter 7 uses time-series methods with dummy variables to find the existence of seasonal daily and monthly anomalies such as the day of the week effect and the January effect. An analysis of the causes of anomalies is also provided.

Chapter 8 employs the Autoregressive Conditionally Heteroscedasticity (ARCH) and Generalized ARCH (GARCH) models to capture the volatility of the Thai stock market. A new approach is developed to identify the volatility of the stock price on various seasonal factors, which uses five GARCH models with 27 seasonal variables. This approach has not been previously undertaken. The five GARCH type models such as GARCH(1,1), EGARCH(1,1), GARCH-M(1,1), GJR-GARCH(1,1) and PGARCH(1,1) have been used in comparison and confirm the level of volatility for the stock market index.

Chapter 9 concludes with the major findings and suggests areas for further study. Policy implications of the results and findings along with the limitations of the study are also given in this chapter.

1.10.2 General Structure

The general structure of the chapters, focused on various financial issues, follows the format shown below:

a)   a discussion of the relevant issues;
b)   a discussion of the alternative methods and models available for studying these issues, the models and methods chosen in this study and the justifications for this choice;
c)   a description of the applications of the relevant models and methods to the Thai stock market;
d)   a discussion of the implications of the econometric studies for financial issues and a comparison of the findings of the present study with other studies; and
e)   a presentation of the conclusion (about the issue, methodologies and finance theory).

2 The Thai Financial System: Characteristics of the Emerging Thai Stock Market

2.1 Introduction

This chapter focuses on the Thai financial system. However, details regarding the development patterns and characteristics of the financial system in East Asian economies are discussed in Masuyama, Vandenbrink and Yue (1999) and Rodan, Hewison and Robison (2001).

The financial system in Thailand started to improve from about 1987 onwards when exports grew rapidly at the rate of 20 per cent per annum and real GDP grew at double-digit rates for many consecutive years. Following financial liberalisation in 1990, Thailand's economy was one of the fastest growing in the world and was considered an economic miracle. The economy recorded an average growth rate in excess of seven per cent with a moderate inflation rate and stable exchange rate due to a high savings rate and a tradition of conservative monetary and fiscal policy. The financial system has been in the public focus since the announcement of a currency devaluation and since changing its exchange system from a fixed to a managed floatation system in 1997. This chapter overviews the development of the Thai financial system and its emerging and enduring issues.

2.2 Financial and Capital Markets

Thailand's organized financial markets are made up of eight major types of financial institutions: (a) commercial banks; (b) finance, securities, and credit companies; (c) specialized banks; (d) development finance corporations; (e) the stock exchange; (f) insurance companies; (g) saving cooperatives; and (h) a variety of mortgage institutions. Commercial banks dominated most of the financial assets in terms of total assets, credit extended and savings mobilized, followed by finance companies. In 1990, commercial banks accounted for 71 per cent of the financial assets in the country (Warr 1996). After a comprehensive financial reform plan was introduced in 1990, there was significant growth in the financial market, particularly in the banking system. The reform focused on the development of financial deregulation and liberalisation, the improvement of supervision and examination of financial institutions, and development of financial instruments, services and the payments system. Again, a second financial development plan was introduced in 1993, which focused on the establishment of the Bangkok International Banking Facilities (BIBF) along with the development of savings mobilization, extension of financial services to rural areas and the development of Bangkok as a financial center (Masuyama et al. 1999; Lewis 1998). The structure of the financial institutions in Thailand is shown in Appendix 1.

According to the Bank of Thailand (2000a), the Thai government established a number of specialized financial institutions for developmental purposes. These included the Government Saving Bank, the Government Housing Bank, the Bank for Agriculture and Agricultural Cooperatives, the Industrial Finance Corporation of Thailand, the Small Industry Credit Guarantee Corporation, the Small Industry Finance Corporation, and the Export-Import Bank of Thailand (EXIM Bank).

Table 2.1 lists financial institutions in Thailand ranked by asset (1997) where commercial banks dominate as the top asset holders followed by finance and securities companies.

Table 2.1. Financial institutions in Thailand ranked by asset, 1997

Financial Institution	Assets*
Commercial Banks	7,279,365
Finance and Securities Companies	1,616,948
Government Housing	310,195
Government Savings Bank	280,933
Saving Cooperatives	276,230
Bank for Agriculture and Agricultural	236,432
Industrial Finance Corp. of Thailand	217,499
Life Insurance Companies	173,243
Mutual Fund	102,462
Credit Foncier Companies	74,161
Export – Import Bank of Thailand	61,377
Agricultural Cooperatives	38,790
Securities Companies	32,423
Pawnshops	16,900
Small Industry Finance Corporation	1,765
Small Industry Credit Guarantee Corporation	580

*Unit: Million baht.
Source: Bank of Thailand 2000b.

2.2.1 The Central Bank and Commercial Bank

The Central Bank

The Central Bank or the Bank of Thailand was established in 1939 and was originally called the Thai National Banking Bureau under the supervision of the Ministry of Finance. However, in 1942 the Bureau changed its name to the Central Bank as per the Bank of Thailand Act.

There are two main reasons for having a Central Bank. The first is that the Central Bank could be seen as the last resort to prevent systemic financial crises. The second is that there is a need for the government to have its reserve policies, which often are in the form of a standard unit of account such as the gold reserve (Mctaggart et al. 1996). The role of the Thai Central Bank is to: (a) formulate monetary policy to maintain monetary stability; (b) supervise financial institutions to ensure that they are secure and supportive of economic development; (c) act as banker and recommend economic policy to the government; (d) act as banker to financial institutions; (e) manage the international reserves; and (f) print and issue bank notes (Bank of Thailand 2002b).

The Central Bank attempts to influence the economy by using monetary policy to control money supply and interest rates. A change in monetary policy settings can also have an effect on the exchange rate; a tightening of monetary policy leads to an appreciation of the exchange rate.

The Commercial Banks

During 1990s commercial banks dominated the majority of all financial activities and absorbed roughly three-quarters of all deposits placed with financial institutions. From 1972 to 1986, the commercial banks total assets increased by around 19.5 per cent annually. After financial liberalisation in 1988 and until 1994, the average annual growth rate was as high as 22.85 per cent with the total assets of the banking system increasing more than twelvefold.

The ownership of commercial banks in Thailand was characterised by a high degree of concentration and dominated by sixteen families. However, the concentration of ownership was reduced after the crisis in 1997 when the fifteen banks reduced to twelve, five of which were bought by foreign institutions (Asia Week 2000; Masuyama et al. 1999; Lewis 1998; Warr 1996). Table 2.2 shows the performance of the top ten Thai commercial banks compared to the rest of the world in term of total assets.

Table 2.2. Top 10 commercial banks in Thailand compared to the rest of the world, 1999

	Institution	HQ	Assets [US Mil]	Profits [US Mil]	Rank in world top 500
1	Bangkok Bank	Bangkok	31,495	-1,594.6	74
2	Krung Thai Bank	Bangkok	26,458	-2,451.3	85
3	Thai Farmer Bank	Bangkok	19,539	-1,253.2	112
4	Siam Commercial Bank	Bangkok	18,445	-947.5	118
5	Bank of Ayudhya	Bangkok	11,901	-585.6	160
6	Thai Military Bank	Bangkok	8,929	-309.8	183
7	Siam Cty Bank	Bangkok	7,187	-204.3	206
8	Bank Thai	Bangkok	6,291	-512.3	229
9	Bangkok Metropolitan Bank	Bangkok	4,298	-159.6	279
10	Bank of Asia	Bangkok	4,183	-299.0	284

Source: Asia Week 2000.

2.2.2 Money and Capital Markets

On the basis of the original maturity length of the financial instruments traded, financial markets can be divided into two general types: money markets and capital markets. The money market is the market for short-term funds (usually one year or less) and includes instruments such as treasury bills, banker's acceptances, and commercial paper, while the capital market is the market for securities of long-term funds (usually more than one year to maturity) and instruments such as bonds, notes, and stocks. The money market rate is usually calculated as (Nikolova 2002):

$$mr_t = \left(\frac{d_t}{1-(d_t/365)} \right)\left(\frac{365}{M} \right) \qquad (2.1)$$

where, mr is the money market rate, d is the discount and M is the days to maturity. The Thai money market rate for the period 1992–2001 is shown in Figure 2.1.

Although Thailand's financial system growth rate is high compared to other countries and is considered one of the South East Asia financial centers, some of its financial markets are not yet well developed. Some commentators have highlighted that the lack of government securities and regulations undermines the efficiency of the financial market (Masuyama et al. 1999). Apart from an inter-bank market, which may be considered a mature market, many financial areas are still developing. The level of money market rates could impact investment in the stock market where investors will have more choices among stock market returns and money market instruments.

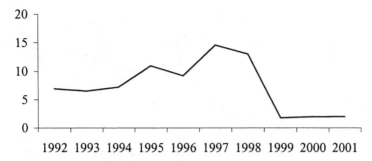

Source: International Monetary Fund, International Financial Statistics 2002.

Fig. 2.1. Money market rate, 1992–2001

2.2.3 Foreign Exchange Market

Ho (1991) states that the existence of a well-developed foreign exchange market is a major element in the development of a country's sound financial system. An efficient foreign exchange market would attract foreign banks to engage in exchange transactions and at the same time strengthen the link between domestic and foreign financial markets.

The foreign exchange market in Thailand grew significantly after the liberalisation of foreign exchange controls and the setting up of the Bangkok International Banking Facilities (BIBFs) in the early 1990s. Most of the transactions are now under the structure of Thai baht per US dollar that takes place in the inter bank market and exchange rate can be calculated from the spot transactions and forward exchange contract. At present, the process of a spot transaction usually takes place instantly by either a direct telephone contact or indirectly through the Reuters dealing system, where the confirmations are printed out instantly and automatically (EMEAP 2002). A forward exchange contract is a transaction in which a specified quantity of a stated foreign currency is bought or sold at the rate of exchange fixed at the time of making the contract, and to be delivered at a future time agreed upon while making the contract (Ho 1991). Figure 2.2 shows the average exchange rate during 1992–2001. The Thai government announced the devaluation of the Thai baht in July 1997.

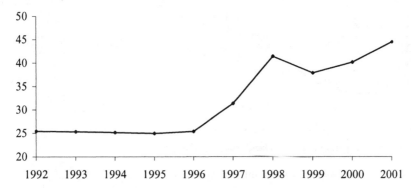

Source: International Monetary Fund, International Financial Statistics 2002.

Fig. 2.2. Average exchange rate, Thai baht per US dollar, 1992–2001

According to CSES (1998), devaluation of the Thai currency had an immediate contractionary impact on the domestic demand in Thailand as it exacerbated the external debt burden of banks and other financial institutions, and aggravated the debt burden of many companies, which led to a reduction in their investment spending.

2.2.4 Stock Market: General Characteristics

The Thai stock market is becoming an increasingly important component of the Thai financial system and capital market. A stock market is an elaborate structure designed to bring together buyers and sellers of securities. The performance of the stock market can determine the functioning of the national economy, since it provides information that facilitates effective decisions in production activities and has a profound influence on the allocation of capital resources.

The Stock Exchange of Thailand (SET) was established on 30th April 1975. There were fourteen listed companies on the market at the time. Subsequently, the number of securities listed on the market increased to 384 companies by 31st May 2002. The role of the SET is to provide facilities for trading of listed securities and undertaking activities relating to the stock market such as a clearing house, securities depository center and securities registrar (Stock Exchange of Thailand 2002b).

Although stock trading activities began in the stock exchange of Thailand in May 1975, the transactions on the stock market greatly increased from the 1980s onward. There was a minor boom in the stock market during 1977 to 1979 as industrial development turned to the stock market for temporary investment. A capital gains tax of ten per cent was introduced on profits from stock trading in May 1978 which removed some of the arbitrage opportunities in the Thai stock market and hence reduced fluctuation in stock prices. In April 1981, the corporate tax rate was lowered by five per cent for companies listed on the stock exchange.

The major boom in the stock market occurred during 1987 to 1994 following financial liberalisation and the reforms introduced by the government in February 1987. The boom continued and reached the highest SET Index of 1,753.73 points in 1994. The Asian economic crisis and the subsequent devaluation of the Thai currency in 1997 caused a significant loss in the SET Index of over seventy per cent to 342.56 points in December 2001. The movement of stock prices during the period 1975 to 2001 is shown in Table 2.3 and Figure 2.3.

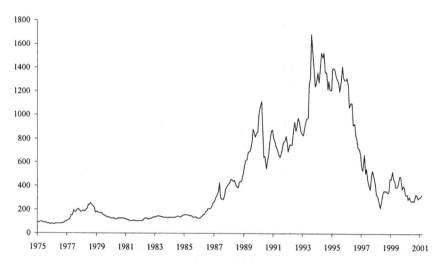

Source: Stock Exchange of Thailand 2002a.

Fig. 2.3. Movement of the SET Index, 1975–2001

As at 30th June 2001 the SET Index comprised some 379 stocks from all sectors of the market. The SET Index reflects the aggregate market value of all the covered stocks. Figure 2.3 shows a monthly chart for the SET going back to the opening of the market in 1975 to the end of 2001. Table 2.3 is calculated from the regional indices available at the time.

Table 2.3 shows the movements of the SET Index from 1975 to 2001. There was a major boom in the stock market during the period 1987–1995. In this period, the SET Index rose 4.49 times reaching 1682.85 points by the end of 1993. Stock prices then fell dramatically by 70 per cent by the end of 1997 as a consequence of the Asian economic crisis and devaluation of the baht.

During the pre-crisis period of 1987 to 1996, a number of favourable factors were responsible for the major boom in the stock market. These factors were financial liberalisation and reforms, the remarkable consistent performance of the Thai economy, the significant growth rate and profits in most listed companies, the inflows of foreign capital, and the high performance of the banking sector.

On the other hand, one of the major factors contributing to the sharp decline in stock prices after 1997 was the Asian economic crisis. Many have argued that the causes of the crisis could be summarized as the loss of competitive ability especially the slowdown in exports, over investment in the property sector, and lack of effective regulation and policies for the Thai financial system (Dixon 1999; Mishkin 1999).

Table 2.3. SET Index of stock prices, 1975–2001

End of Year	High	Low	Close	Chg	%Chg	Volume [mil shares]	Value [mil bath]
1975	100	84	84	84.0		2	547
1976	83	76	82	-1	-1	5	971
1977	205	82	181	98	119	96	26,226
1978	266	180	257	76	41	173	54,412
1979	259	146	149	-108	-42	92	21,139
1980	148	113	124	-24	-16	57	6,386
1981	129	103	106	-18	-14	28	2,206
1982	138	102	123	16	15	58	5,537
1983	148	122	134	10	8	63	7,393
1984	144	128	142	7	5	74	8,802
1985	158	132	134	-7	-5	72	11,091
1986	207	127	207	72	53	142	23,376
1987	472	203	284	77	37	883	115,637
1988	471	287	386	101	35	1,562	152,653
1989	879	391	879	492	127	3,253	377,037
1990	1,143	544	612	-266	-30	8,244	626,307
1991	908	582	711	98	16	10,425	793,068
1992	963	667	893	182	25	27,848	1,860,070
1993	1,682	818	1,682	789	88	32,544	2,201,148
1994	1,753	1,196	1,360	-322	-19	23,051	2,113,860
1995	1,472	1,135	1,280	-79	-5	20,874	1,534,899
1996	1,415	816	831	-449	-35	19,359	1,303,143
1997	858	357	372	-458	-55	29,902	929,597
1998	558	313	318	-54	-14	18,643	335,061
1999	545	313	481	126	35	96,322	1,609,787
2000	498	250	269	-212	-44	60,502	923,696
2001	342	265	303	34	12	180,317	1,577,757

Source: Stock Exchange of Thailand 2000a.

2.3 Recent Issues

2.3.1 Financial Liberalisation

Financial liberalisation in Thailand was first introduced in 1990 along with national economic policies aimed at liberalisation and deregulation. Throughout the liberalisation period – the first phase in 1990–1992 and the second phase in 1993 with the establishment of new banking facilities to serve as international financial intermediates – the Thai government implemented credit allocation, interest rate liberalisation, loan portfolio, business lines, market entry including entry by foreign institutions, and development and reform of the securities markets (Masuyama et al. 1999). The key actions taken by the Thai government in liberalizing its financial system were interest rate liberalisation, exchange control deregulation and the establishment of the Bangkok International Banking Facilities (BIBF). Williamson and Mahar (1998) believe that liberalisation has been an important contributing factor to the boom and crash cycles in emerging economies.

2.3.2 Economic Crisis

Economic and financial crisis, market instability and high volatility in the stock market have become worldwide phenomena in recent years. In early 1997, macroeconomic conditions had seriously deteriorated in most Asian countries. The crisis affected trade, investment and financial linkages, increasing risk premiums between many developing countries, especially Asian countries, and the rest of the world. Thailand was the first to experience the effects of the crisis (CSES 1998; Mishkin 1997).

The Thai government was forced to implement a devaluation policy, moving from a fixed to a managed float currency system in July 1997. Many finance companies, 56 out of 91, closed down in December 1997. The crisis caused a sudden and unprecedented collapse in asset prices, corporate and financial fragility, and a drastic economic slowdown in East Asian markets. In just over 12 months, the region's stock markets shrunk by as much as 85% in US dollars. At the same time, East Asian currencies depreciated sharply beyond the levels needed to maintain export competitiveness, while the credit rating of government bonds fell from AA+ to CC- and unemployment jumped 370 per cent in 1998 compared to 1997 (IMF 2002; International Financial Risk Institute 2001; Bank of Thailand 2000c; Leightner 1999).

2.3.3 Focus on Foreign Capital Flows

Foreign capital has played an important role in developing economies. It has filled the gap when domestic savings were insufficient to finance the country's investment activities. Foreign capital flows have the components of direct foreign investment, portfolio investments, foreign loans and short-term foreign loans. Notwithstanding the availability of domestic savings, Thailand's economy also depended relatively heavily on foreign investment in order to secure its high rates of growth. The composition of foreign capital has changed over time as dependence on official sources gradually declined and foreign direct investment became the main source of foreign capital. Table 2.4 shows the net foreign capital inflows to Thailand.

Many developing countries implemented financial liberalisation and globalization to attract international capital flows. However, in most cases capital flows were of the form of financial and portfolio investments rather than real investment and consumption (Siamwalla et al. 1999; Akrasanee et al. 1993).

Table 2.4. Net capital inflows to Thailand's economy (US$ millions), 1980–1997

	1980	1985	1990	1995	1996	1997
Official transfer	141	119	187	42	30	14
Direct investment	187	159	2404	1169	1455	2354
Portfolio investment	96	141	457	3485	4351	4451
Other long-term capital	1824	1326	793	3718	5935	2625
Other short-term capital	-64	227	4489	2310	2460	-9306
Deposit money banks	N/A	-533	1603	11239	5003	-5340
Net errors and omissions	-180	113	1182	-1479	-2985	235

Source: Masuyama et al. 1999, p. 9.

2.3.4 Unstable Exchange Rate in an Open Economy

Exchange rates are important for macroeconomic policy in an open economy for a number of reasons. The exchange rate is used as an instrument of monetary and fiscal policies, affecting real income and domestic price levels. It can be viewed as a deterrent to the external shocks that could affect the domestic economy. Finally, the short-run dynamics of an exchange rate adjustment is used in formulating and implementing aggregate demand policies (Grabbe 1996; Gay and Kolb 1984).

After the devaluation of the Thai baht against international currencies in 1997, the Thai exchange rate had fluctuated severely immediately after the announcement of the devaluation policy and consequently created uncertainty and discouraged international trade and investments. Figure 2.4 shows the price volatility in the exchange rate between 1997 and 2001.

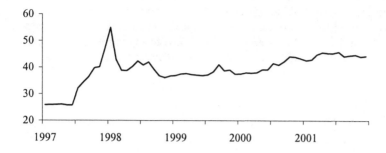

Source: International Monetary Fund, International Financial Statistics 2002.

Fig. 2.4. Exchange rate during 1997–2001, Thai baht per US dollar

2.3.5 Market Imperfection

The sudden crisis in Thailand revealed the shortcomings of traditional open economy models, which assume efficient global financial markets. Financial market imperfection could be seen as asymmetric information, adverse selection, moral hazard and incomplete markets. Information asymmetry can severely restrict financial market transactions. Adverse selection would create inequality or inefficiency in the exchanges on the market caused by information asymmetry between the two parties. Moral hazard is the risk resulting from misleading information about a company's assets, liabilities, or credit capacity, or by an incentive to take unusual risks in a desperate attempt to earn a profit before the contract settles. These imperfections harm long-term development and account for many characteristics of the recent crisis (Dixon 1999).

2.4 Conclusions

This chapter describes and provides an overview of the financial characteristics of Thailand and its financial system. Finance, money and capital, foreign exchange, and stock markets are all major components of the Thai financial system.

This study focuses on the time period between 1992 and 2001, which includes the pre-crisis period of 1992–1996 and the post-crisis period of 1997–2001. The ordinance of the financial system in 1996–1997 is a clear example of the result of the Asian economic crisis. Although many government policies such as devaluation and financial intervention took place immediately after the crisis, the Thai economy is still recovering. This situation affects the behaviour of investors and, ultimately, market prices. The Thai stock market performance is still very poor,

measured by the closing index at the end of 2001 at around 300 index points compared to the end of 1999 and 2000 at around 540 and 500 points respectively.

The following chapter applies some descriptive statistics and univariate time
series models on the SET Index and market returns to highlight further more the
financial market characteristics of the Thai financial system and stock market.

3 Descriptive Statistics and General Characteristics of the Stock Market

3.1 Introduction

A stock market index is a tool for measuring the performance of an entire stock market or group of related stocks. It plays an important role in finance, as it is often associated with particular stock exchanges or industries, which is used in many finance and econometric applications and models (Gourieroux and Jasiak 2001) for analyzing the empirical characteristics of the financial system and the stock market.

It is stated in Section 1.3 that there is a large number of financial econometric methods, which can be applied to investigate issues in the theory of financial and stock markets. While more specialized advanced techniques will be used in the later chapters, relatively simple methods of the following forms are adopted in this chapter: 1) descriptive statistics such as mean, median, standard deviation, skewness and kurtosis (Section 3.2); and 2) univariate time series econometric models such as the moving average, exponential smoothing, Holt Winters and Autoregressive Integrated Moving Average (ARIMA) models (Sections 3.2 to 3.4). These methods are applied to investigate the empirical characteristics of the Thai stock market. Formal tests will also be undertaken to identify which is the best model to describe the time series behaviour of the Thai stock market. The implications of these econometric exercises will also be discussed (Section 3.5).

Some crucial properties of financial time series data such as fair game, martingale, white noise, random walk and stationarity will be analysed in other chapters of this book (especially Chapters 4 and 5).

3.2 Descriptive Statistics

Stock market returns are calculated from the monthly index performance of the Stock Exchange of Thailand. The SET Index is intended to provide investors with a general idea about the stock price movements in the Thai stock market and is computed by comparing the current total market value of the issued shares of the constituent stocks with their corresponding value on the base day as:

$$I_t = \frac{\sum MC_t}{\sum MC_{t-1}} \times 100 \tag{3.1}$$

where I is the index at date t, and MC is the market capitalization of constituent stocks at dates t, and base day $t-1$.

Stock market returns are calculated assuming that stock prices and returns follow a geometrical random walk (geometric average prices/returns). Denoted by I_t is the price of the closing index at time (day/month) t and l_n is the logarithm neperiano. We assume that the model's variable α is a constant with a zero mean and is a normal random variable. The simple net return, R_t, on the asset between dates $t-1$ and t, is defined as:

$$R_t = \ln\left(\frac{I_t}{I_{t-1}}\right) \times 100 = \alpha + u . \tag{3.2}$$

Geometric average return is used through out this book in the notation of general continuously compounded multi-period returns. Campbell et al. (1997) give two reasons for focusing on returns rather than on prices. First, for the average investor, financial markets may be considered close to perfectly competitive, so that the size of the investment does not affect price changes. Therefore, since the investment is "constant-returns-to-scale", the return is a complete and scale free summary of the investment opportunity. In addition, for theoretical and empirical reasons, returns have more attractive statistical properties than prices, such as stationarity and ergodicity. In particular, the dynamic general-equilibrium model often yields nonstationary prices, but stationary returns.

For univariate statistics, mean, median, standard deviation, skewness, and kurtosis are computed in order to determine the central tendency, dispersion and shape of frequency distributions of the return on the stock exchange of Thailand. Mean μ is calculated by the following formula:

$$\mu = \frac{\sum R}{n} \tag{3.3}$$

where $\sum R$ refers to the sum of all the observation returns, and n refers to the number of observations in the population. The median could be seen as:

$$Median = L + \frac{n/2 - F}{fm} c \tag{3.4}$$

where L is lower limit of the median class, F is sum of the frequencies up to but not including the median class, fm is frequency of median class, and c is width of the class interval.

The monthly and daily stock volatility of the stocks trading on the SET could be estimated from the stock returns (simple net return) of the Stock Exchange of

Thailand composite portfolio from January 1992 through December 2001. The estimates from January 1975 through December 2001 use monthly returns on the SET composite portfolio. The estimator of the variance σ^2 of the yearly return is the sum of the squared monthly returns (after subtracting the average monthly return). It is important to note that it is possible to estimate the monthly variance by finding the daily returns on the selected composite portfolio.

Standard deviation σ is calculated by the following formula:

$$\sigma = \sqrt{\frac{\sum (R_{it} - \mu)^2}{N_t}} \tag{3.5}$$

where there are N_t monthly or daily returns R_{it} in month t. Using nonoverlapping samples of monthly data to estimate the yearly variance creates an estimation error that is uncorrelated through time.

Figure 3.1 plots the estimated standard deviations from monthly mean/average returns between May 1975 to December 2001. Volatility estimations are much higher following October 1997 to December 1999 (marked by the arrow). High volatility fluctuation is present in the period when Thailand experienced the economic crisis and the crash in the Thai stock market. The overall volatility of the individual stocks had increased substantially immediately after the crisis.

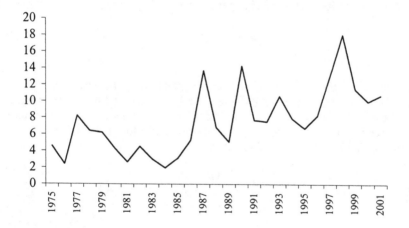

Fig. 3.1. Volatility of the SET Index, 1975–2001

The market risk premium is a broad measure that covers the stock markets as a whole. However, not all companies are equally risky. Investors would demand more return for investing in a risky venture than in a company that has stable and predictable earnings. The beta coefficient is an adjustment to the market risk premium based upon the risk perception of the company. Therefore, if a company is perceived to be no more or no less risky than the stock market as a whole, its beta coefficient would be 1. Similarly, firms more risky than the average will have a beta coefficient greater than 1 and companies with less risk will have a beta coefficient value of less than one. The beta coefficient is an individual risk measure for a given firm, identifying how responsive the stock's return is relative to movements in the entire stock market (Lie, Brooks and Faff 2000). Beta is estimated by:

$$R_i = \alpha_i + \beta_i \; (SET)_m + \varepsilon_i \; . \tag{3.6}$$

By deriving the covariance between the returns on stock i and the market index, we are able to identify the systematic and non-systematic risk. By definition, the firm-specific or non-systematic component is independent of the systematic component, that is, $Cov(SET_m, \; \varepsilon_i) = 0$. From this relationship, it follows that the covariance of the excess rate of return on security i with that of the market index is:

$$
\begin{aligned}
Cov(R_i, \; SET_m) \quad &= Cov(\beta_i \; SET_m + \varepsilon_i \; SET_m) \\
&= \beta_I \; Cov \; (SET_m) + Cov(\varepsilon_i \; SET_m) \\
&= \beta_i \sigma_m^2 \; .
\end{aligned}
\tag{3.7}
$$

Note that it is possible to drop α_i from the covariance terms because α_i is a constant and thus has zero covariance with all variables. Because $Cov(R_i, \; SET_m) = \beta_i \sigma_m^2$, the sensitivity coefficient, β_i, in equation $R_i = \alpha_i + \beta_i \; (SET)_m + \varepsilon_i$, is the slope of the regression line representing the index model, equals:

$$\beta_i = \frac{Cov(R_i, SET_m)}{\sigma_m^2} \; . \tag{3.8}$$

The market model beta coefficient turns out to be the same beta as that of the Capital Asset Pricing Model (CAPM) for a well-specified and observable market index. We can test the beta of individual stock to see whether that particular stock has a greater risk. However, the beta is not modeled here for individual stocks.

Skewness and kurtosis can be defined as:

$$Skewness = \frac{\sum f(R-\mu)^3}{\sigma^3} \tag{3.9}$$

$$Kurtosis = \frac{\mu_4}{\mu_2^2} - 3 \tag{3.10}$$

where μ denotes the ith central moment.

In this chapter, the monthly market index was observed from May 1975 to December 2001. The time interval of 1992 to 1996 has been regarded as the boom in the Thai financial and stock market followed by a tumultuous period of economic crisis from 1997 to 2001. We hypothesize that the statistical characteristics are different in each time interval: whereas the pre-crisis results would produce more positive returns, the post-crisis period is hypothesized to produce negative returns with higher standard deviation. Thus, the comparison between the periods of May 1975 to December 2001 (referred to as *Overall* period), January 1992 to December 1996 (referred to as *Pre-Crisis* period), and January 1997 to December 2001 (referred to as *Post-Crisis* period) is shown in Table 3.1, which presents a number of descriptive statistics calculated for the monthly return series of the SET closing index over the period 1975 to 2001. In particular, the return over the whole ten-year period starting from 1992 to 2001 is the focus of the analysis to capture the effect of economic crisis. The mean, median, standard deviation, skewness and kurtosis were estimated and are reported in Tables 3.1 and 3.2.

Table 3.1. Descriptive statistics for monthly return on the SET Index

Period	Mean	Median	Standard deviation	Skewness	Kurtosis
1975–2001 (Overall)	0.3815	0.2231	8.8641	-0.2197	2.3113
1992–1996 (Pre-Crisis)	0.2602	0.0019	8.5283	0.5426	1.1602
1997–2001 (Post-Crisis)	-1.6780	-2.1431	12.9072	0.3222	-0.0586
1992	1.8990	2.8589	7.2041	-0.2121	2.2764
1993	5.2766	3.7574	10.1528	1.1599	0.7747
1994	-1.7745	-1.3858	7.5528	0.1006	-1.4915
1995	-0.5005	-1.2123	6.4481	0.7773	2.2531
1996	-3.5994	-1.3811	7.9116	-0.5269	-0.1699
1997	-6.6881	-6.8083	12.4969	0.8473	1.9644
1998	-0.3863	-2.1297	17.2904	0.3491	-1.1387
1999	2.5282	1.7722	10.9680	0.6248	0.4093
2000	-4.8530	-2.2471	9.5303	-0.7489	-0.2242
2001	1.0093	1.6694	10.2452	-0.0371	0.5100
1992–2001	-0.7089	-0.8735	10.9819	0.2793	0.5092

The monthly return during the overall period is higher than the pre-crisis and post-crisis period. The stock exchange performed best over the period of financial liberalisation in 1988 to 1996. The significant effect of the Asian economic crisis results in negative returns in the subsequent years with the highest risk level, measured by standard deviation, in 1997 and 1998 of 12% and 17% respectively. A higher degree of risk in the exchange market could also be interpreted as a higher degree of speculation over the stocks and consequently generating greater volatility in the market as shown in Figure 3.2.

Table 3.2. Descriptive statistics for daily return on the SET Index

Period	Mean	Median	Standard deviation	Skewness	Kurtosis
1992–1996 (Pre-Crisis)	0.0127	0.0151	1.4489	-0.1920	4.9080
1997–2001 (Post-Crisis)	-0.0820	-0.2174	2.2383	0.6318	2.7615
1992	0.0923	0.0826	1.6157	0.0058	9.0352
1993	0.2042	0.1424	1.1882	0.5779	1.1866
1994	0.0006	0.0704	1.6676	-0.6639	3.0638
1995	-0.0111	-0.1245	1.2615	0.3288	1.4969
1996	-0.2047	-0.1589	1.3551	-0.3649	2.7480
1997	-0.3121	-0.4524	2.2737	0.7017	1.4035
1998	-0.0190	-0.0880	1.8891	0.4559	4.0141
1999	0.1238	-0.0338	2.1975	1.0905	3.1830
2000	-0.2358	-0.2462	1.8965	-0.2398	4.0205
2001	0.0494	-0.0317	1.6612	-0.3562	2.8353
1992–2001	-0.0347	-0.0802	1.8863	0.4537	4.0283

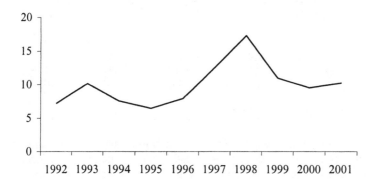

Fig. 3.2. Volatility of the SET Index measured by standard deviation, 1992–2001

The stock market during the post-crisis period was very volatile, measured by standard deviation, especially in 1997–1998 when there was high fluctuation in stock returns. The monthly returns data shows a positive skewness for both periods. The shape of kurtosis for both periods is leptokurtic distribution. The kurtosis for both monthly and daily SET returns suggests that this distribution is quite far from normal (gaussian). This means that the periods of relatively modest change are interspersed with higher-than-predicted changes, especially in both pre- and post-crisis periods. Considering monthly and daily returns (Table 3.1 and Table 3.2), the basic characteristics of these descriptive statistics are very similar. However, the monthly returns and risk are much higher than those in the daily data to the extent that the mean and standard deviation have a large range.

From these financial market indicators, the P/E and dividend yield (DY) are relatively important in the Thai stock and obtained below. P/E ratio for the stock is the ratio of the stock's price to the stock's annual earnings:

$$P/E = \frac{P}{E}. \qquad (3.11)$$

P/E ratio can present a very useful measure of the market sentiment regarding a stock. Stocks which have great expectations but small earnings can have P/Es of 30 or more, while solid but uninspiring companies may have P/Es below 10. In general, some investors wishing to invest in growth stocks usually avoid companies with a P/E above 20. Similarly, the DY is the ratio of the annual dividend per share to the stock price.

The values of these financial market indicators provide useful information for investors, policy makers and financial analyst and can be used for financial market forecasting and prediction. The implications of these indicators for various financial issues are discussed in Chapter 5 and other parts of the book.

3.3 Univariate Time Series Modelling

The stock market indices are often in the form of non-stationary series. These series wander widely, rarely return to an earlier value and are also called random walk (Abelson and Joyeux 2000). Time series analysis is the set of statistical methodologies that are appropriate to analyse non-stationary data series. Time series methods identify the regularity patterns present in the data to forecast future observations. Campbell, Lo and MacKinlay (1997) comment that one of the earliest and most enduring questions of financial econometrics is whether financial asset prices are forecastable. Efficient market hypothesis provides the view that stock prices cannot be predicted because they stagger up and down over time, which is often described as a random walk, $Y_t = Y_{t-1} + \varepsilon_t$ with random up and down prices called the martingale property (or drift), $Y_t = Y_{t-1} + \alpha + \varepsilon_t$.

Since a pure time series model does not include explanatory variables, these forecasts of future observations are simply extrapolations of the observed series at the end of the sample. In this section, we consider a single variable in the stock market index analysis which is called a *univariate time series model*.

A univariate time series model for y_t is formulated in terms of past values of y_t and/or its position in relation to time. Time series of economic data display many different characteristics and one easy way of starting the analysis of a series is to display the data by means of a time plot in which the series of interest is graphed against time. The basic characteristics of univariate time series are trends (long-run movements of the series), seasonalities (see also Chapter 7), and cycles.

The trend is specified as a deterministic function of time which is usually denoted as a random walk model with drift and can be formulated as follows:

$$y_t = \alpha + \beta t + \varepsilon_t \tag{3.12}$$

where ε_t is the error term that may be correlated. The variable t is constructed artificially as a seasonal variable (trend) that takes the value of 1 in the first period of the sample, 2 in the second period and so on.

A time series with seasonality can be easily modelled as a deterministic function of time by including in the regression model a set of n seasonal dummies:

$$D_{it} = \begin{cases} 1 & t \in season(i) \\ 0 & otherwise \end{cases} \quad i=1,2,\ldots,n \tag{3.13}$$

where n is the number of seasons in a year, thus, $n=4$ if we have quarterly data, $n=12$ if we have monthly data, and so forth. A linear regression model for a time series with a linear trend and seasonal behaviour can be formulated as follows:

$$y_t = \alpha + \beta t + \sum_{i=1}^{n} \gamma_i D_{it} + \varepsilon_t \tag{3.14}$$

where γ_i are the seasonal coefficients constrained to sum zero.

A linear regression model is simple and could be easily estimated by least squares. Trends and seasonalities estimated by these models are represented by a deterministic function of time which holds at all points throughout the sample.

The alternatives to these models are the Exponential Smoothing Modelling and Holt Winters' Model. These models fit trends and seasonalities placing more weight on the more recent observations. In addition, these methods allow the components to change slowly within the sample and the most recent estimate of these components are extrapolated into the future in forecasting. These models are easy to implement and can be quite effective. Finally, modelling time series with a trend and/or seasonal behaviour within the ARIMA framework is a popular approach to forecast stock market returns.

However, if we are dealing with two or more variables in the stock market analysis, a *multivariate time series* model is necessary which will be discussed in Chapter 5. This technique is based on the relationship between one dependent variable and one or more independent variables. This technique involves more sophisticated forecasting models. This category of time series modelling technique is called *causal technique* where the model is called a multi-factor model. The model generated in this book is called the Thai Stock Market Multi-Factor Model (TSMM, see Chapter 5).

This section provides an understanding of univariate time series analysis, models, smoothing and forecasting techniques. By doing so, we use historical data for stock prices to forecast future prices. Monthly data for the stock market index and returns during January 1992 to December 2001 were used in the analysis. The discussed time series techniques are moving average, exponential smoothing, Holt Winters' model, and ARIMA. Moving average is used as a smoothing technique and trading rules. Exponential, Holt Winters and ARIMA are used as forecasting techniques.

3.3.1 Moving Average

A moving average of ten months is used on the SET Index to determine the medium-term trends, to smooth the time series and to develop a new trading rule. The method of moving average is highly subjective and dependent on the length of the period (L) selected for constructing the averages. The methods of moving averages are well established, are considered reliable, and are simple to understand and to calculate (Temby 1998). Figure 3.3 shows the moving average of 10 consecutive months on SET Index, while Figure 3.4 shows the moving average on the SET returns.

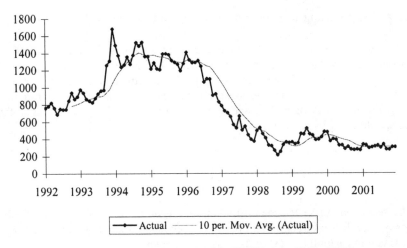

Fig. 3.3. Single moving average on monthly SET Index, 1992–2001

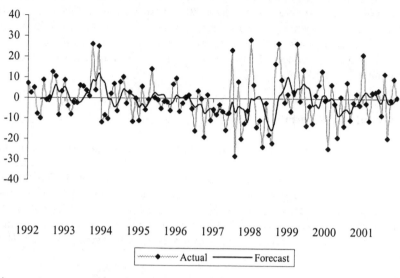

1992   1993   1994   1995   1996   1997   1998   1999   2000   2001

⋯⋯◆⋯⋯ Actual ———— Forecast

Fig. 3.4. Single moving average on the monthly stock returns, 1992–2001

Both figures are computed ten-month moving averages from a series of 10 years starting from January 1992 to December 2001. The ten-month moving averages consist of a series of mean values obtained over time by averaging over consecutive sequences containing ten observed values. The first of these ten-month moving averages is computed by adding the values for the first ten months in the series and dividing by ten as follows:

$$Mov(10) = \frac{\sum_{t=1}^{10} M_t}{10}.$$ (3.15)

The second of these ten-month moving averages is computed by adding the values of month two through to eleven in the series and then dividing by ten. The process continues until the last of the moving averages.

Double and Triple Moving Average

The moving average concept can be extended to double and triple moving averages. The double moving average (DMA) comprises an additional single moving average (SMA), while triple moving average (TMA) adds two additional SMAs. TMA is a useful *technical analysis* technique for investors.

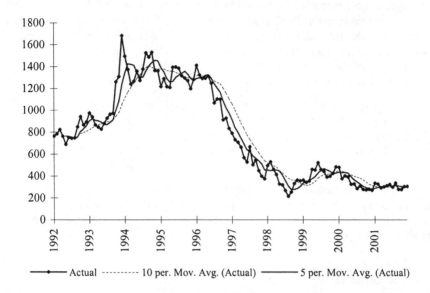

Fig. 3.5. Double moving average on the monthly SET Index, 1992–2001

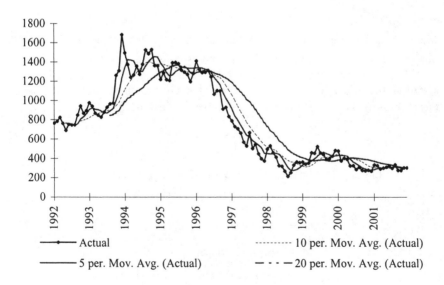

Fig. 3.6. Triple moving average on the monthly SET Index, 1992–2001

Observing the SMA lines in Figures 3.5 and 3.6, it is apparent that the longer the length of the period (L) the smoother the SMA line produced. DMA and TMA are useful for investors as these models give the signal when to purchase and when to quit the trade. Basically, the TMA indicator uses one pair of SMAs to open a trade, and a second, more agile, pair of SMAs to close the trade (Temby 1998).

Applying Temby's theory of "Basic TMA" (1998, pp. 55-58), the new trading rules that could apply to the Thai stock market are:

a) An uptrend is signaled when the 5-month SMA crosses above the 10-month SMA. This happened in January 1993 to January 1995 and January 1999 to July 2000.

b) A downtrend is signaled when the 5-month SMA crosses below the 10-month SMA especially in January 1995 and January 1999.

As a statistical measure of the market between 1992 to 2001, 56 per cent of the SET Index was below its 20 months moving average and 52 per cent was below its 10 months moving average. However in 1996, 1997 and 1998, these numbers were around 89 per cent.

3.3.2 Exponential Smoothing

Exponential smoothing uses only past values of a time series to forecast future values of the same series. It is a form of moving average of time series forecasting, and is defined as:

$$F_{t+1} = \alpha y_t + (1-\alpha)F_t \qquad (3.16)$$

where F_t is the forecast for period or time t, y_t is the actual value of the present time period, and α is the exponential smoothing constant.

With exponential smoothing, the forecast value at any time is a weighted average of all the available previous values which decline geometrically over time. If this process uses more than one period of time, the forecast F_t will be:

$$F_t = \alpha y_{t-1} + (1-\alpha)F_{t-1} . \qquad (3.17)$$

Substituting F_t into the preceding equation for F_{t+1}, we get:

$$
\begin{aligned}
F_{t+1} &= \alpha y_t + (1-\alpha)[\alpha y_{t-1} + (1-\alpha)F_{t-1}] \\
&= \alpha y_t + \alpha(1-\alpha)[\alpha y_{t-2} + (1-\alpha)^2 F_{t-1}] \\
&= \alpha y_t + (1-\alpha)[\alpha y_{t-1} + (1-\alpha)F_{t-1}] \\
&= \alpha y_t + \alpha(1-\alpha)[\alpha y_{t-2} + (1-\alpha)^2 F_{t-1}] .
\end{aligned}
\qquad (3.18)
$$

However, $F_{t-1} = \alpha y_{t-2} + (1-\alpha)F_{t-2}$.

Then we substitute this expression for $F_{t\,1}$ into the preceding equation for F_{t+1} and repeat to F_{t+n}, to get:

$$F_{t+1} = [\alpha y_t + \alpha(1-\alpha)][y_{t-1} + (1-\alpha)^2 F_{t-1}] \qquad (3.19)$$
$$F_{t+2} = [\alpha y_t + \alpha(1-\alpha)]\{y_{t-1} + (1-\alpha)^2[\alpha y_{t-2} + (1-\alpha)F_{t-2}]\}$$
$$F_{t+3} = [\alpha y_t + \alpha(1-\alpha)]\{y_{t-1} + \alpha(1-\alpha)^2[y_{t-2} + (1-\alpha)^3 F_{t-2}]\}$$
$$\cdots\cdots\cdots\cdots\cdots\cdots\cdots\cdots\cdots\cdots\cdots\cdots\cdots\cdots\cdots\cdots\cdots\cdots$$
$$F_{t+n} = [\alpha y_t + \alpha(1-\alpha)]\{y_{t-1} + \alpha(1-\alpha)^2[y_{t-2} + (1-\alpha)^n F_{t-2}]\}.$$

Usually, the weight value α is determined by the forecaster, Table 3.3 shows the values of α, $(1-\alpha)$, $(1-\alpha)^2$, $(1-\alpha)^3$, and $\alpha(1-\alpha)^3$, which is the weight value on the actual value for three previous periods.

Table 3.3. Selected weight value property

α	$1-\alpha$	$(1-\alpha)^2$	$(1-\alpha)^3$	$\alpha(1-\alpha)^3$
0.2	0.8	0.64	0.512	0.1024
0.5	0.5	0.25	0.125	0.0625
0.8	0.2	0.04	0.008	0.0064

According to Black and Eldreadge (2002), the value of α determines the impact level that the error has on the new forecast. If α is small, there will be less impact on the new forecast. On the other hand, if α is equal to 1.0, the new forecast is likely to be the same as the last actual value.

In choosing α, we selected an α value close to 0 if the series has a great deal of random variation, while we selected an α value close to 1 if the forecast values depend strongly on recent changes in the actual values.

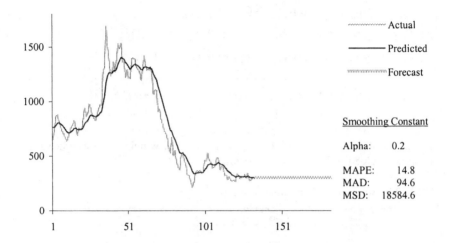

Fig. 3.7. Single exponential smoothing of the SET Index, $\alpha = 0.2$, 0.5 and 0.8

Figure 3.7 shows the forecast of the next 50 months on the SET Index data, 1992–2001. The weight value of 0.2, 0.5 and 0.8 is used, however the results indicate a close match between actual and predicted values as in Figure 3.7 and Figure 3.8.

Single exponential smoothing projects the forecast of the next 50 periods of the stock market index and returns simply by imitating the last period outcome. Because of this it is limitated in that its forecast lags behind the actual data and has no ability to adjust for any trend or seasonality. A model that can accommodate trends is required.

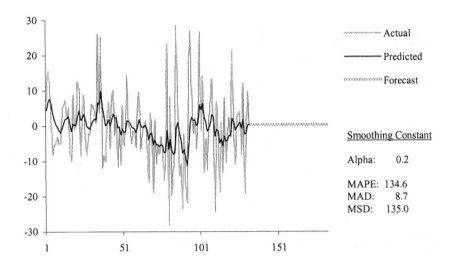

Fig. 3.8. Single exponential smoothing of the SET returns, $\alpha = 0.2$

The double exponential smoothing[1] model is more complicated than the simple exponential smoothing model because it includes trend components that may be present in the data. Double exponential smoothing is defined as:

$$F_t = [\alpha y_{t-1} + (1-\alpha)F_{t-1}] + \{\beta[\alpha y_{t-1} + (1-\alpha)F_{t-1}][\alpha y_{t-2} + (1-\alpha)F_{t-2}]\} + (1-\beta)T_{t-1} \qquad (3.20)$$

where $T_t = \beta[\alpha y_{t-1} + (1-\alpha)F_{t-1}][\alpha y_{t-2} + (1-\alpha)F_{t-2}] + (1-\beta)T_{t-1}$.

Figures 3.9, 3.10 and 3.11 present the forecast for the next 50 months on the SET Index data and Figures 3.12, 3.13 and 3.14 forecast for the next 50 months on the returns on SET (when $\alpha = 0.2$, 0.5, and 0.8 respectively).

---

[1] Sometimes called trend adjusted exponential smoothing.

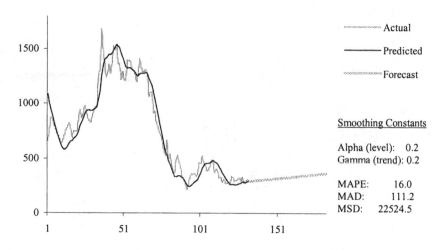

Fig. 3.9. Double exponential smoothing of the SET Index, α, $T = 0.2$

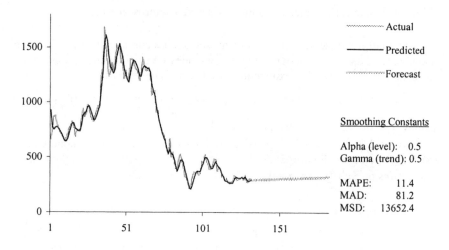

Fig. 3.10. Double exponential smoothing of the SET Index, α, $T = 0.5$

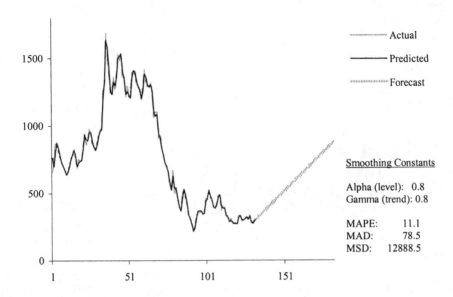

Fig. 3.11. Double exponential smoothing of the SET Index, α, $T = 0.8$

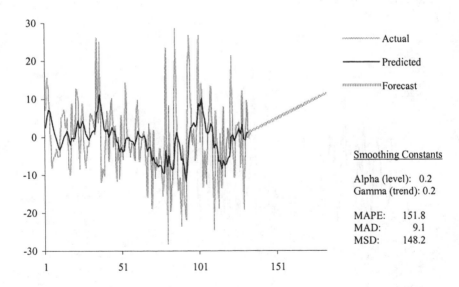

Fig. 3.12. Double exponential smoothing of the SET returns, α, $T = 0.2$

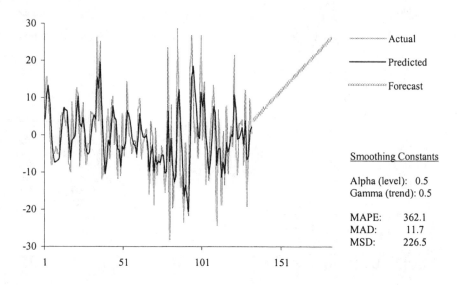

Fig. 3.13. Double exponential smoothing of the SET returns, α, $T = 0.5$

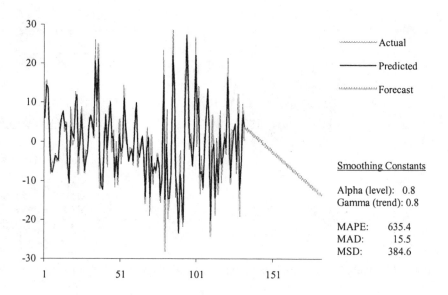

Fig. 3.14. Double exponential smoothing of the SET returns, α, $T = 0.8$

Several techniques are used as assessment measures in evaluating the forecast accuracy of the above fitted time series. These are *mean absolute percentage error* (MAPE) and *mean absolute deviation* (MAD), and *mean squared deviation* (MSD).

Mean absolute percentage error measures the accuracy of fitted time series values. It is defined as:

$$MAPE = \frac{\sum_{t=1}^{n} \left| (y_t - \hat{y}_t) / y_t \right|}{n} \qquad (3.21)$$

where $y_t \neq 0$, y_t = the actual value, $\hat{y}_t$ = the forecast value, and n equals the number of forecasts.

Mean absolute deviation is also used to measure the accuracy of fitted time series values. It expresses accuracy in the same units as the data, which helps conceptualize the amount of error and is expressed as:

$$MAD = \frac{\sum_{t=1}^{n} \left| y_t - \hat{y}_t \right|}{n}. \qquad (3.22)$$

Finally, mean squared deviation is a commonly used measure of accuracy of fitted time series values and is very similar to mean squared error (MSE). Because MSD is always computed using the same denominator, n, regardless of the model, it is very useful and effective in comparing MSD values across models. On the other hand, MSE is computed with different degrees of freedom for different models which makes it harder to compare MSE values across models and will not be used here. MSD is defined as:

$$MSD = \frac{\sum_{t=1}^{n} (y_t - \hat{y}_t)^2}{n}. \qquad (3.23)$$

Table 3.4. Summary of the forecasting assessment measures results

	MAPE	MAD	MSD
Single Exponential [$\alpha = 0.2$]			
SET Index	14.8	94.6	18584.6
SET Returns	134.6	8.7	135.0
Double Exponential			
SET Index [$\alpha, T = 0.2$]	16.0	111.2	22524.5
SET Index [$\alpha, T = 0.5$]	11.4	81.2	13652.4
SET Index [$\alpha, T = 0.8$]	11.1	78.5	12888.5
SET Returns [$\alpha, T = 0.2$]	151.8	9.1	148.2
SET Returns [$\alpha, T = 0.5$]	362.1	11.7	226.5
SET Returns [$\alpha, T = 0.8$]	635.4	15.5	384.6

Comparing MAPE, MAD, and MSD across all models, we find that it is better to use a smoothing constant value α and trends T that are close to 1 to forecast the SET Index for the future periods, as this minimizes the value of MAPE, MAD and MSD. On the other hand, as shown in Table 3.4, when the smoothing and trends level values are close to 0, the value of these forecasting assessment measures is minimized.

3.3.3 Holt Winters' Multiplicative Method

Winters (1960) proposes forecasting techniques for seasonal time series which are additive seasonality (additive Holt Winters method) and multiplicative seasonality (multiplicative Holt Winters method). The additive Holt Winters method does not depend on the current level of the time series and can simply be added to or subtracted from a forecast that depends only on level and trend. On the other hand, the multiplicative Holt Winters shows that the effect of seasonal influences increases with an increase in the level of the time series. It is important to note that while the multiplicative Holt Winters method provides reasonable point forecasts, it is very difficult to justify the choice of prediction intervals because no underlying statistical model on which to base the variance of the forecast error has been found (Koehler and Snyder 1999).

Assuming that the initial conditions and the parameters are the same, the Holt Winters method adds a third smoothing constant and smoothed seasonal indices to the double exponential smoothing model. This method uses weights to smooth the trend that is similar to single and double exponential smoothing.

The Holt Winters method uses the following four equations:

a) seasonal smoothed values (S):

$$S_t = \alpha X_t + (1-\alpha)(S_{t-1} + T_{t-1})$$
(3.24)

b) trend (T):

$$T_t = \beta(E_t - E_{t-1}) + (1-\beta)T_{t-1}$$
(3.25)

c) forecast (F):

$$F_{t+1} = S_t + T_t$$
(3.26)

d) for f periods:

$$F_{t+f} = S_t + fT_t.$$
(3.27)

Applying the multiplicative property to the model, the new Holt Winters Exponential Smoothing Model requires the following equations:

a) level (L):

$$L_t = \alpha\left(\frac{y_t}{S_{t-s}}\right) + (1-\alpha)(L_{t-1} + T_{t-1}) \tag{3.28}$$

b) trend:

$$T_t = \beta(L_t - L_{t-1}) + (1-\beta)T_{t-1} \tag{3.29}$$

c) seasonal smoothed values:

$$S_t = \gamma\left(\frac{y_t}{L_t}\right) + (1-\gamma)S_{t-s} \tag{3.30}$$

d) forecast:

$$F_{t+f} = (L_t + T_{t+f})S_{t-s+f}. \tag{3.31}$$

Now we complete the Holt Winters multiplicative model; the forecasts of the SET Index for the next 50 periods are presented in Figures 3.15, 3.16 and 3.17, and the returns on SET are shown in Figures 3.18, 3.19 and 3.20 for various weightings.

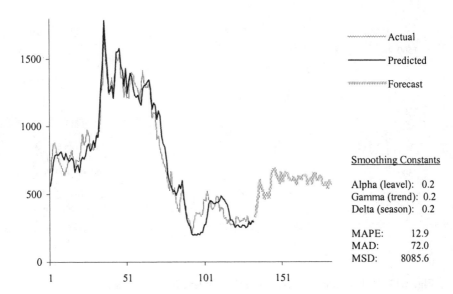

Fig. 3.15. Holt Winters model of the SET Index, L, T, S = 0.2

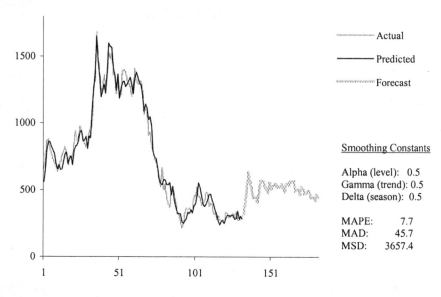

Fig. 3.16. Holt Winters model of the SET Index, *L, T, S* = 0.5

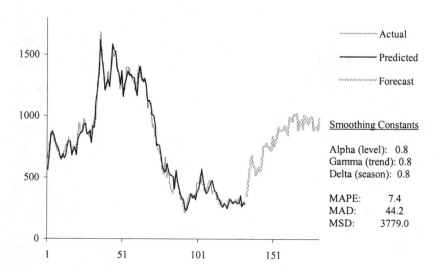

Fig. 3.17. Holt Winters model of the SET Index, *L, T, S* = 0.8

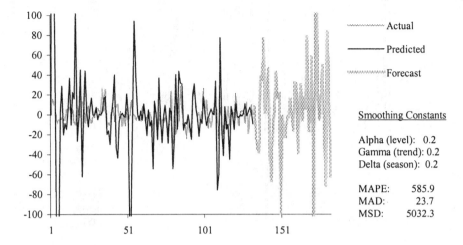

Fig. 3.18. Holt Winters model of the SET returns, *L, T, S* = 0.2

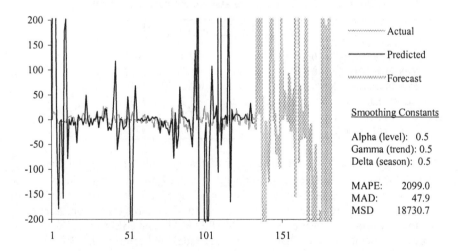

Fig. 3.19. Holt Winters model of the SET returns, *L, T, S* = 0.5

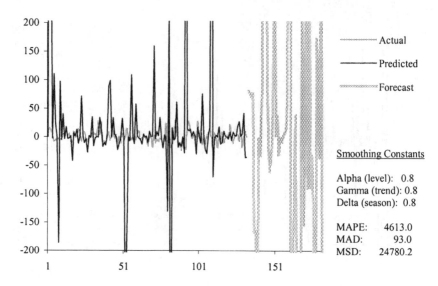

Fig. 3.20. Holt Winters model of the SET returns, L, T, $S = 0.8$

Table 3.5. Summary of the forecasting assessment measures results

	MAPE	MAD	MSD
Holt Winters			
SET Index (α, T, S = 0.2)	12.9	72.0	8085.6
SET Index (α, T, S = 0.5)	7.7	45.7	3657.4
SET Index (α, T, S = 0.8)	7.4	44.2	3779.0
SET Returns (α, T, S = 0.2)	585.9	23.7	5032.3
SET Returns (α, T, S = 0.5)	2099.0	47.9	18730.7
SET Returns (α, T, S = 0.8)	4613.0	93.0	24780.2

The results are consistent with the findings on double exponential smoothing where the use of smoothing constant value α, trend T and seasonal value S that are close to 0 is appropriate for the prediction of the SET Index, whereas the use of these values that are close to 1 is appropriate for the returns prediction. According to the assessment measures such as MAPE, MAD and MSD in evaluating the forecast accuracy of the Thai stock market index and returns, the Winter Holts model is superior to all exponential models. We can conclude that the Winter Holts model (α, T, $S = 0.2$) produces a better forecasting accuracy for the Thai stock market index, and it is clear that the model (α, T, $S = 0.8$) produces a better forecasting accuracy for the Thai stock market returns.

The smoothing exercises here show that in future Thai stock indices and returns will have a positive trend, although with some fluctuation.

3.3.4 ARIMA Models

We will now discuss how to apply the autoregressive integrated moving average (ARIMA) process to predict future movements by using past movements of the stock index. The characteristics of an ARIMA process will be a combination of those from the autoregressive (AR) and moving average (MA) part in differenced d times (or being integrated, I). This model is well grounded in financial or economic theory despite its limitation to forecast unusual movement in prices or returns. Usually, variables are exploited solely for their time series properties to achieve a forecast.

Autoregression in order p, [AR(p)] can be expressed as:

$$y_t = \gamma_1(y_{t-1}) + \gamma_2(y_{t-2}) +,...,+ \gamma_p(y_{t-p}) + \varepsilon_t \tag{3.32}$$

where y_t = the actual or data value at time t, γ = the constant value, and ϵ = the residual or error term.

Moving average of order q, [MA(q)] can be expressed as:

$$y_t = \varepsilon_t - \theta_1(\varepsilon_{t-1}) - \theta_2(\varepsilon_{t-2}) -,...,- \theta_q(\varepsilon_{t-q}). \tag{3.33}$$

Combining both (AR) and (MA) processes, an autoregressive moving average is expressed as:

$$y_t = \gamma_1(y_{t-1}) + \gamma_2(y_{t-2}) +,...,+ \gamma_p(y_{t-p}) + \varepsilon_t - \theta_1(\varepsilon_{t-1}) - \\ \theta_2(\varepsilon_{t-2}) -,...,- \theta_q(\varepsilon_{t-q}). \tag{3.34}$$

ARIMA estimates a model of dependent variables on independent variables where the disturbances are allowed to follow a linear autoregressive moving average (ARMA) specification. However, in using the Thailand stock market index when the independent variables are not specified, these models are reduced to autoregressive integrated moving average models in the dependent variable. The persistence of error terms could be identified through the autocorrelation function (ACF) and the partial autocorrelation function (PACF) which will be discussed in Chapter 4.

We will use the ARIMA(p,d,q) model applied to the Thailand stock market index between 1992–2001, where p denotes the number of autoregressive terms, d is the number of times the series has to be differenced before it becomes stationary, and q is the number of moving average terms. Thus the result of ARIMA(1,1,1) is reported as follows (for details, see Appendix 2).

Observing the autocorrelation function, we see one large positive correlation at 1 lag, and 3 large negative correlation at 3 lags, compared to the partial autocorrelation which contains 2 large positive correlations at 2 lags and 1 negative at 1 lag. Therefore, after accounting for the ACF and PACF, the overall lags show a very small correlation, since our model of AR(1) process shows correlations at a 5 per cent level of significance. The critical value for the chi-square distribution with 10 *DF* (Dickey Fuller's unit root test) at the 5 per cent level of significance is 18.31. Since the Modified Box-Pierce (Ljung-Box) Q is 16.1, which is less than 18.31, we accept the null hypothesis and there is scant evidence of correlation. However, the AR(1) process is statistically significant at the 10 per cent level where 16.1 is greater than *DF* 15.99. Therefore, according to the results, we can forecast the SET Index at time *t* by using the following formula:

$$y_t = 6.54 + (-.6925)y_{t-1} + (-0.6282)\varepsilon_{t-1} . \tag{3.35}$$

We can conclude that the autocorrelation function for the residuals shows only white noise with no significant values in any of the 48 lags. The value from the chi-square table is about 16.1 for 12 lags, 22.5 for 24 lags, 36.5 for 36 lags, and 51.0 for 48 lags.

3.5 Implications and Empirical Characteristics

This chapter presents a variety of descriptive statistical techniques and models that have been developed and applied in an attempt to understand the overall picture of the Stock Exchange of Thailand. Various descriptive statistics of the SET for both monthly and daily stock returns were calculated. The results of these statistics imply that during the Thai economic miracle years of the pre-crisis period the expected mean return was highly positive. During this period, Thailand maintained sound macroeconomic policies and carried out financial liberalisation presumably removing government intervention and its distortionary effects from the financial markets.

However, what Thailand should have done was to first develop a sound financial system and policy instruments before fully implementing financial liberalisation. The Thai economic crisis of 1997–1998 was an unfortunate outcome of the confluence of a weak domestic financial system and volatile international capital movements where the post-crisis period yields a negative mean return and the standard deviation or risk is also higher, as shown by other descriptive statistics and univariate time series methods. Higher standard deviation in the post-crisis period means greater volatility, which in turn could mean extraordinary gains or losses, thus greater uncertainty in the Thai stock market. In addition, the shape of the kurtosis suggests that the unconditional distribution of the volatility is nearly a normal distribution.

Univariate time series econometrics models such as moving average, exponential smoothing, Holt Winters and ARIMA models have shown that the stock market had exhibited historically a fair bit of seasonal movements and fluctuations. The stock returns time series produced useful results for technical analysts and investors to monitor the market and determine changes in trends of the key indicators of the Thai stock market performance. The use of multiple models and techniques will enhance the accuracy of the forecasting process and thus improve the decision making of investors. The implication of the financial models and technical analysis in forecasting is that if these models are used by investors to earn extraordinary returns, it reflects that the market is not efficient. Under EMH, historical data for stock prices cannot be used in order to predict future prices. A discussion of market efficiency follows in the next chapter.

3.6 Conclusion

Simple financial econometric analyses using descriptive statistics and univariate time series methods can provide useful insights into the operation of the financial systems in emerging financial markets. The time series results in this chapter provide useful information for predicting the behaviour of the financial market in Thailand. The results on kurtosis and skewness indicate, however, some general lack of applicability of the normal distribution based econometric and financial models in this book. For understanding the controversial financial issues in depth, it is necessary to focus on the specific issues and adopt more advanced methods and models. Such an exercise for the Thai stock market is undertaken in Chapters 4 to 8 before summarizing the major findings from all these exercises and their implications in Chapter 9.

4 Market Efficiency Models and Tests

4.1 Introduction

Possibly the most controversial issue in finance is whether the financial market is efficient in allocating or using economic resources and information or not. Other financial theory issues such as volatility, predictability, speculation and anomalies are also related to the efficiency issue and are all interdependent (Islam and Oh 2003; Mills 1999; Cuthbertson 1996). An investigation of the Efficient Market Hypothesis (EMH) of the Thai stock market is provided in this chapter while the other related issues of finance theory and their implications for EMH are included in subsequent chapters.

"An efficient capital market is a market that is efficient in processing information... In an efficient market, prices 'fully reflect' available information" (Fama 1976, p. 133). In the broadest terms of EMH, there are three types of market efficiency. Firstly, in *weak form efficiency*, the information set is that the market index reflects only the history of prices or returns themselves. Secondly, in *semi-strong form efficiency*, the information set includes most information known to all market participants. Finally, in *strong form efficiency*, the information set includes all information known to any market participant.

In the 1960s and early 1970s, the controversy focused on the extent to which successive changes in prices of the stocks were independent of each other or whether stock prices followed a random walk. The early tests to answer this question were conducted by Fama (1965) and Samuelson (1965b), in which they concluded that most of the evidence seems to have been consistent with the efficient market hypothesis (EMH). Stock prices followed a random walk model and the predictable variations in equity returns, if any, were found to be statistically insignificant. Other studies in the US with similar findings included those of Sharpe (1966), Friend et al. (1970), and Williamson (1972).

Throughout the 1980s, EMH has provided the theoretical basis for much of the research, and most empirical studies during these years focused on predicting prices from historical data, while also attempting to produce forecasts based on variables such as P/E ratios (Campbell and Shiller 1987), dividend yield (Fama and French 1988), term structure variables (Harvey 1991), and announcement of various events, i.e. earnings, stock splits, capital expenditure, divestitures, and takeovers (Jensen and Ruback 1983; McConnell and Muscarella 1985).

The issue of EMH in relation to stock prices is fundamental for an investigation of the characteristics of the Thai stock market. The results from testing the EMH can assist in the identification of the factors, which could be seen as the influence of anomalies (Nassir and Mohammad 1987; Ho 1990; Berument and Kayimaz 2001), insider trading and asymmetric information (Jaffe 1974; Jagadeesh, and Titman 1993), stock splits (Ikenberry, Ranikine and Stice 1996), dividend initiations and omissions (Michaely, Thaler, and Womack 1995), etc.

The major challenges to EMH are mainly in the following forms: empirical tests for EMH showing no evidence in favour of EMH, limitations of the statistical and mathematical models for EMH, and the evidence of the excess volatility mean reversion predictability, existence of bubbles, and non-linear complex dynamics and chaos in the stock market. While the empirical tests for EMH are reported here, other challenges to EMH will be examined in the subsequent chapters.

Various methods for testing market efficiency of the stock market have been used in this book such as the run-test, autocorrelation test, rational speculative bubble test, seasonal anomalies test and autoregressive (AR) test. Our focus in this chapter is to build a theory-free paradigm of non-parametric testing of market efficiency. The non-parametric run-test and autocorrelation test target consistent statistical characteristics of the price and returns process using few interlinkages with a specific model of asset pricing. If the stock exchange of Thailand was efficient, the stock prices would correctly and fully reflect all relevant information and hence, no arbitrage opportunities would exist. Thus in this type of test, the rejection of the null hypothesis would reject market efficiency for the Thai stock market. The implication of efficiency, in its broadest sense, is that stock prices always reflect their intrinsic worth and can be taken at their face value.

EMH has two dual aspects of the rational expectation hypothesis and the risk-neutral behaviour of investing agents. The tests of EMH relates to the issues of predictability, anomaly, seasonality, volatility and the existence of bubbles. Studies of all these issues enable an analyst to draw a conclusion about the efficiency of a financial market of a country.

This chapter is structured as follows: Section 4.2 provides a literature review of the market efficiency hypothesis. Section 4.3 discusses and applies the most common non-parametric methods such as the run-test and the autocorrelation function (ACF) test in testing the EMH. The results are also shown in this section. The implications of these tests for EMH in the Thai stock market are discussed in Section 4.4. A conclusion is given in Section 4.5.

4.2 Market Efficiency Hypothesis

4.2.1 The Concept

To examine the efficiency issues of the Stock Exchange of Thailand, we need to define EMH. The EMH is a statement about: (1) the theory that market stock prices reflect the true value of stocks (alternately, the expected value of stock prices are their true or actual values, which is the rational expectation (RE) hypothesis); (2) the absence of arbitrage opportunities in an economy populated by rational, profit-maximizing agents; and (3) the hypothesis that market prices always fully reflect available information (Fama 1970). In Jensen (1978), an efficient market is defined with respect to an information set Φ_t if it is impossible to earn economic profits by trading on the basis of Φ_t. Fama (1970) presented a general notation describing how investors generate price expectations for stocks. This could be explained as (Cuthbertson 1996):

$$E(p_{j,t+1} \mid \Phi_t) = [1 + E(r_{j,t+1} \mid \Phi_t)] p_{jt} \qquad (4.1)$$

where E is the expected value operator, $p_{j,t+1}$ is the price of security j at time $t+1$, $r_{j,t+1}$ is the return on security j during period $t+1$, and Φ_t is the set of information available to investors at time t.

The left-hand side of the formula $E(p_{j,t+1} \mid \Phi_t)$ denotes the expected end-of-period price on stock j, given the information available at the beginning of the period Φ_t. On the right-hand side, $1 + E(r_{j,t+1} \mid \Phi_t)$ denotes the expected return over the forthcoming time period of stocks having the same amount of risk as stock j.

Under the efficient market hypothesis (EMH), investors cannot earn abnormal profits on the available information set Φ_t other than by chance. The level of over value or under value of a particular stock is defined as:

$$x_{j,t+1} = p_{j,t+1} - E(p_{j,t+1} \mid \Phi_t) \qquad (4.2)$$

where $x_{j,t+1}$ indicates the extent to which the actual price for security j at the end of the period differs from the price expected by investors based on the information available Φ_t. As a result, in an efficient market it must be true that:

$$E(x_{j,t+1} \mid \Phi_t) = 0. \qquad (4.3)$$

This implies that the information is always impounded in stock prices. Therefore the rational expectations of the returns for a particular stock according to the EMH may be represented as:

$$P_{t+1} = E_t P_{t+1} + \varepsilon_{t+1} \qquad (4.4)$$

where P_t is the stock price; and ε_{t+1} is the forecast error. $P_{t+1} - E_t P_{t+1}$ should therefore be zero on average and should be uncorrelated with any information Φ_t. Also $E(x_{j,t+1} \mid \Phi_t) = 0$ when the random variable (good or bad news), the expected value of the forecast error, is zero:

$$E_t \varepsilon_{t+1} = E_t (P_{t+1} - E_t P_{t+1}) = E_t P_{t+1} - E_t P_{t+1} = 0 . \tag{4.5}$$

Underlying the efficiency market hypothesis, it is opportune to mention that expected stock returns are entirely consistent with randomness in security returns. This position is supported by the *law of iterated expectations* (Campbell, Lo and MacKinlay 1997; Samuelson 1965b). The expectational difference equation can be solved forward by repeatedly substituting out future prices and using the law of iterated expectations:

$$E_t [E_t + I_t (X)] = E_t(X). \tag{4.6}$$

Campbell, Lo and MacKinlay state that:
…if one has limited information I_t, the best forecast one can make a random variable X is the forecast of the forecast one would make of X if one had superior information J_t, rewritten as $E_t [X-E[X| J_t]| I_t$ is equal to zero. One cannot use limited information I_t to predict the forecast error one would make if one had superior information J_t. (1997, p. 23)

Non-parametric testing of market efficiency is based on the premise of no arbitrage opportunities, i.e., that opportunities for earning unusual returns do not exist (Fama 1970; Jensen 1978). Along with other empirical studies, some authors (Ball 1978; Charest 1978; Banz 1981; Schwert 1983; Fama and French 1989; Fama 1991; Fama et al. 1993; Lo 1996) have also jointly tested the market efficiency with an asset pricing model. If the null hypothesis is rejected, the failure of either market efficiency or the model does exist. However, the authors have often preferred to conclude that difficulties in asset pricing theory, rather than market efficiency, underlie the rejection of the null which have been uncovered in tests of asset pricing. In addition, the rejection of the null hypothesis is likely to have resulted from the misspecification of the asset pricing theory and not market efficiency itself.

4.2.2 EMH and Time Series Behaviour

Broadly speaking, the incident of white noise, random walk, martingale and fair game properties of financial time series is evidence in favour of EMH. To reiterate, the absence of arbitrage opportunities expresses the idea that the only chance for speculators to gain an opportunity to earn abnormal profits occurs if mispriced stocks exist in an economy populated by rational agents. In fact, the mispriced stocks will be automatically adjusted.

Since this scenario will be replayed every time an arbitrage opportunity arises, price levels will be continuously maintained according to the Samuelson's fair game theory or martingale difference. Samuelson (1965a) modeled this property of prices as the random walk:

$$Y_t = Y_{t-1} + \varepsilon_t \tag{4.7}$$

and random walk with drift (time trend):

$$Y_t = \mu + Y_{t-1} + \varepsilon_t. \tag{4.8}$$

Random walks also exhibit Markov and martingale properties. A Markov property is the information for determining the probability of a future value of the random variable already contained or expressed in the current status of that variable. The martingale property is the conditional expectation of a future value of the random variable. The positive drift (called sub-martingale) in random walk exists when α is greater than zero. On the other hand, negative drift (called super-martingale) in random walk exists when α is less than zero. However, if α is equal to zero, then it would be a normal random walk. The martingale property is defined as:

$$Y_t = Y_{t-1} + \alpha + \varepsilon_t. \tag{4.9}$$

Campbell, Lo and MacKinlay (1997, p. 29) summarize the classification of random walk and martingale hypotheses as in Table 4.1.

Table 4.1. Classification of random walk and martingale hypotheses

$Cov[f(r_t), g(r_{t+k})] = 0$	$g(r_{t+k}), \forall g(.)$	$g(r_{t+k}), \forall g(.)$
$f(r_t), \forall f(.)$ Linear	Uncorrelated Increments, Random Walk 3: $Proj[r_{t+k} \mid r_t] = \mu$	
$f(r_t), \forall f(.)$	Martingale/Fair Game: $E[r_{t+k} \mid r_t] = \mu$	Independent Increments, Random Walks 1 and 2: $pdf[r_{t+k} \mid r_t] = pdf(r_{t+k})$

Source: Campbell, Lo and MacKinlay 1997, p. 29.

If the stock prices follow a random walk, then price changes are white noise. Therefore, testing whether returns are white noise is observationally equivalent to the test of random walk in stock prices. Given r_t as the percentage change in Y_t, the null hypothesis of market efficiency is thus formed as testing for the standard statistical properties of a homoscedastic white noise process as follows:

$$
\begin{aligned}
H_0 : E(r_t) &= 0; \\
E(r_t r_t) &= \sigma_r^2; \\
E(r_t r_s) &= 0; \forall t \neq s.
\end{aligned}
\tag{4.10}
$$

Generally, if stock prices and returns are not predictable then these time series have the properties of martingale, fair game, random walk and white noise implying the validity of EMH. Since the empirical tests in Chapter 5 show the possibility of predictability of stock prices and returns, it can be argued that the stock prices and returns time series in Thailand during the study period did not show those properties of time series – evidence against EMH.

4.3 Stock Market Efficiency Tests

Keane (1983, p. 31) provides some basic explanations of what makes markets inefficient. One of his ideas is called "Gambler's Fallacy". This may be described as the belief that what "goes up must come down". This phenomenon exhibits itself amongst investors whose stocks' price has risen for a period of time and so is deemed to be "due for a fall".

Generally speaking, by knowing the relationship of the current price to recent price movements, one can better estimate the likely direction of future price movements, i.e. historical data such as price movement can be used to predict future prices. This provides credibility to the argument that the market is predictable and inefficient. Therefore, the issue is to see whether the stock market is predictable or not by detecting the autocorrelation of stock returns. In this chapter, some of the popular tests of market efficiency are applied, which are the run test and autocorrelation function (ACF) test. We have tested the semi-strong form of the EMH since this is the most commonly adopted form in empirical tests (Cuthbertson 1996).

4.3.1 Run Test

The run test, also called Geary test, is a non-parametric test whereby the number of sequences of consecutive positive and negative returns is tabulated and compared against its sampling distribution under the random walk hypothesis (Campbell, Lo and MacKinlay 1997; Gujarati 2003). A run is defined as the repeated occurrence of the same value or category of a variable. It is indexed by two parameters, which are the type of the run and the length. Stock price runs can be positive, negative, or have no change. The length is how often a run type occurs in succession. Under the null hypothesis that successive outcomes are independent, the total expected number of runs is distributed as normal with the following mean:

$$\mu = \frac{N(N+1) - \sum_{i=1}^{3} n_i^2}{N} \qquad (4.11)$$

and the following standard deviation:

$$\sigma_\mu = \left[\frac{\sum_{i=1}^{3} [\sum_{i=1}^{3} n_i^2 + N(N+1)] - 2N(\sum_{i=1}^{3} n_i^3 - N^3)}{N^2(N-1)} \right]^{\frac{1}{2}} \qquad (4.12)$$

where n_i is the number of runs of type i. The test for serial dependence is carried out by comparing the actual number of runs, a_r in the price series, to the expected number μ. The null proposition is:

$$H_0 : E(runs) = \mu. \qquad (4.13)$$

In this section, runs in the monthly SET Index for the total period, pre-crisis, and post-crisis are studied. The test results are tabulated in Table 4.2.

Table 4.2. Run tests for the monthly data SET Index

Period	Observed no. of runs	Expected no. of runs	Negative	Positive	Test value
1975–2001	13	145.99	209	111	454.26
1992–1996 (Pre-crisis)	3	30.70	27	33	1132.62
1997–2001 (Post-crisis)	10	29.37	37	23	399.33

A remarkable aspect of runs of all periods is that the observed number of runs is significantly less than the expected number of runs, approximately only ten per cent of the expected number of runs, especially in the overall period (1975–2001), and the pre-crisis period (1992–1996). This is evidence that the residuals change sign frequently, thus indicating a strong positive serial correlation. Table 4.3 shows the test results for the daily SET Index. Two periods, pre-crisis and post-crisis, are studied.

Table 4.3. Run tests for the daily data SET Index

Period	Observed no. of runs	Expected no. of runs	Negative	Positive	Test value
1992–1996 (Pre-crisis)	551	613.99	611	615	0.01
1997–2001 (Post-crisis)	570	611.99	657	571	-0.82

A run test using daily data produces a similar result to the monthly results in the degree of autocorrelation. It is noticed that the observed and expected numbers of runs for both the pre-crisis and post-crisis periods are different. In addition, the test value is not significant and we can generally conclude that, for both periods, the null hypothesis of market efficiency is rejected and there is an evidence of autocorrelation.

Many papers on market efficiency have employed run tests in a similar framework for verification of the weak-form efficiency of the U.S. and other countries' stock markets, such as the studies by Fama (1965), Sharma and Kennedy (1977), Cooper (1982), Chiat and Finn (1983), Wong and Kwong (1984), Yalawar (1988), Ko and Lee (1991), Butler and Malaikah (1992), and Thomas (1995). These typically find that in most markets (except Hong Kong, India, Kuwait and Saudi Arabia), the null hypothesis is not rejected. Thailand, as elsewhere in developing countries, experiences relative underdevelopment of the capital market especially the stock market, which can be attributed to inadequate market and legal infrastructure. Therefore, the results of the run tests indicate that Thailand's stock market is not efficient.

4.3.2 Autocorrelation Function Test

The autocorrelation function (ACF) test is examined to identify the degree of autocorrelation in a time series. It measures the correlation between the current and lagged observations of the time series of stock returns, which is defined as:

$$p_k = \frac{\sum_{t=1}^{n-k}(R_t - \overline{R})(R_{t+k} - \overline{R})}{\sum_{t=1}^{n}(R_t - \overline{R})^2} \tag{4.14}$$

where k is the number of lags, and R_t represents the real rate of return calculated as:

$$R_t = \ln\left(\frac{I_t}{I_{t-1}}\right) \times 100 = \alpha + u . \tag{4.15}$$

Two important elements for estimating of autocorrelation are the standard error test and the Box Pierce Q (BPQ) test. The standard error test measures the autocorrelation coefficient for individual lags and identifies the significant one, while the Box Pierce Q test, measures the significant autocorrelation coefficients at the group level.

The standard error σ_k is defined as:

$$\sqrt{\frac{1 + 2\sum_{t=1}^{k-1}\theta_t^2}{N}} \tag{4.16}$$

where N is the total number of observations and θ_k is the autocorrelation at lag (k).

Box Pierce Q is identified as:

$$N(N+2)\sum_{t=1}^{k}\frac{R_t^2}{N-t}.$$ (4.17)

One hundred lags length have been run, as Gujarati (2003) suggests, computing ACF of around one-quarter to one-third of the length of the time series. The calculation results of the autocorrelation function and partial autocorrelation for both monthly and daily returns are reported in Figures 4.1 and 4.2.

ACF Results of Monthly Returns

We use monthly data of the stock return to calculate ACF. Figures 4.1 and 4.2 show the correlograms of the autocorrelation and partial correlation function on stock returns during 1992–2001.

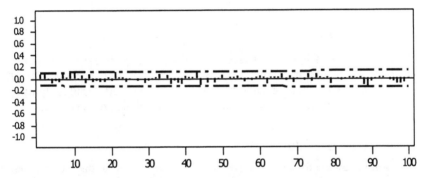

Fig. 4.1. Correlogram of the autocorrelation function on stock returns, 1992–2001

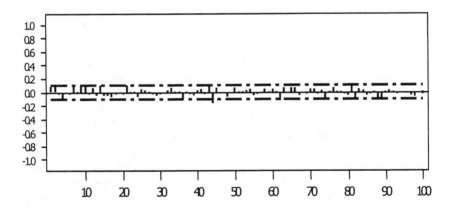

Fig. 4.2. Correlogram of the partial autocorrelation function on stock returns, 1992–2001

According to the results, there are movements of autocorrelation at various lags that hover around positive numbers and zero. This explains the non-stationarity time series. The results exhibit the small level of positive autocorrelation of the monthly returns on the stock during 1992–2001. The ACF and run test of monthly return are similar in that both tests produce a positive autocorrelation, however, the run test produces much stronger positive correlation evidence for the returns on the stock exchange of the Thailand index.

To see if ACF is significant, we calculate the Q statistics for 100 lags. The critical value for the chi-square distribution with 100 DF at the 5 per cent level of significance is 124.3. The ACF result at lag 100 yields 122.86. With the ACF test on the monthly stock price, the test statistic is significant at a 10 per cent level, when $Q = 122.86 > 118.5$. Therefore, we can accept the null hypothesis of the presence of autocorrelation at the 10 per cent level of significance.

ACF Results of Daily Returns

a) Pre-Crisis, 1992–1996

It is clear that the ACF test produces evidence supporting the existence of auto-correlation when the Q statistic at lag 100 is 136.23 which is greater than 100 DF at the 5 per cent level. We conclude that the autocorrelation is stronger by using the daily data. Therefore, we accept the null hypothesis of the presence of autocorrelation.

b) Post-Crisis, 1997–2001

The result pertaining to the post-crisis period is very similar to the pre-crisis period. In fact, during this period, there is a strong autocorrelation existed in the data. The Q statistic at lag 100 yields 161.33, which is considered very significant.

4.4 The Market Efficiency of the Thai Financial System

The implication of the tests for the efficient market hypothesis of the Thai stock market is that the market was not efficient during the study period (1992-2001). There was a chance that investors or stock analysts could use historical data to earn extraordinary gains by purchasing and selling stocks. Under strong-form efficiency, it suggests that security prices always reflect all available information, including private information. The semi-strong form of EMH asserts that stock prices reflect all publicly available information, thus there are no undervalued or overvalued securities, and trading schemes are capable of producing superior returns. The weak form of the hypothesis incorporates all the information in past prices. However, in all forms of the EMH, technical analysts could not use various forecasting models and technical analysis, discussed in Chapter 3, to predict the stock movement and make extraordinary gains. However, Fama (1991) expanded the concept of the weak form to include the test of predictability of returns with the use of accounting or macroeconomic variables (see Chapter 5).

Studies such as Islam and Oh (2003), Fama (1991), and Seyhun (1986) agree that the weak and semi-strong form of EMH have formed the basis for most empirical research. The result of the tests confirms the presence of autocorrelation on the Thai stock market returns, which implies that the stock market did not conform with the EMH. Moreover, the other forms of stock market behaviour such as anomalies, volatility and predictability, which will be discussed in subsequent chapters, provide evidence against the EMH.

4.5 Conclusions

The theoretical and empirical studies of the Efficient Market Hypothesis have made an important contribution to the understanding of the stock market. The results show that there is an autocorrelation on the Thai stock market returns especially during the post-crisis period. The result from the run test on daily return data, rejects the null hypothesis that the market is efficient. From this we may conclude that the stock market is inefficient.

The inefficiency of the Thai stock market follows from the violation of the necessary conditions for an efficient market with a developed financial system (see Chapter 1) and also implies financial and institutional imperfections. This leads to the conclusion that Thai financial policies and regulations (such as those concerning liberalisation, deregulation and privatization) perceived inconsistency and tendency to produce instability. The implication is that the benefits of a well functioning stock market are not being realized in the economy. Indeed, the weak-form inefficiency of the stock market demonstrated in this study is most likely caused by a combination of the lack of its development and the implication of policy choices.

It is necessary to gain more insights into the operation and characteristics of the stock market of Thailand in terms of its efficiency and the valuation processes to make an informed assessment of the empirical characteristics of the Thai financial market. The next chapter will introduce the fundamental methods of stock valuation such as discounted cash flow methods, capital asset pricing theory, and arbitrage pricing theory. A new muti-factor valuation model is developed by incorporated relevant economic and international factors to model the appropriate valuation processes in the Thai stock market and to gain an in depth understanding of the operation of the Thai market. Further analysis and the use of econometric models such as multiple regression with dummy variables (anomalies), predictability and volatility models are necessary to identify the level of EMH in the Thai stock market (Chapters 6 to 8).

5 Stock Valuation Models

5.1 Introduction

There are many different emerging and enduring financial issues in the financial sectors of developing countries, however a central issue is the valuation of stocks, i.e. the mechanism (process and factors) for determining the values of stocks. Substantial progress has been made towards understanding the relationship of different variables determining stock prices and returns in particular markets such as the U.S. stock market (Dhalkal, Kandil and Sharma 1993), U.K. stock market (Cheng 1995), and some Asian stock markets (Wongbangpo and Shama 2002) (see also Islam and Oh 2003; Cuthbertson 1996).

Valuation is closely related to market efficiency – if the market is efficient then stocks should be valued approximately by market forces and factors at their fundamental/efficient values. There are various models for determining values of stocks such as the discounted cash flow model (DCFM), the capital asset pricing model (CAPM), and the arbitrage pricing model (APM). In recent years multifactor modelling has become prominent (Islam and Oh 2000; Dabek 1999; Mishkin 1997). These models can also be applied to developing countries.

The objective of this chapter is to analyse the principles of valuation of stocks in a developing economy, especially in Thailand. A valuation is an estimate of the value of some financial assets. There are many approaches in stock valuation such as DCFM, CAPM, and APM. Limitations of the existing models are based on their assumptions of market equilibrium and the existence of a perfect market. In many developing countries, there are market imperfections and other market characteristics, which make the existing models unsuitable for countries like Thailand and other developing countries. Therefore, there is a need to develop a suitable approach to valuation of stocks trading on the Thai stock exchange.

This chapter reviews the existing theories of valuation of financial assets in Section 5.2 and also proposes a new valuation model which supports the existence of a significant, long-run relationship between stock prices and macroeconomic factors affecting stock prices on the Stock Exchange of Thailand. The valuation model is developed and empirically applied to the data gathered between 1992 and 2000 in Sections 5.3 to 5.5 The implications of the model results are also stated in Section 5.6.

5.2 Literature Review: Why a Multifactor Model?

In this section we look at models that seek to determine how investors decide what is the real value V_t of a particular stock. We start with the basic valuation models of analysis used in finance and econometrics literature. The most commonly used models are the Rational Valuation Model, the Capital Asset Pricing Model and the Arbitrage Pricing Model.

5.2.1 The Rational Valuation Model

According to Bodie et al. (1993), Peirson et al. (1995) and Chew (1997), the rational valuation model is one of the most widely used valuation models for determining the market values of firms and is based on the Discounted Cash Flow (DCF) method. The DCF Model is widely accepted as a basic valuation model for a security that is expected to generate cash payments. According to the *Efficient Market Hypothesis*, stock prices should always fully reflect all relevant information. Therefore, the fundamental value under expected discounted present value of future cash flow and dividends should always underline the expected value of the stock. The value of a particular stock is defined as:

$$V_0 = \frac{CF_1}{(1+K)^1} + \frac{CF_2}{(1+K)^2} + \frac{CF_3}{(1+K)^3} + \ldots \frac{CF_n}{(1+K)^n} \tag{5.1a}$$

or:

$$V_0 = \sum_{n=1}^{\infty} \frac{CF_n}{(1+K)^n} \tag{5.1b}$$

where V_0 is the present value of the anticipated cash flows from the security, its current value, $CF_{1,2,3\ldots n}$ is cash flows expected to be received, and K is the discount rate or the required rate of return.

The periodic cash flows from an investment in shares are dividends D. Valuating common stock by estimating the present value of the expected future cash flows or dividends from the common stock could be done by applying the general valuation model to common stocks as follows:

$$P_0 = \frac{D_1}{(1+K_s)^1} + \frac{D_2}{(1+K_s)^2} + \frac{D_3}{(1+K_s)^3} + \ldots \frac{D_n}{(1+K_s)^n} + \frac{P_n}{(1+K_s)^n} \tag{5.2a}$$

or:

$$P_0 = \sum_{n=1}^{n} \frac{D_n}{(1+K)^n} + \frac{P_n}{(1+K)^n} \tag{5.2b}$$

where P_0 is the current price of the common stock, D_1, D_2 ... D_n are dividends expected to be received at the end of the periods, P_n is the anticipated selling price of the stock in n periods, and K_s is the required rate of return on this common stock investment.

This model takes into account the source of return (anticipated selling price of the stock) from an investment in stock P. Hence, the capital gain or loss is the difference between P_n and P_{n-1}. The price of the stocks when they are sold is the discounted value of all future dividends from year $n+1$. Therefore, after substituting the equation, we obtain the DCFM expression on the stock price:

$$P_0 = \sum_{n=1}^{\infty} \frac{D_n}{(1+k)^n} . \tag{5.3}$$

The basic model for stocks valuation is the discounted cash flow or present value model. A key proposition running through this model is that stock returns and stock prices are closely linked (for details, see Cuthbertson 1996). This model relates the price of a stock to its expected future cash flow and dividends discounted to the present using a time-varying discount rate. Since cash flows in all future periods enter the discounted rate, the cash flow in any one period is only a component of the stock price. Therefore, persistent movements in cash flows have much larger effects on prices than temporary movements. The simple net return formula for a stock with constant expected return is defined as:

$$R_{t+1} = \frac{(P_{t+1})(D_{t+1})}{P_t} - 1 \tag{5.4}$$

where R_{t+1} is the return on the stock held from time t to time $t+1$, P_t is the price of a share of stock measure at the end of period t or equivalently an ex-dividend price, and D_t is dividends or cash flow at the period $t+1$.

An alternative measure of return is the log or continuously compounded return:

$$r_{t+1} = \log (1 + R_{t+1}). \tag{5.5}$$

Law of Iterated Expectations

It is assumed that the expected stock return is equal to a constant R:

$$E_t [R_{t+1}] = R . \tag{5.6}$$

Taking expectations of the identity (5.4), imposing (5.6), and rearranging, the equation relating the current stock price to the next expected stock price and dividend is:

$$P_t = E_t \left[\frac{P_{t+1} + D_{t+1}}{1 + R} \right]. \tag{5.7}$$

The most commonly used discounted cash flow (DCF) valuation approaches are those based on either intrinsic financial reports or on earnings (Islam and Oh 2000). The intrinsic method is based on the present value of expected cash flows projected from data that is considered subjective and associated with specific strategic or management choices. The earnings method is generally characterised by the use of profits, dividends or free cash flows for valuing the firm. The use of future cash flows to determine stock prices is consistent with the randomness in security returns under the Efficient Market Hypothesis (Campbell, Lo, and MacKinlay 1997).

This position is supported by the *law of iterated expectations* (Campbell, Lo and MacKinlay 1997; Samuelson 1965). In (5.7), the expectational difference equation can be solved forward by repeatedly substituting out future prices and using the law of iterated expectations:

$$E_t \{E_t + I_t (X)\} = E_t(X). \tag{5.8}$$

To eliminate future-dated expectations, after solving for the forward k periods we have:

$$P_t = E_t \left[\sum_{i=1}^{k} \left(\frac{1}{1+R} \right)^i D_{t+1} \right] + E_t \left[\left(\frac{1}{1+R} \right)^k P_{t+k} \right]. \tag{5.9}$$

The second term on the right-hand side of (5.9) is the expected discounted value of the stock price k periods from the present.

In some circumstances, dividends can grow at different rates. Applying the DCF and the Dividend Discount Model (DDM) incorporating growth may be difficult because these models assume stock dividends are paid regularly and grow at a constant rate (FitzHerbert 1998, p. 172). When constant growth occurs, the model could be seen as:

$$P_0 = \frac{D_1}{k-g} \tag{5.10}$$

where P_0 is the Current price of the stock, D_1 is the Dividend in period 1, k is the discount rate, and g is the growth rate. In addition, the discount rate k acts as proxy for the expected rate of return required by investors.

5.2.2 Capital Asset Pricing Model (CAPM)

According to Cuthbertson (1996), the Capital Asset Pricing Model (CAPM) is interpreted as a model of *equilibrium asset return*. It is one of the economic models and relevant to business valuation where businesses and business interests are subsets of investment opportunities available in the total capital market. It predicts a trade off between expected return under specific conditions and systematic risk β (Pratt et al. 1996). Sharpe (1964) suggests that much of the nonsystematic (or security specific) risk is not relevant to investors in the company's stock, as this risk could be diversified away in a well-managed portfolio.

Many studies such as Chen et al. (1986), Fama (1990) and Balvers et al. (1990) use CAPM to explain the relationship between interest rates, macroeconomic activity and stock returns. Theoretically, the determination of stock prices should be subject to the same economic forces and relationships that determine the prices or values of other investment assets (Peirson et al. 1995; Pratt et al. 1996; Brigham and Gapenski 1994).

According to Sharpe (1964) and Lintner (1965), CAPM is defined as:

$$E(Ri) = R_f + \beta \ (E(Rm) - Ri) \tag{5.11}$$

where ER_i is the expected return on investment, R_f is the risk free rate of return, β is the investment's systemic risk, and $E(R_m) - R_i$ is the expected risk premium in the market.

Some of the assumptions behind the CAPM need to be followed in order to apply CAPM to the valuation of stocks (Sharpe 1995; Fama 1970). These assumptions are:

a) investors evaluate portfolios by looking at the expected returns and standard deviations of the portfolios over a one-period horizon;
b) investors are never satiated, so when given a choice between two portfolios with identical standard deviations, they will choose the one with the higher expected return;
c) investors are risk averse, so when given a choice between two portfolios with identical expected returns, they will choose the one with the lower standard deviations;
d) individual assets are infinitely divisible, meaning that an investor can buy a fraction of a share if he or she so desires;
e) there is a risk-free rate at which an investor may either lend or borrow money;
f) taxes and transaction costs are irrelevant;
g) all investors have the same one-period horizon;
h) the risk-free rate is the same for all investors;
i) information is freely and instantly available to all investors; and
j) investors have homogeneous expectations regarding the expected returns, standard deviations, and covariances of stocks.

Throughout this and subsequent chapters the following equivalent ways of expressing expected returns, variances and covariances will be used.

Expected return: $\mu_i = ER_i$

Variance of returns: $\sigma_i^2 = \mathrm{var}(R_i)$

Covariance of returns: $\sigma_i = \mathrm{cov}(R_i)$

CAPM is a conceptual cornerstone of modern capital market theory and stock valuations. Sharpe and Cooper (1992) and Black, Jensen and Scholes (1972) have provided evidence on the stability of betas by holding the stocks of 10 particular classes over the entire period and found that the relationship between strategy and return whilst not perfect is close. Black (1986) comments that correlation of stock prices and return are observable. It is also possible to observe the correlations among the returns on different stocks.

The CAPM is specified ex-ante the event and is a theory based on investors' unobservable beliefs about future returns on securities in equilibrium. The CAPM proves that the relationship between asset prices in general equilibrium, where the investors select assets to maximize the mean-variance utility, is linear (Islam and Oh 2000).

According to Oh (2001), and Islam, Oh and Watanapalachaikul (2001), the capital asset pricing equation from the microeconomic foundations of portfolio choice could be explained as:

$$V_t(s) = \sum_{k=1}^{K} r_{tk} s_k \tag{5.12}$$

where vector s is (s1, s2,..., sk), v is the value of the portfolio, s is the quantities of each of the K assets held in portfolio, and r_{tk} is the return of the assets in each period t.

The expected value of the portfolio s equals the sum of the expected returns from the individual assets weighted by the quantities of the assets held in the portfolio:

$$\mu(s) = \sum_{k=1}^{k} \mu_k s_k \tag{5.13}$$

where μ_k is the expected return from asset k $(k=1, ..., k)$. The variance of the value of holding portfolio s for a specific period is denoted by:

$$\sigma^2(s) = \left[\sum_{k=1}^{K} s_k \right] \left[\sum_{j=1}^{J} s_j \sigma_{jk} \right]. \tag{5.14}$$

When we differentiate $\mu(s)$ and $\sigma^2(s)$ with respect to asset s_H we get:

$$\mu_H(s) = \mu_H \tag{5.15}$$

where $\mu_H(s) = \partial\mu_H(s)/\partial\mu_H$ denotes the partial derivative of $\mu_H(s)$ with respect to s_H, and denoting the partial derivative of $\sigma^2(s)$ with respect to s_H by $\sigma_H^2(s) = \partial\sigma^2(s)/\partial\sigma_H$:

$$\sigma_H^2(s) = 2\left(\sum_{k=1}^{K} s_k \sigma_{HK} \right) \tag{5.16}$$

or:

$$\sigma_H^2(s) = 2\sigma(s, H).$$

Thus, $\sigma(s,H) = \sum_{k=1}^{k} s_k \sigma_{Hk}$, is the covariance between the return of the entire portfolio and the return of the single asset H.

In optimising the value of the asset portfolio of some investor $i \in (1,2,\ldots\ldots, i)$:

$$\text{Max } s = V^i(\mu(s), \sigma^2(s)) \tag{5.17}$$

subject to $\sum_{k=1}^{K} p_k s_k = \sum_{k=1}^{K} P_k \bar{s}_k$, and denoting that $V^i_1 = \partial V^i / \partial \mu$ and $V^i_1 = \partial V^i / \partial \sigma^2$, the first order conditions for this problem are as follows:

$$\left| V^i_1 \left(\mu(s), \sigma^2(s) \right) \left(\mu_H(s) \right) \right| + \left| V^i_2 \left(\mu(s), \sigma^2(s) \right) \left(\sigma^2_H(s) \right) \right| - \left[\lambda(P_H) \right] = 0 \tag{5.18}$$

for $H = 1, \ldots, k$, and:

$$\sum_{k=1}^{k} p_k s_k = \sum_{k=1}^{k} P_k \bar{s}_k \tag{5.19}$$

where λ is the Lagrange multiplier of the budget constraint. The CAPM is derived from the first order condition of equation (5.18) at equilibrium, and assuming that one of the assets is riskless.

The first order conditions implicitly define share demand as follows:

$$s^i_H = f^i_H(p_1, p_2, \ldots, p_k; \bar{s}^i_1, \bar{s}^i_2, \ldots, \bar{s}_k) = \sum_{i=1}^{i} \bar{s}^i_k = S_k \tag{5.20}$$

where S_k is the aggregate quantity of the asset (stocks) available in the market. If we assume all the assets to be stocks, then the quantity of stocks demanded is the equilibrium with the available supply.

To derive the CAPM equation from equation (5.18), we assume asset k is risk-free, then the return is $r_{tk}=r$ for all $t=1, \ldots, t$. The partial derivatives of the expected return and variance function with respect to the changes in the size of asset k in the portfolio are:

$$\mu_k(s) = r \tag{5.21}$$

and:

$$\sigma^2_H(s) = \sigma(s, k) = 0. \tag{5.22}$$

Substituting these values into the first-order conditions and choosing the riskless asset as numeraire $p_k=1$, we solve the k th first order condition for the Lagrange multiplier as:

$$\lambda = V_{i1}[\mu(s^{*i}), \sigma^2(s^{*i})](r). \tag{5.23}$$

Substituting for λ, $\mu_H(s)$ and $\sigma_H^2(s)$, the first K-1 first-order condition of equation (5.18) becomes:

$$\left| V_1^i\left(\mu(s^{*i}), \sigma^2(s^{*i})\right)\left[\mu_H - p_H^*(r)\right]\right| + \tag{5.24}$$

$$2\left| V_1^i\left(\mu(s^{*i}), \sigma^2(s^{*i})\right)\left[\sum_{j=1}^{k} s_j^{*i}(\sigma_{jH})\right]\right| = 0$$

Rewriting this equation as:

$$\Phi^i(s^{*i})(\mu_H - p_H^*(r)) = \sum_{j=1}^{k} s_j^{*i}(\sigma_{jH}) \tag{5.25}$$

where:

$$\Phi^i(s^{*i}) = -\frac{V_1^i(\mu(s^{*i}), \sigma^2(s^{*i}))}{2V_1^i(\mu(s^{*i}), \sigma^2(s^{*i}))} . \tag{5.26}$$

This could be seen as the marginal rate of substitution along an investor's indifference curve in (μ, σ) space.

In equilibrium and over all investors:

$$\sum_{i=1}^{I} s_k^{*i} = S_k \tag{5.27}$$

and:

$$\theta(s^*)(\mu_H - p_H^*(r)) = \sigma(S, H) \tag{5.28}$$

where:

$$\theta(s^*) = \sum_{i=1}^{I} \Phi^i(s^{*i}) \tag{5.29}$$

$$\theta(S, H) = \sum_{j=1}^{k} S_j \sigma_{jH} . \tag{5.30}$$

The covariance of asset H with the aggregate of assets A is $(A_1, \ldots, A_k)$. Multiplying equation (5.28) by S_H and summing up all risky assets $H=1, \ldots, K-1$, we obtain:

$$\theta(s^*)[(\mu(S) - r)(V_0(s)] = \sigma^2(S). \tag{5.31}$$

The mean return on aggregate assets is defined as:

$$\mu(S) = \sum_{H=1}^{k} \mu_H S_H \tag{5.32}$$

and the market value of the market portfolio is defined as:

$$V_0(S) = \sum p_H A_H .$$ (5.33)

Solving equation (g) for $\theta(s^*)$ and substituting into equation (5.28) we are able to obtain the CAPM equation for asset units:

$$\left[(\mu - r)(p_H^*)\right] = \frac{\sigma(S,H)}{\sigma^2(S)}\left[\mu(S) - rV_0(S)\right] .$$ (5.34)

In financial economics, the pay-off unit of investment is measured by the expected rate of return in equilibrium represented by:

$$(E)\mu_k = \frac{\mu_k}{p_k^*}$$ (5.35)

and by the optimal investment share in total expenditure on asset k, instead of the optimal quantity of assets in investment. Expected investment in asset k is measured by:

$$(E)A_k^* = A_k^* \frac{p_k^*}{V_0^i} .$$ (5.36)

Dividing equation (5.34) by p_H and $V_0(S)$ on the right-hand side, we have:

$$(\hat{\mu}_H - r) = \frac{\hat{\sigma}(s,H)}{\hat{\sigma}^2(S)}(\hat{\mu}(S) - r)$$ (5.37)

where:

$\hat{\mu}(S) = \dfrac{\mu(S)}{V_0(S)}$ = the average return on the market portfolio per unit of investment;

$\hat{\sigma}(S,H) = \dfrac{\sigma(S,H)}{p_h V_0(s)}$ = the covariance between the asset H and the market portfolio per unit of investment; and

$\hat{\sigma}^2(S) = \dfrac{\hat{\sigma}^2(S)}{V_0(S)^2}$ = the variance of the market portfolio per unit of investment.

Replacing $\dfrac{\hat{\sigma}(S,H)}{\hat{\sigma}^2(S)}$ with β_H in equation (5.37), we have the CAPM expression for the expected return on a particular stock:

$$(\hat{\mu}_H - r) = \beta_H(\hat{\mu}(S) - r)$$ (5.38)

or:

$$(\hat{\mu}_H) = r + \beta_H(\hat{\mu}(S) - r) .$$

The above equation, which states that in equilibrium, the expected return of each risky asset is equal to the riskless rate of return plus the difference between the expected rate of return on the market portfolio and the riskless rate for each individual risk class.

Finally, expected return is $\mu_i = ER_i$ then the CAPM expression is:

$$ER_i = R_f + \beta (ER_m - R_i). \tag{5.39}$$

The CAPM is a useful method and relevant to stock valuation where it posits a simple and stable linear relationship between an asset's systematic risk and expected returns. Three factors need to be determined in order to use the CAPM for estimating the required rate of return: the risk-free rate, the market risk premium and the systematic risk (beta, β).

According to Islam and Oh (2003, 2000), the standard procedure for estimating beta is simply to regress stock returns against market returns and to use the slope of the regression as the beta. However, some studies such as Akdenis, Salih and Caner (2002), and Fama and French (1992), have found weak or non statistical evidence in support of this simple relationship between an asset's systematic risk and expected return. Criticisms against the CAPM include the suggestion that since the market portfolio could never be observed, the CAPM could never be tested and that all tests of the CAPM were effectively joint tests of the model and the market portfolios used in the tests (Islam and Oh 2003). Stimulated by these findings, a number of researchers have sought to find alternative explanations for the risk and return trade off.

5.2.3 The Arbitrage Pricing Theory

The Arbitrage Pricing Theory (APT)[2] can be seen as an alternative to the CAPM to determine the expected rate of return on particular stocks and on portfolios of stocks. In the CAPM there is only one factor that influences expected return which is the covariance between the return on the stock and the return on the market portfolio (Cuthbertson 1996). However, the APT incorporates a larger number of factors that affect the rate of return on a particular stock (Madala 2001; Cuthbertson 1996). Empirical evidence suggests that the APT explains expected returns better than the single factor CAPM (Cuthbertson 1996; Berry, Burmeister and McElroy 1988; Chen Ross and Roll 1986; Chen 1983). The APT is defined as:

$$R_{it} = R_{it}^e + u_{it} \tag{5.40}$$

where R_{it} is the actual rate of return on the ith stock, R_{it}^e is the expected rate on the ith stock and u_{it} is the unexpected, surprise and news element. The element

---

[2] The APT is often referred to as a *multi-factor* or *multi-index* model (Madala 2001; Cuthbertson 1996).

u_{it} could also be seen as a combination of *systematic* or *market risk* m_t, and *unsystematic*[3] risk ε_{it}. This could be written as:

$$u_{it} = m_t + \varepsilon_{it} \tag{5.41}$$

given that, $m_{it} = \sum_j \beta_{ij}(F_j - EF_j)_t$, where F is the economy-wide factors (indexed by j).

The crucial assumption of the APT worth mentioning is that the unsystematic risk is uncorrelated across different stocks:

$$\text{cov}(\varepsilon_i, \varepsilon_j) = 0. \tag{5.42}$$

Assuming that all investors have homogeneous expectations E and that the return R_{it} on any stock is linearly related to a set of k factors F_{ij}, the return will be defined as:

$$R_{it} = \alpha_i + \sum_{j=1}^{k} \beta_{ij} F_{ij} + \varepsilon_{it} \tag{5.43}$$

where β_{ij} is the factor weights or the sensitivity of the stock return. Taking the expectations E of (j) and assuming $E\varepsilon_{it} = 0$, and subtracting it from actual value of F_{jt}:

$$R_{it} = ER_{it} + \sum_{j=1}^{k} \beta_{ij}(F_{jt} - EF_{jt}) + \varepsilon_{it}. \tag{5.44}$$

Equation (5.44) shows that the impact of any particular F_j depends on the value of β_{ij} being different for each stock.

According to Cuthbertson (1996), the APT could be summed up in two equations. One is (5.43) and the other is:

$$ER_{it} = \lambda_0 + \sum_{j=1}^{k} \beta_{ij}\lambda_j. \tag{5.45}$$

It is possible to interpret λ_j assuming that the value of β_{ij} is known. Then $\lambda_0 = r_t$ or the risk free rate.[4]

---

[3] Sometimes called idiosyncratic or specific risk.
[4] For details see Cuthbertson (1996, pp. 64–65).

5.2.4 Estimation of the Valuation Model

For estimating and testing valuation models of Thai stocks involving the relationships between stock prices, the dependent variable, and one or more of the identified independent variables, the multiple regression methods were used (Islam 2001; Mills 1999; Campbell, Lo and MacKinlay 1997). For such econometric estimation of valuation models of Thai stocks, the valuation model for T observations is specified as follows:

$$Y = X\beta + e \qquad (5.46)$$

where Y = a vector of a dependent variable (stock price) to be observed; $X = (t*k)$ non-stochastic design matrix of explanatory variables; $\beta = (k*1)$ unknown (to be estimated) matrix of explanatory variables such as income, inflation, the exchange rate, etc., which are known; and $e = (1*t)$ unobservable random error vector.

The usual assumptions in this model are the following: $E(e) = 0$; and a constant variance: $E(e'e) = \sigma^2 I_t$.

If X has k rank and $X'X$ is non-singular, the econometric estimation by the least squares method involves the estimation of β by minimising the squared equation errors and the minimisation rule provides the vector of estimated β coefficients as:

$$\hat{\beta} = (X'X)^1 XY. \qquad (5.47)$$

The classical least squares method is based on some crucial assumptions: normal distribution, no autocorrelation, constant variance, no simultaneous dependence, identifiability and no multicollinearity. In econometric modelling of valuation models, it should be determined whether these assumptions are valid in observations so that the use of the classical least squares method for estimating the model can be justified. Some statistics used for model selection and hypothesis testing are t-statistic, R^2 and standard error.

Several econometric computer programs were used including Excel and Stata to estimate the valuation models in this book.

5.2.5 Limitation of Current Models

Today, most stocks earning history has fluctuated in recent years and stock prices are too volatile to be rational forecasts of future dividends (Islam and Oh 2003). The DCFM and CAPM do not fully reflect all the important factors for valuating the stocks such as the changes in economic conditions and technology. These factors or variables include: changes in the financial market; the money and capital market; the foreign exchange market; goods; the gold and commodities market; the stock market; changes in government regulation and policies; and changes in consumer behavior. A multi-factor model can overcome these limitations of the equilibrium models. Therefore a multi-factor modelling approach is adopted.

5.2.6 Relation between Macroeconomic Factors and Stock Prices

There is a growing number of empirical studies regarding the fundamental connection between stock price and key macroeconomic factors. Fama (1981) found a positive relationship between stock returns and economic factors such as GNP, money supply, capital expenditure, industrial production and interest rates. Chen, Roll and Ross (1986) also found a correlation between stock market returns and macroeconomic factors such as inflation, industrial production, money supply, the exchange rate, and interest rates by using an APT model.

Other recent studies that focus on the relationship between stock prices or returns and macroeconomic, microeconomic and international factors in different countries include: Dhakal, Kandil and Sharma (1993) and Abdullah and Hayworth (1993) on the US stock market; Cheng (1995) studies U.K. stock price returns and macroeconomic factors; Fung and Lie (1990) investigate the Taiwanese stock market and macroeconomic factors; Sukhamongkhon (1994) studies the relationship between Thai stock returns and microeconomic factors; Brown and Otsuki (1990) study the stock returns and macroeconomic factors in Japan; and Kwon, Shin and Bacon (1997) examine the Korean stock market and macroeconomic factors. Wongbangpo and Sharma (2002), Nasseh and Strauss (2000), and Kiranand (1999) study the relationship between stock returns and macroeconomic factors in five or more Asian countries. Finally, Islam and Oh (2003) study the relationship between the return of e-commerce stocks and macroeconomic and international factors.

5.3 Models, Econometrics Methodology and Data

5.3.1 Variable Selection, Macroeconomic and International Factors

In Chapter 2, we hypothesized the need for a new stock valuation model that can represent the interrelationships among different markets, which are components of the Thai financial system. These markets are the money and capital markets, foreign exchange market and stock market. In addition, since we expect our model to operate in an open economy including factors at the international level, real goods markets such as goods, gold and commodities markets, along with government investment, have been added to the analysis. All these factors are listed under separate categories in Table 5.1.

Table 5.1. Factors categories

Categories	Regressor code
a) Financial market factors	
Bank deposit	BD
Bank loan	BL
Interest rate	IR
b) Money and capital market factors	
Money market instruments	MMI
Bonds	BND
c) Foreign exchange market factors	
Exchange rate	FX
d) Stock market factors	
Stock market index	SMI
Price earning ratio	PE
Dividend yield	DY
Market capitalization	MC
e) Goods, gold and commodities market factors	
Gross domestic product	GDP
Gold reserve value	GLD
Export	EX
Import	IM
Consumer price index	CPI
f) Government investment factors	
Government expenditure	GE

Financial Market Factors

Commercial banks play a major role in the Thai financial market where they hold around seventy per cent of the total financial assets; therefore, bank deposits, bank loans and interest rates are chosen as variables for the model. Generally, bank deposits reflect household saving levels and bank loans reflect household investment levels which are also dependent on the interest rate. The ability of interest rates to affect returns is regarded as an important factor in the understanding of investments (Peiro 1996).

Money and Capital Market Factors

Money market instruments consist of securities that are used to transfer funds from one party to the other and usually are short-term funds. Some money market instruments are provided by the Central Bank of Thailand, but most are private sector securities. On the other hand, bonds are usually long-term capital market funds with more than one year to maturity (Juttner and Hawtrey 1997).

Foreign Exchange Market Factors

In addition to the discussion in Chapter 2, the exchange rate expresses the price of the US dollar in terms of the Thai Baht. The devaluation of the Thai currency in July 1997 had an immediate impact on: 1) the national balance of trade – a devaluation is expected to stimulate an economy by encouraging the growth of net exports; 2) the inflation rate – aggravating pre-existing problems with inflation; and 3) international liabilities – increasing the country's external debts especially the lending from international banks, mainly in Japan and the U.S. (CSES 1998).

Stock Market Factors

The stock market index measures the market value of all local and foreign companies which have their stocks listed on the stock exchange of Thailand. Price changes in each security cause a rise or a fall of the SET Index, in proportion to the security's market value. The P/E ratio is a measure of the market sentiment regarding the attractiveness of a particular stock, in this case, the P/E ratio is measured for all stocks listed on the SET. Several studies such as those by Ball (1978), Shiller (1984) and Fama and French (1988) find evidence that dividend yields and returns are correlated. According to Oh (2001), market capitalization represents the total market value of listed domestic equities calculated at month-end for all equities listed on the SET including preference shares and excluding overseas domiciled stocks compiled by the Central Bank of Thailand.

Goods, Gold, and Commodities Market Factors

The basis of the relationship between stock prices, returns and future economic growth rates of real activities is evident in the studies of Tongzon (1998) and Chia and Pacini (1997), who measure gross domestic product (GDP). The gold and commodities market in Thailand has given rise to opportunities for investors, brokers, and overseas bullion dealers to trade, hedge or arbitrage gold and other commodities in Thailand. Exports and imports are commonly used in identifying the relationship between stock prices/returns and international trade. Finally, the consumer price index measures the average level of prices of goods and services.

Government Investment Factors

Government expenditure, especially transfer payments, is the most important economic stabilizer particularly when the economy goes into recession or crisis. Government expenditure is one effective way to stimulate the economy, and hence it could stimulate the stock prices.

5.3.2 Multi-Factor Model

The development of this valuation model makes a valuable contribution to our understanding of the effects of the internal and external factors that influence stock prices and return. Significant factors that influence the value of stocks are identified using the multiple regression technique. Hypothesis testing is conducted to find a basis for making a probability statement about the true values of population regression coefficients (Islam and Watanapalachaikul 2001; 2002c; 2002d).

We argue that the standard valuation models DCFM and CAPM are based on the assumption of perfect financial market. However, as we have discussed in Chapter 2, there are market imperfections in the Thai financial system. Therefore, a valuation model for Thai stocks will be developed based on the multiple-factor modelling approach incorporating key factors/variables. Factor modelling provides identification of the key factors and variables and proves the time convergence at an appropriate rate by model simulation as well as identifying the relationship between an exogenous variable and multiple endogenous factors. Mathematically, a linear multiple factor model can be expressed as follows:

$$R_{it} = \alpha_i + (\beta_1)_i (F_1)_t + (\beta_2)_i (F_2)_t + \ldots + (\beta_n)_i (F_n)_t + \varepsilon_{it} \tag{5.48}$$

where R_{it} is the return of stock i in period t, α_i is the expected value if each factor has a value of zero, $(F_1)_t$ and $(F_2)_t$ are the values of factors 1 and 2 with pervasive influence in period t, $(F_n)_t$ is the value of factor n, $(\beta_1)_i$ and $(\beta_2)_i$ are the prices of factors 1 and 2 (the risk premium) for stock i, $(\beta_n)_i$ is the price of factor n (the risk premium) for stock i, and ε_{it} is the stock specific return.

For the initial development of this new model, the correlation coefficient, unit root and cointegration were tested using Islam and Oh's (2003) process. If macroeconomic variables are significant and consistently priced on the index, they should be cointegrated. This cointegration relationship between the index price and the underlying factors is a necessary condition of the equilibrium model of the stock market price and return. The cointegration analysis takes place in two stages: first, the unit root test is applied to determine their stationarity or nonstationarity, and when the results indicate that the first differenced series of each variable is stationary, a subsequent test is used to determine whether these two variables are cointegrated. The test for unit root is done by using the augmented Dickey Fuller (ADF) test.

5.3.3 Data

Monthly data for the closing SET Index from 1992 to 2001 are used in this study. The choice of time period corresponds to the pre- and post-crisis period. These stock price indexes are obtained from the Stock Exchange of Thailand CD-ROMs and SET Data Service Department. The economic factors are gathered from the Bank of Thailand, the United Nations Research Department, and the International Monetary Funds (International Financial Statistics CD-ROM).

5.4 Results and Implications for Valuation

5.4.1 Unit Root and Cointegration Test

Islam and Watanapalachaikul (2001) have provided an exercise to determine the factors that are considered to have influence on the value of Thai stocks, which can be repeated to see which ones have a relatively higher impact on the valuation of Thai stocks. This was done by examining the correlation coefficient and cointegration of each factor (see Appendix 3 for details). The correlation coefficient gives the quality of a Least Squares Fitting to the original data. The results show that market capitalization, P-E ratio and gold deposit rate have a positive correlation of more than 70 per cent, which means that these variables should tend to increase or decrease together with the stock market index, while bond rate, money market instruments, foreign exchange rate, export and consumer price index have negative correlation of more than 70 per cent.

Table 5.2 summarises the estimation of the correlation coefficients of stock prices and macroeconomic factors, numbers in bold are regarded as having a high correlation coefficient.

Table 5.2. Summary of correlation coefficients for the study

	1992–2001	Pre-Crisis	Post-Crisis
BD	-64%	68%	-66%
BL	22%	51%	72%
IR	39%	-65%	36%
PE	**93%**	**91%**	48%
MMI	**-76%**	49%	-34%
BND	-64%	52%	**-75%**
FX	**-84%**	-47%	**-73%**
DY	4%	**-95%**	40%
MC	**85%**	**88%**	**79%**
GDP	-19%	36%	-14%
EX	**-75%**	56%	-70%
IM	-55%	52%	-45%
GLD	**86%**	62%	**78%**
CPI	**-77%**	46%	**-88%**
GE	-51%	35%	-14%

In addition, we use the augmented Dickey-Fuller (ADF) test to identify the stationarity of each factor. Using the following regression, we can determine the unit root as:

$$\Delta y_t = \alpha_o + \sum \alpha_j (\Delta y_{t-j}) + \beta t + \gamma (y_{t-j}) + \mu_t \qquad (5.49)$$

where μ_t is a pure white noise error term. The Model 1 proposition is defined as:

$$y_t = \mu + \varepsilon_t \qquad (5.50)$$

and the trend stationary (Model 2) is defined as:

$$y_t = \mu + \beta(t) + \varepsilon_t . \qquad (5.51)$$

Model 1 is the model with a non-zero mean and with white noise stationarity, while Model 2 represents the model with a non-zero mean and with trend stationarity. Test statistics are shown in parentheses in Table 5.3.

The optimal lag length for each of the autoregressive processes of the ADF test is determined by Schwert's (1987) formula:

$$L = Int\left[4\frac{n}{100} \right]^{\frac{2}{9}} \qquad (5.52)$$

where n is the number of the observations in the series.

The results of the unit root test for macroeconomic factors are shown in Table 5.3.

Table 5.3. Unit root test for stock prices and macroeconomic factors

	Augmented Dickey Fuller (ADF) test						
	ADF test (model 1)			ADF test (model 2)			
Factors	α_t	α_{t-1}	F	$(\alpha_t)\tilde{}$	$(\alpha_{t-1})\tilde{}$	$(y_{t-1})\tilde{}$	F
BD	192.98	-0.01	0.37	247.71	-0.09	11.90	5.21
	(1.49)	(0.01)		(1.90)	(-2.28)	(2.20)	
BL	220.54	-0.01	0.88	1051.56	-0.002	-15.89	0.13
	(1.02)	(-0.94)		(4.34)	(-0.36)	(-5.61)	
IR	-0.29	-0.01	0.29	0.39	-0.03	-0.002	1.75
	(0.17)	(-0.54)		(1.28)	(-1.32)	(-1.43)	
MMI	5.23	-0.02	1.28	2.11	-0.03	0.08	1.55
	(1.25)	(-1.13)		(0.32)	(-1.24)	(0.62)	
BND	3.08	-0.01	4.08	3.15	-0.02	0.01	0.53
	(3.43)	(-2.02)		(2.90)	(-0.73)	(0.12)	

Table 5.3. (cont.)

FX	0.78	-0.02	0.85	2.06	-0.10	0.02	6.60
	(1.12)	(-0.92)		(2.40)	(-2.57)	(2.43)	
SMI	7.18	-0.01	0.61	81.30	-0.01	-0.70	4.45
	(0.45)	(-0.78)		(2.17)	(-2.13)	(-2.19)	
PE	0.44	-0.04	1.84	2.64	-0.12	-0.02	7.81
	(1.03)	(-1.36)		(2.71)	(-2.78)	(-2.50)	
DY	0.13	-0.06	3.83	0.17	-0.06	-0.001	3.84
	(1.65)	(-1.96)		(1.39)	(-1.96)	(-0.42)	
MC	80.22	-0.04	2.46	17.04	-0.05	-11.02	4.04
	(1.52)	(-1.57)		(2.32)	(-2.01)	(-1.74)	
GDP	11.03	-0.94	1.02	66.20	-1.02	8.36	1.18
	(7.43)	(-1.03)		(3.21)	(-1.09)	(2.99)	
EX	4.92	-0.02	1.21	13.53	-0.28	0.48	18.99
	(1.46)	(-1.10)		(3.60)	(-4.35)	(4.20)	
IM	8.96	-0.05	2.89	21.91	-0.26	0.31	17.34
	(1.90)	(-1.70)		(3.88)	(-4.16)	(3.76)	
GLD	13.30	-0.02	0.87	56.42	-0.06	-0.18	3.71
	(0.81)	(-0.93)		(1.89)	(-1.92)	(-1.73)	
CPI	0.92	-0.01	2.63	-0.04	-0.01	-0.004	0.12
	(2.53)	(-1.62)		(-0.02)	(0.34)	(-0.66)	
GE	18.63	-0.30	2.10	29.01	-0.74	2.96	6.71
	(4.52)	(-4.58)		(7.37)	(-8.19)	(6.26)	

The results show that all the Model 1 ADF tests with white noise stationarity fail to reject the null hypothesis of the existence of a unit root in log levels except GE, since the test statistics in α_{t-1} is greater than (-3.33) (the variables are non-stationary). However, the correct procedure is then to take first differences of y before using it in a regression. Therefore, according to the Model 2 ADF tests with trend stationarity, we can reject the null of a unit root for all factors except EX and IM (since most of the factors yield F statistics which are less than 7.24, where as EX and IM yield 18.99 and 17.34 respectively). As a result, EX and IM are discarded in the further analysis.

Generally, cointegration is used in analysing the relationship between groups of economic factors over time and gives a more conceptually and empirically valid measure of that relationship in the light of nonstationarity of the time series (Watsham and Parramore 1997). Applying the ordinary least square (OLS) regression in the following model, we now have the cointegration regression:

$$y_t = \alpha_0 + \alpha x_t + \mu_y.$$ (5.53)

Table 5.4. Unit root test for macroeconomic factors residuals

Augmented Engle-Granger (AEG) test		
AEG test (model 1)		
Factors	α_t	α_{t-1}	F
BD	2.69 (0.32)	-0.05 (-1.77)	3.16
BL	-4.13 (-0.54)	-0.02 (-1.93)	0.86
IR	-0.72 (-0.09)	-0.04* (-2.18)	1.40
MMI	-0.05 (-0.01)	-0.08* (-2.11)	4.47
BND	2.98 (0.38)	-0.05** (-2.82)	3.50
FX	2.92 (0.28)	-0.13** (-2.97)	8.83
PE	2.01 (0.25)	-0.19** (-3.43)	11.75
DY	-3.67 (-0.46)	-0.02 (-0.85)	0.72
MC	-5.59 (-2.17)	-0.02* (-2.07)	2.46
GDP	-3.35 (-0.28)	-0.05 (-1.60)	1.02
GLD	1.48 (0.17)	-0.11** (-2.631)	6.92
CPI	3.89 (0.52)	-0.06* (-2.25)	2.63
GE	1.84 (0.12)	-2.85** (-4.58)	2.10

Note: (*) indicates rejection of the null hypothesis at the 5 per cent significant level and (**) indicates rejection of the null at the 1 per cent significant level.

To obtain the *error correction model*, we need to estimate residuals of the long-run relationship; where $\mu_y = y_t - \alpha_0 - \alpha x_t$ (results are shown in Appendix 3, Table A3.4, where α is the coefficient). These ADF tests in the present context are known as *augmented Engle-Granger* (AEG) tests. Then we repeat the unit root process on the residuals.

Next, we regress the error corrected factors with statistical significance between 1 and 5 per cent. As a result, BD, BL, DY, and GDP were dropped in the cointegration regression. Therefore, *the cointegration regression* of the remaining variables can be expressed as seen below.

Interest Rate (IR)

$$\Delta \hat{y}_t = 297 + 52.9\Delta x_t - 0.04 e_{t-1} \qquad\qquad R^2 = 15.1\%$$

Money Market Instrument (MMI)

$$\Delta \hat{y}_t = 1048 - 172\Delta x_t - 0.08 e_{t-1} \qquad\qquad R^2 = 57.8\%$$

Bonds (BND)

$$\Delta \hat{y}_t = 1409 - 4.83\Delta x_t - 0.05 e_{t-1} \qquad\qquad R^2 = 41\%$$

Foreign Exchange Rate (FX)

$$\Delta \hat{y}_t = 2172 - 43.7\Delta x_t - 0.13 e_{t-1} \qquad\qquad R^2 = 70.5\%$$

Price Earning Ratio (PE)

$$\Delta \hat{y}_t = -119 + 64.6\Delta x_t - 0.19 e_{t-1} \qquad\qquad R^2 = 86.5\%$$

Market Capitalisation (MC)

$$\Delta \hat{y}_t = -49 + 0.001\Delta x_t - 0.02 e_{t-1} \qquad\qquad R^2 = 71.7\%$$

Gold (GLD)

$$\Delta \hat{y}_t = -1639 + 2.92\Delta x_t - 0.11 e_{t-1} \qquad\qquad R^2 = 73.7\%$$

Consumer Price Index (CPI)

$$\Delta \hat{y}_t = 3269 - 23.19\Delta x_t - 0.06 e_{t-1} \qquad\qquad R^2 = 58.5\%$$

Government Expenditure (GE)

$$\Delta \hat{y}_t = 1566 - 0.01\Delta x_t - 2.85 e_{t-1} \qquad\qquad R^2 = 26.3\%$$

5.4.2 The Factors Determining the Values of the Stocks

The new valuation model, named the Thai Stock Multi-factor Model (TSMM), is described as follows:

$$Y = \alpha + \beta_1 IR + \beta_2 BND + \beta_3 FX + \beta_4 PE + \beta_5 MC + \beta_6 CPI + \varepsilon_t \qquad (5.54)$$

A new stock valuation model is developed, based on a generic six-factor model, the factors being selected from the significant results of the cointegration test.

All six factors in the estimated equation are the highest factors which are significant at the 5 per cent significance level. The result shows an $\bar{R}^2$ of 0.987 which is regarded as very significant (Appendix 3, Table A3.5). It is interesting to see that TSMM includes at least one factor from each of the five different markets identified in Table 5.5.

Table 5.5. Classification of significant factors

Markets in Financial System	Significant Factors
1. Financial Market	⟹ Interest Rate (IR)
2. Money and Capital Market	⟹ Bonds (BND)
3. Foreign Exchange Market	⟹ Foreign Exchange Rate (FX)
4. Stock Market	⟹ Price Earning Ratio (PE) Market Capitalisation (MC)
5. Goods, Gold and Commodities Market	⟹ Consumer Price Index (CPI)

According to the regression result, the systematic risk measured by the multi-factor model explains 98.7 per cent of the Thai stock market index. The estimated equation of the TSMM model is shown below (t-statistics are shown in parentheses):

$$Y = 760.18 + 8.58(IR) - 2.24(BND) + 6.49(FX) + 7.548(PE) + 0.0003(MC) - 7.11(CPI) + \varepsilon_t$$
$$\quad (2.953) \quad (3.894) \quad (-3.156) \quad (4.301) \quad (3.711) \quad (22.734) \quad (-2.245)$$

This study used the cointegration test to investigate the relationship between the SET Index and the underlying economic and financial variables. All six factors in the estimated equation are statistically significant at the 10 per cent significance level and this confirms the evidence of their pervasiveness on the stock price. The unit root test is conducted in identifying the stationarity of the factors and the results indicated that the first differenced series of each factor of the TSMM model are stationary. The TSMM model implies that the financial market, money and capital market, foreign exchange market and goods, gold and commodities market are determinants of stock price value.

5.5 Cointegration Test of the Six-Variable Model

Section 5.4.1 shows the integration of the individual explanatory factors cointe-grated with the dependent variable by using the ADF and AEG tests. There is a need to test the TSMM to see whether all six factors are integrated in long-run equilibrium. In Islam and Oh (2003), the cointegration technique was used in the multi-factor model in which the authors conclude that e-commerce stock returns are cointegrated with the combination of three macroeconomic variables at a 5 per cent significance level in a long-run equilibrium. In addition, it is suggested that the stationarity of the individual explanatory factors can be checked by the means of an ADF test. A similar technique can be applied to the TSMM. From a single-equation perspective of the multi-factor model considerable use has been made of the cointegration specification where a cointegration analysis can be conducted between the dependent variable or stock price and interest rate, bond rate, foreign exchange rate, price earning ratio, market capitalisation, and consumer price in-dex.

Cointegration Test Summary for the TSMM model

$$Y = 760.18 + 8.58(IR) - 2.24(BND) + 6.49(FX) + 7.548(PE) + 0.0003(MC) - 7.11(CPI) + \varepsilon_t.$$
$$ (2.953) \quad (3.894) \quad (-3.156) \quad (4.301) \quad (3.711) \quad (22.734) \quad (-2.245)$$
$$\bar{R}^2 = 0.987$$

Augmented Dickey-Fuller

$$\text{ADF } \varepsilon_t = -0.5784\varepsilon_{t-1} - 0.8474\varepsilon_{t-2} - 0.4738\varepsilon_{t-3} - 0.4321\varepsilon_{t-4} - 0.6451\varepsilon_{t-5} - 0.9741\varepsilon_{t-6}.$$
$$\phantom{\text{ADF }} (-1.231) \quad (-0.7454) \quad (-1.0069) \quad (-2.1452) \quad (-1.6521) \quad (-0.0451)$$

We can conclude that the individual factors of the TSMM are cointegrated and there is no spurious unit root in the test (using the t-statistics of the ADF test for the unit root of the lagged cointegrated residuals). The test for cointegration be-tween IR, BND, FX, PE, MC and CPI, which in the long run reveals a sufficient condition for a joint cointegration among the variables in a long-run regression, is that the error ε_t should be stationary. The residuals based on the ADF test statistics for ε_t suggest the rejection of the null of no cointegration at a 5 per cent signifi-cance level. The cointegrating relation of the linear combination of the six vari-ables is interpreted as an equilibrium relationship.

5.6 The Real Value of Stocks

In this chapter, we have investigated the factors which determine the value of stocks in Thailand. Currently, some organisations are still using financial statements such as ratio analysis, and growth models such as the Gordon growth model or a historical and fundamental growth rate as the basic methods of analysis in determining the real value of businesses or stocks. Generally, there are a large number of investors and stakeholders who rely on financial statements to evaluate the performance of firms and managers (Palepu, Healy and Bernard 2000). However, these methods sometimes contain noisc (Black 1986) where communication by the corporations to investors is not completely credible because of the existence of inside information, moral hazard, asymetric information and adverse selection problems. This considerably affects outside parties' valuation of firms' current and prospective performances, and hence lead to an inaccurate valuation of the firms and their stocks. Furthermore, since these methods can only be applied to individual stocks (as opposed to the aggregate stock market index), they have not been applied in this study.

This study adopts a multi-factor model for valuation of Thai stocks. The results of this multi-factor valuation model show a strong relationship between the financial and real sectors. This implies that macroeconomic, financial and international factors are interdependent. It is clear that all six significant variables appear to play an important role in explaining as much as 98.7 per cent of stock values in the Thai stock market. The results therefore support the premise that macroeconomic, financial and international factors such as interest rate, bonds price, foreign exchange rate, price-earning ratio, market capitalisation and consumer price index are important forces in determining Thai stock values and these factors are interdependent. The interdependence between each factor makes the issue of valuation even more complex to understand by some relatively simple theoretical statements of the financial market such as DCFM and CAPM. Therefore, the estimated TSMM model provides a better valuation model of Thai stocks by incorporating macroeconomic, financial and international factors.

Whilst this finding is consistent with recent studies such as Islam and Oh (2003), Fifield, Power and Sinclair (2002), Wongbangpo and Sharma (2002), Nasseh and Strauss (2000), and Kiranand (1999), which have found a significant role for macroeconomic and international factors in explaining the returns of emerging markets, it does contradict the results of Harvey (1995a, 1995b) who suggested that international factors were not significant in explaining share returns in emerging financial markets.

5.7 Conclusions

The TSMM model revealed a strong, significant long-run relationship during 1992–2001 between stock prices and macroeconomic factors such as the interest rate, bonds price, foreign exchange rate, price-earning ratio, market capitalisation and consumer price index. In addition, these factors explain 98.7 per cent of the stock price, which is regarded as very significant.

We observe that in the long run, the stock indices/prices are positively related to the interest rate, foreign exchange rate, price-earning ratio, and market capitalisation, while a negative long-run relationship is present for the bonds price and consumer price index. The unit root, augmented Dickey Fuller and augmented Engle Granger tests detected the causal relationships between the selected factors to the stock index prices.

6 Models for Rational Speculative Bubbles

6.1 Introduction

Possibly the most controversial issue in finance is whether the financial market is efficient in transmitting information and the allocation of resources or not. A generation ago, a positive view known as the Efficient Market Hypothesis (EMH) was widely accepted by academic financial economists. Many crucial financial issues such as volatility, predictability, speculation and anomalies are also related to the efficiency issue and are all interdependent. The existence of bubbles has been especially controversial since the existence of bubbles contribute to market inefficiency. Binswanger states that "speculative bubbles are thought of as having a negative overall impact on the economy. They are supposed to create additional price risk and increase the instability of the economy" (1999, p. 116). Therefore, in recent years there have been a number of empirical studies attempting to identify rational speculative bubbles in stock prices and returns.

Several studies such as Rappoport and White (1993) and West (1987) found evidence of rational bubbles in stock prices and returns. On the other hand, Diba and Grossma (1988) show empirical evidence to prove the absence of rational bubbles in stock prices. Surprisingly, Harman and Zuehlke (2001) found both existence and non-existence of rational bubbles in the New York Stock Exchange by applying different empirical models, resulting in contradicting conclusions.

Since many studies in this area are non-conclusive and controversial, there is a need to correctly identify and analyse the existence of rational speculative bubbles in the Thai stock market by applying a suitable approach (such as the Weibull Hazard model). The objective of this paper is to empirically investigate the existence of rational bubbles in an emerging stock market, the Thai stock market, to provide a conclusive study on the evidence of bubbles in a stock market. Since many studies on bubbles cannot provide conclusive evidence (see Cuthbertson 1996), this definitive study makes a useful contribution to the literature, especially to the literature on the emerging financial markets. Furthermore, no study on the existence of bubbles in the Thai stock market has been undertaken yet; therefore this paper makes a useful contribution to the Thai literature on finance.

This chapter is organized in five sections. Section 2 provides an overview of bubbles and financial market behaviour. Section 3 underlines the theoretical background, literature reviews and discusses the methods used to identify the existence of bubbles. Section 4 describes the selected models used in the analysis of the Thai stock market. Section 5 contains the source of data used in this analysis and reports the empirical findings on rational speculative bubbles. Section 6 discusses the rational speculative bubbles related issues in the Thai stock market. Finally, Section 7 provides the conclusions of the chapter.

6.2 Rational Speculative Bubbles and Financial Market Behaviour

6.2.1 The Concept of Bubbles

In studies of speculative behaviour (e.g. Cuthberson 1996), there are multiple forms and definitions of speculation. However in this case, the stock market speculation could be explained as the process of buying and selling stocks in order to create capital gains resulting in a process of movements in stock prices which are generally not justifiable on the basis of any economic and financial principles and cannot be sustained. There are four generally adopted concepts of bubbles: rational, irrational, endogeneous and collasing bubbles.

Rational bubbles can exist in a rational valuation model where it is assumed that the traders are perfectly rational, so the stock price contains an element of bubbles resulting in a divergence between the market stock price and the fundamental value of the stock (Cuthbertson 1996).

Rational speculative bubbles are often used by behavioral finance theorists in an attempt to identify behaviour of investors who act irrationally, such as when 'herding' occurs (Cuthbertson 1996). Statman (1988) identifies irrational behaviour of investors as: 1) trading for both cognitive and emotional reasons; 2) trading because they think they have information when they have nothing but noise; and 3) trading because it brings personal satisfaction.

In the theoretical literature on bubbles, studies have been undertaken to determine the conditions and limits of the existence of bubbles in a general equilibrium framework. The rational bubbles literature assumes that stock prices can diverge from economic fundamentals and that a bubble will emerge due to excessive optimism with respect to these fundamentals. Investors (called noise traders) may not trade in a fully rational way (when their stocks are known to be overvalued relative to fundamentals) and therefore sustain the presence of significant bubbles in share prices.

Bubbles in the stock market arise when stock prices are not at the levels consistent with economic fundamentals or stocks are over-valued in comparison with real economic activity. Bubbles b_t can be written in the form of:

$$b_t = p_t - f_t \tag{6.1}$$

where p_t is the stock price at time t, and f_t is the fundamental value.

In the rational bubble concept, a bubble is consistent with rational behaviour of agents. The agents know that stock prices are higher than fundamentals by b_t but still they trade since they know that they can make profit by trading in the market.

Another form of a bubble is an irrational bubble which is a mean-reverting deviation from the fundamentals of stocks caused by irrational behaviour of agents in the form of a feedback trading strategy in which agents buy when the stock prices have already risen with a hope of further rises and sell when the prices have started to fall for a fear that they will fall more. Stochastic bubbles are also discussed in the literature.

Bubbles cause stock price fluctuations, which create stock market instability and inefficiency. Generally when the stock prices diverge from economic fundamentals, bubbles will emerge due to excessive optimism with respect to fundamentals. In some cases, investors might recognize an excess in stock prices compared with economic fundamentals, and they might find an arbitrage opportunity and believe that the excess will continue. However, in the long term, it is quite impossible that such rises in stock prices can be sustained beyond levels consistent with economic fundamentals. Therefore, when stock prices are inflated by a bubble, sooner or later, there will be an inevitable collapse or bursting of the bubble.

6.2.2 Issues about Bubbles

Rational bubbles can exist in a rational valuation model where it is assumed that the traders are perfectly rational, still the stock price contains an element of bubbles resulting from a divergence between the market share price and the fundamental value of the stock (Cuthbertson 1996).

A wide range of controversial issues regarding the existence and influence of bubbles in the stock market have dominated the literature of the economic analysis of the stock market including the following:

(1) What is a bubble and what are the different forms of bubbles?
(2) Can bubbles exist in the stock market and the economy?
(3) Do bubbles contribute to volatility in the stock market?
(4) What is the relative importance of economic fundamentals (as represented by the discounted net present values of stocks) and bubbles in determining stock returns?
(5) What are the different tests for the existence of bubbles?
(6) How conclusive are the standard tests of bubbles about the existence of bubbles?
(7) In addition to the evidence of the various bubble tests, what are the other characteristics of the stock market such as predictability, valuation, mechanism, volatility, anomalies, etc., considered as evidence of the existence of bubbles?
(8) If bubbles do exist in the stock market, what are the financial theory and regulatory implications of their existence?

Research on the behaviour of stock market indices (or prices) and returns has focused on addressing the above issues and providing information about these issues so that an improved understanding of the stock market dynamic is possible by academics, analysts and the policy makers.

6.3 Different Models

Many approaches have been developed to identify the existence of rational bubbles in stock prices and returns. One of the earlier and most popular approach is the cointegration and the unit-root process (see Diba and Grossman 1988; Campbell and Shiller 1987) where the unit-root process is tested for stationarity or non-stationarity of the residuals between asset prices and market fundamentals. This process has been criticized by Wu and Xiao (2002) and Charemza and Deadman (1995) for having serious drawbacks in detecting bubbles. They found that the unit root process could not identify bubbles correctly when the market price contains *collapsible bubbles*, so that the hypothesis of a bubble is not equivalent to the hypothesis of a unit root by conducting a Monte Carlo simulation.

Other approaches include the two methods of West (see Mills 1999; Cuthbertson 1996), the Duration Dependence test (McQueen and Thorley 1994), the Weibull Hazard model (Mudholkar, Srivastava and Kollia 1996) and Simulation Time Series Analysis (Wu and Xiao 2002; Fung 2001). The two methods of West and simulation time series analyses have several limitations in testing bubbles. The use of time series simulation is considered to be in the early stages of model development, and hence, this approach is not yet fully accepted. The Duration Dependence test and Weibull Hazard model are more widely accepted (Fung 2001; Harman and Zuehlke 2001), because of their robustness in testing for rational speculative bubbles. Therefore these two models will be adopted in testing the existence of rational bubbles in this study.

Two classical models of rational speculative bubbles are *rational expectation model* (see Mills 1999; Campbell, Lo and MacKinlay 1997; Wu 1997; Cuthbertson 1996) and a stochastic model of bubbles (see Fung 2001).

The rational expectation model is defined as:

$$P_t = \frac{1}{(1+r)} E_t(P_{t+1} + D_{t+1}) \qquad (6.2)$$

where P_t is the real stock price at t, r is the constant rate of return and thus $1/(1+r)$ is the discount factor, and D_{t+1} is the dividend paid to the owner of the stock between t and $t+1$.

According to Campbell, Lo and MacKinlay (1997), if the conditional distribution of prices is normal, then there will always be a positive probability of obtaining a negative price (violation of limited liability). Therefore, the price and dividend could be interpreted in terms of a logarithm or logarithm neperiano:

$$p_t + q = k + \delta E_t p_{t+1} + (1-\delta)E_t d_{t+1} \tag{6.3}$$

where p_t and d_t are logarithms of P_t and D_t, q is the log gross return rate and is the average ratio of the stock price to the sum of the stock price and dividend, and k is a function of δ (Wu 1997). Under the following transversality condition:

$$\lim_{k \to \infty} \delta^k E_t p_{t+k} = 0. \tag{6.4}$$

If the transversality condition does not hold, the logarithm of the price has the following form:

$$p_t = f_t + b_t \tag{6.5}$$

where b_t is a rational speculative bubble generated by extraneous events, and f_t is the market fundamental given by:

$$f_t = \eta + (1-\delta)\sum_{j=0}^{\infty} \delta^j E_t d_{t+1+j} \tag{6.6}$$

and:

$$E_t b_{t+1} = \frac{1}{\delta} b_t. \tag{6.7}$$

The second type of bubble is a stochastic process (see Fung 2001) where the next period bubbles grow with a random error. Rational speculative bubbles are b_t, and u_{t+1} is an error term which can either be additive or multiplicative. Addictive random errors are defined as:

$$b_{t+1} = \lambda_{t+1} b_t + u_{t+1} \tag{6.8}$$

where λ_{t+1} is the random variable such that the expected value of λ_t, $E\lambda_t$ is $1+r$. In addition, bubbles with a multiplicative random error are defined as:

$$b_{t+1} = \lambda_{t+1}(b_t u_{t+1}). \tag{6.9}$$

The rational bubbles with a multiplicative error must satisfy sub-martingale and non-negativity conditions. The sub-martingale condition assumes that $E_{t-1}(b_t) = (1+r)b_{t-1}$. The non-negativity is achieved by assuming that $\lambda_t = \exp(\Theta_t)$ and $u_t = \exp(U_t)$, where $\Theta_t \sim IIN(\ln(1+r) - \frac{\sigma_\theta^2}{2}, \sigma_\theta^2)$ and $U_t \sim IIN(-\frac{\sigma_\theta^2}{2}, -\sigma_\theta^2)$ (Fung 2001).

6.4 Adopted Models

To investigate the existence of rational speculative bubbles, we employ the Duration Dependence test using the Discrete Log Logistic model developed by McQueen and Thorley (1994) and the Weibull Hazard model by Mudholkar, Srivastava and Kollia (1996).

6.4.1 Discrete Log Logistic Model

The discrete log logistic model is defined as (Harman and Zuehlke 2001; Zorn 2000):

$$\ln L(\alpha, \beta) = \sum_{i=1}^{N} \{J_i \ln[g(t_i)] + (1 - J_i) \ln[1 - G(t_i)]\} \tag{6.10}$$

where α is the shape parameter of the lognormal distribution, β is the duration elasticity of the hazard function, J_i is a duration of the process or time to exit from a state, g_t is the discrete density function for duration, and G_t is the corresponding distribution function. The discrete density and distribution functions for duration are related as:

$$G(t_i) = \sum_{k=1}^{t_i} g(k). \tag{6.11}$$

However, if the law of conditional probability is applied (Harman and Zuehlke 2001), the density for completed duration is:

$$g(k) = h(k) \prod_{m=0}^{k-1} [1 - h(m)]. \tag{6.12}$$

In addition, McQueen and Thorley (1994) use the logistic distribution function ψ evaluated at a linear transformation of log-duration as:

$$h(k) = \psi[\alpha + \beta \ln(k)] = \{1 + \exp[-\alpha - \beta \ln(k)]\}^{-1}. \tag{6.13}$$

6.4.2 Weibull Hazard Model

The Weibull model is defined as (Harman and Zuehlke 2001):

$$S(t) = \exp(-\alpha t^{bt+1}) \tag{6.14}$$

where S(t) is the probability of survival in a state to at least time (t) and the corresponding hazard function is:

$$h(t) = \alpha(\beta + 1)t^{\beta} \tag{6.15}$$

where α is the shape parameter of the Weibull distribution, and β is the duration elasticity of the hazard function. The fundamental assumption of the Weibull Hazard model is a linear relationship between the log of the hazard function and the log of duration, where:

$$\ln[h(t)] = \ln[\alpha(\beta + 1] + \beta \ln(t) . \tag{6.16}$$

To demonstrate the existence of rational speculative bubbles using the Duration Dependence and Weibull Hazard tests, the closing stock index of the Stock Exchange of Thailand and dividend yield are required. Fama and French (1989) argue that the dividend yield is useful in predicting time-varying risk primia. The dividend yield is the value weight of the SET portfolio. The corresponding sequence of runs is determined by the length of the runs, which is the number of consecutive periods.

It is hypothesized that rational speculation bubbles exist when the rate of return of the stock price between the period t-1 and t is growing faster than the rate of return of the dividend yield at the same period. According to the rational expectation theory, we hypothesize that:

$$E_t P_t = P_t + b_t \tag{6.17}$$

given that:

$$P_t = \delta(P_{t+1} + D_{t+1}) . \tag{6.18}$$

Therefore, the gap between the expected return and the real return is considered to be caused by a bubble.

6.5 Data and Empirical Results

Both monthly and daily data for the closing SET Index during 1992 to 2001 is used in this study. Four time periods are analysed, which can be described as:

1) Overall period   1992 to 2001
2) Pre-crisis period   1992 to 1996
3) Post-crisis period   1997 to 2001
4) Yearly period   1992 to 2001

The model, $\ln L(\alpha, \beta) = \sum_{i=1}^{N} \{J_i \ln[g(t_i)] + (1 - J_i) \ln[1 - G(t_i)]\}$, lays the foundation for the Duration Dependence test, and $\ln[h(t)] = \ln[\alpha(\beta + 1] + \beta \ln(t)$, lays the foundation for the Weibull Hazard test. The empirical results of the estimates of the Duration Dependence test are shown in Tables 6.1 and 6.2.

The estimates of Weibull Hazard model are presented in Tables 6.3 and 6.4, where the maximum likelihood estimates and likelihood ratio tests with one degree of freedom are reported.

Table 6.1. Runs of the duration dependence test for monthly data

Year	α	ln [gamma]	gamma	Log like-lyhood	LR test [p-value]
1975–2001	-0.2554 (0.0111)	-1.1544 (0.0451)	0.3152 (0.0142)	-258.62	341.72 (0.0001)
1992–1996	-0.3437 (0.0141)	-3.2307 (0.1058)	0.0395 (0.0041)	74.81	151.09 (0.0001)
1997–2001	0.0699 (0.0266)	-1.8438 (0.1052)	0.1582 (0.0166)	-7.78	6.91 (0.0086)
1992	-0.2823 (0.0267)	-4.0761 (0.2466)	0.0169 (0.0041)	24.87	25.80 (0.0001)
1993	-0.4348 (0.0353)	-3.4347 (0.2508)	0.0322 (0.008)	16.91	29.44 (0.0001)
1994	-0.4166 (0.028)	-4.6747 (0.2397)	0.0093 (0.0022)	32.30	35.74 (0.0001)
1995	-0.3755 (0.0505)	-4.285 (0.2608)	0.0137 (0.0035)	26.73	18.16 (0.0001)
1996	-0.3670 (0.0070)	-5.157 (0.236)	0.0057 (0.0013)	38.21	68.16 (0.0001)
1997	-0.2860 (0.0184)	-3.5304 (0.2443)	0.0292 (0.0071)	18.38	36.79 (0.0001)
1998	0.1261 (0.0737)	-1.9673 (0.2396)	0.1398 (0.0335)	-0.21	2.25 (0.1338)
1999	-0.4735 (0.0801)	-3.2906 (0.238)	0.0372 (0.0088)	15.74	17.05 (0.0001)
2000	0.9217 (0.0491)	-3.9724 (0.2535)	0.0188 (0.0047)	23.34	40.07 (0.0001)
2001	-0.1912 (0.037)	-3.9974 (0.2439)	0.0183 (0.0044)	23.90	16.14 (0.0001)
1992–2001	0.0988 (0.0517)	-1.0232 (0.0732)	0.3594 (0.0263)	-112.06	3.63 (0.0566)

Note: α is the size of the bubbles, *gamma* is the instantaneous exit rate and *ln(gamma)* is the instantaneous hazard rate. Numbers shown in parentheses are standard errors except those in LR test column which are p-values. The log likelihood is the logarithm of the joint probability density function. The LR test is for null hypothesis of no duration dependence. The LR statistic is asymptotically x^2 with 1 degree of freedom.

Table 6.2. Runs of the duration dependence test for daily data

Year	α	ln [gamma]	gamma	Log likelihood	LR test [p-value]
1975–2001	n/a	n/a	n/a	n/a	n/a
1992–1996	-0.2916	-3.7723	0.0395	1325.94	1670.61
	(0.0033)	(0.0299)	(0.0041)		(0.0001)
1997–2001	0.07247	-1.8013	0.165	-210.60	139.49
	(0.0061)	(0.0232)	(0.0038)		(0.0001)
1992	-0.0134	-3.0828	0.0458	271.17	0.2
	(0.0304)	(0.0523)	(0.0023)		(0.6577)
1993	-0.2925	-2.477	0.0839	102.12	28.94
	(0.0517)	(0.0576)	(0.004)		(0.0001)
1994	-0.4208	-4.325	0.0132	566.17	553.87
	(0.0092)	(0.0538)	(0.0007)		(0.0001)
1995	-0.3755	-4.285	0.0137	26.73	293.68
	(0.0505)	(0.2608)	(0.0035)		(0.0001)
1996	-0.3694	-5.2895	0.005	804.27	1416.36
	(0.0013)	(0.0532	(0.0002)		(0.0001)
1997	-0.2905	-3.2817	0.0375	324.16	618.41
	(0.0058)	(0.052)	(0.0019)		(0.0001)
1998	0.064	-1.8621	0.1553	-24.71	20.95
	(0.0141)	(0.0517)	(0.008)		(0.0001)
1999	-0.4928	-3.1891	0.0412	298.95	315.92
	(0.0207)	(0.052)	(0.0021)		(0.0001)
2000	-0.5146	-3.7165	0.0243	423.51	723.96
	(0.0078)	(0.0533)	(0.0012)		(0.0001)
2001	-0.1795	-3.7587	0.0233	430.19	198.89
	(0.0106)	(0.0534)	(0.0012)		(0.0001)
1992–2001	0.0525	-0.9375	0.3915	-1991.21	17.7
	(0.0125)	(0.0179)	(0.007)		(0.0001)

Note: α is the size of the bubbles, *gamma* is the instantaneous exit rate and *ln(gamma)* is the instantaneous hazard rate. Numbers shown in parentheses are standard errors except those in the LR test column which are p-values. The log likelihood is the logarithm of the joint probability density function. The LR test is for null hypothesis of no duration dependence. The LR statistic is asymptotically x^2 with 1 degree of freedom.

Table 6.3. Runs of the Weibull Hazard test for monthly data

Year	α	ln [p]	λ	Log likeli-hood	LR test [p-value]
1975–2001	-0.3026	0.871	0.4184	-233.91	400.41
	(0.0082)	(0.0465)	(0.0194)		(0.0001)
1992–1996	-0.3635	2.5682	0.0766	66	124.18
	(0.0171)	(0.0882)	(0.0067)		(0.0001)
1997–2001	0.1004	1.3489	0.261	-10.85	16.01
	(0.0228)	(0.0965)	(0.0252)		(0.0001)
1992	-0.26	3.5709	0.0281	24.43	26.40
	(0.0254)	(0.2184)	(0.0061)		(0.0001)
1993	-0.4404	3.2038	0.0406	18.73	38.95
	(0.0191)	(0.2426)	(0.0098)		(0.0001)
1994	-0.4051	4.2027	0.0149	32.04	34.95
	(0.0288)	(0.2176)	(0.0032)		(0.0001)
1995	-0.4055	4.0446	0.0175	28.62	22.50
	(0.0375)	(0.2442)	(0.0042)		(0.0001)
1996	-0.3645	4.8375	0.0079	39.02	67.23
	(0.0041)	(0.2347)	(0.0018)		(0.0001)
1997	-0.3041	3.0854	0.0457	18.29	35.25
	(0.0141)	(0.2277)	(0.0104)		(0.0001)
1998	0.1296	1.7185	0.1793	1.24	5.02
	(0.0536)	(0.2394)	(0.0429)		(0.025)
1999	-0.4855	2.8422	0.0582	15.65	16.35
	(0.0596)	(0.2179)	(0.0127)		(0.0001)
2000	0.9587	3.297	0.0369	21.68	39.49
	(0.08)	(0.2051)	(0.0075)		(0.0001)
2001	-0.2429	3.3161	0.0362	21.81	11.48
	(0.077)	(0.2156)	(0.0078)		(0.0007)
1992–2001	-0.0383	0.684	0.5045	-107.43	0.39
	(0.0607)	(0.0705)	(0.0378)		(0.534)

Note: α is the size of the bubbles, λ is the instantaneous exit rate and $ln(p)$ is the instantaneous hazard rate. Numbers shown in parentheses are standard errors except those in the LR test column which are p-values. The log likelihood is the logarithm of the joint probability density function. The LR test is for null hypothesis of no duration dependence. The LR statistic is asymptotically x^2 with 1 degree of freedom.

Table 6.4. Runs of Weibull Hazard test for daily data

Year	α	ln [p]	λ	Log like- lihood	LR test [p-value]
1975–2001	n/a	n/a	n/a	n/a	n/a
1992–1996	-0.3437 (0.0141)	3.3786 (0.0288)	0.034 (0.0009)	1339.49	1596.09 (0.0001)
1997–2001	0.1052 (0.0053)	1.3004 (0.0212)	0.2724 (0.0005)	-272	324.15 (0.0001)
1992	-0.1338 (0.0303)	2.5966 (0.0485)	0.0745 (0.0036)	260.56	17.07 (0.0001)
1993	-0.0288 (0.1006)	1.577 (0.0448)	0.2065 (0.0092)	27.78	0.08 (0.7741)
1994	-0.4055 (0.0082)	3.6976 (0.0448)	0.0247 (0.0011)	538.67	526.55 (0.0001)
1995	-0.4067 (0.0106)	3.847 (0.0556)	0.0213 (0.0011)	533.83	384 (0.0001)
1996	-0.3663 (0.001)	4.7839 (0.0476)	0.0083 (0.0003)	794.62	1342.53 (0.0001)
1997	-0.3022 (0.0038)	2.8783 (0.0498)	0.0562 (0.0028)	326.81	606.64 (0.0001)
1998	0.0972 (0.0136)	1.524 (0.0514)	0.2178 (0.0112)	-12.5	48.92 (0.0001)
1999	-0.499 (0.0155)	2.7116 (0.0481)	0.0664 (0.0032)	289.79	306.56 (0.0001)
2000	-0.5732 (0.0133)	3.1575 (0.0501)	0.0425 (0.0021)	399.78	713.58 (0.0001)
2001	-0.2372 (0.0188)	3.2335 (0.0496)	0.0394 (0.0019)	415.13	164.43 (0.0001)
1992–2001	-0.3446 (0.018)	0.5579 (0.018)	0.5723 (0.0103)	-1922.39	4.34 (0.0373)

Note: α is the size of the bubbles, λ is the instantaneous exit rate and *ln(p)* is the instantaneous hazard rate. Numbers shown in parentheses are standard errors except those in the LR test column which are p-values. The log likelihood is the logarithm of the joint probability density function. The LR test is for null hypothesis of no duration dependence. The LR statistic is asymptotically x^2 with 1 degree of freedom.

Table 6.5. Summary of the results of the duration dependence and Weibull Hazard tests

Year	DD – Monthly α	WH – Monthly α	DD – Daily α	WH – Daily α
1975–2001	-0.2554458	-0.3026306	n/a	n/a
1992–1996	-0.3437964	-0.36355	-0.2916168	-0.3010924
1997–2001	0.0699114*	0.1004323*	0.0724716*	0.1052452*
1992	-0.2823224	-0.2600498	-0.0134382	-0.1337965
1993	-0.434855	-0.4404215	-0.2925718	-0.0288201
1994	-0.4166478	-0.4051263	-0.4208818	-0.4055613
1995	-0.3755235	-0.4055728	-0.3604701	-0.4067694
1996	-0.3670404	-0.3645129	-0.3694731	-0.366379
1997	-0.2860517	-0.3041832	-0.2905493	-0.3022275
1998	0.1261683*	0.1296854*	0.0640916*	0.0972772*
1999	-0.473512	-0.4855359	-0.4928002	-0.4990586
2000	0.9217006*	0.9587039*	-0.5146781	-0.5732041
2001	-0.1912209	-0.2429695	-0.1795834	-0.2372162
1992–2001	0.0988104*	-0.0383979	0.0525267*	-0.0344637

Note: (*) indicates the rejection of the null where no rational speculative bubble is present.

The estimates of the Duration Dependence and Weibull Hazard models reported in Table 6.5 are consistent with the presence of rational speculative bubbles. For the overall period (1975–2001), rational bubbles are indicated where α is negative. The presence of bubbles was significantly high before the crisis period, especially in 1993, 1994, 1995 and 1996 with monthly α value of approximately -0.43, -0.42, -0.38, and -0.37 respectively. These results are evidence for the conclusive existence of rational speculative bubbles during the pre-crisis period (1992–1996). The tests of daily data produce similar results in all test periods.

In contrast, estimates of these two models provide evidence against the presence of rational speculative bubbles after the crisis period (1997–2001) where α is positive since the bubbles were burst by this time. The presence of rational bubbles is significant in the years 1993, 1994, 1995, 1996 and 1999 with an average negative α of less than -0.3. In short, this indicates that during these periods there are speculation and arbitrage opportunities which make returns on stock prices grow even faster than the return on dividends. Hence, this influences the bubble to grow over time.

The finding implies that bubbles keep growing until a crisis point is reached where either they burst and are no longer present, or demise to a much smaller size. A simulation of sizes of rational speculative bubbles for the Stock Exchange of Thailand is shown in Figures 6.1 and 6.2.

6.6 Rational Speculative Bubbles in the Thai Stock Market

Thailand's economy has experienced extremely large fluctuations of stock price bubbles during the past decade due to its periods of emergence, expansion and crisis. If stock prices were at levels consistent with economic fundamentals, price fluctuations would not be considered a serious problem for the Thai economy. However, rational speculative bubbles over-expanded during the stock market boom and the rapid decline in stock values which followed had a negative effect on the economy causing instability in the capital market. Rational speculative bubbles were also blamed as one of the reasons for poor market performance during the past few years (Moosa 2003b; Fox 2001).

The results of the rational speculative bubble tests in Figures 6.1 and 6.2 clearly indicate the existence of bubbles in the Thai stock market. The bubbles were driven by various factors especially speculation, and as a result, stock prices rose too high and too fast (from about 600 points in 1990 to 1,700 points in 1994). Eventually when the bubbles burst after the Asian financial crisis (indicated in Table 6.5 where α is positive in 1998), stock prices dropped rapidly to their fundamental values especially in the property, communications and technology sectors.

During 1999 and 2000, the bubbles grew larger because of uncertainty in the stock market, caused by high volatility in stock prices. The increase in uncertainty of the Thai financial market after the crisis and stock market crash, increased the severity of speculation, adverse selection and moral hazard problems in the market. Because of worsening investment conditions and uncertainty about the health of the stock market, investors, especially overseas, began to withdraw their funds and postpone future investment. Regarding the real value of stocks, the existence of bubbles implies that the Thai stock market during the periods of 1992–1997 and 1999–2002 was overvalued.

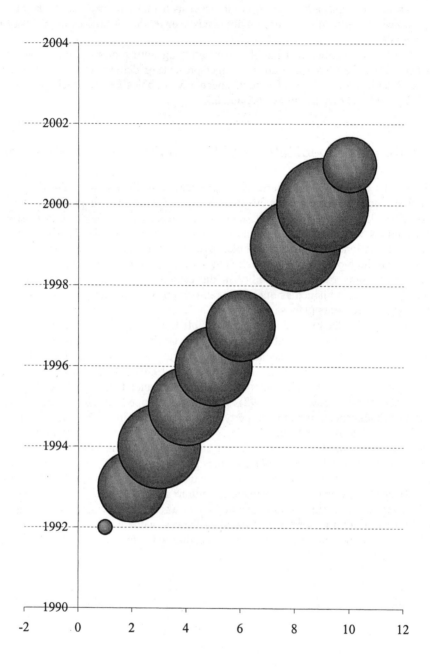

Fig. 6.1. Simulation of sizes of rational speculative bubbles on daily data, the duration dependence test, 1992–2001

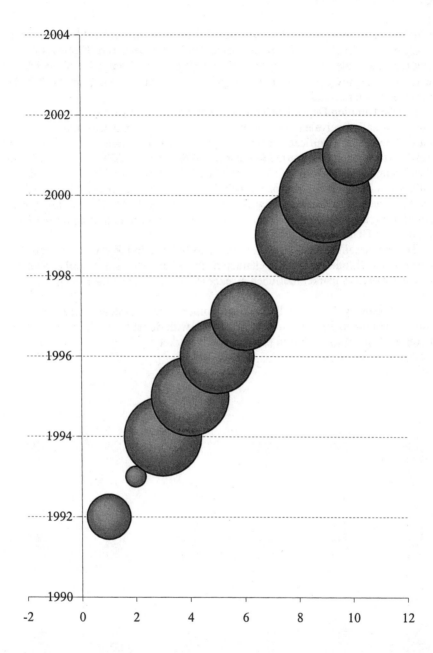

Fig. 6.2. Simulation of sizes of rational speculative bubbles on daily data, the Weibull Hazard model, 1992–2001

6.7 Conclusions

Empirical analyses provide the evidence for the existence of bubbles in the Thai stock market. These results are consistent with McQueen and Thorley's (1994) Duration Dependence Test results, where a rational speculative bubble is present when α is negative. The Weibull Hazard model of Mudholkar et al. (1996) also provides similar results.

For the Duration Dependent Test, the negative value of gamma heterogeneity is observationally equivalent to a Weibull Hazard λ. The presence of rational speculative bubbles is significant during the pre-crisis period especially in 1993 and 1994, before the bubble started to burst in 1996. After the crisis when the price of the closing index was down from an average of 1600 points in 1994 to just around 300 points in 1997, the size of the bubble was much smaller and disappeared in 1998. However, the bubble grew larger again during 1999. This could have resulted from arbitrage and speculative behaviour of investors trading on the Stock Exchange of Thailand.

The empirical evidence of the existence of bubbles in the Thai stock market is consistent with other empirical characteristics of the Thai stock market found in this study such as market inefficiency, excess volatility, anomalies and predictability.

The following chapter will examine another issue regarding market imperfections called anomalies. A multiple regression with dummy variables will be used in the analysis of anomalies in the Thai stock market.

7 Models for Anomalies Studies

7.1 Introduction

One of the implications of the EMH is that stock prices and returns are distributed identically and independently. In one line of research on EMH, the effects of calendar time on stock prices have been examined to determine the empirical relevance of the above proposition of EMH. Although initially four types of investigations were conducted, recently much attention in empirical finance has been focused to study stock market anomalies in more areas including the day of the week effect, the January effect, the weekend and holiday effects, the semimonthly effect, and the turn of the month effect. A considerable number of studies on this issue have often resulted in inconclusive findings. They have found long-term historical anomalies in many stock markets revealing the complexities of the real life financial systems, which seem to contradict EMH.

This chapter examines daily seasonal anomalies (day of the week effect) and the monthly seasonal anomalies (the January effect) for the case of the Thai stock market. A thorough analysis is made using returns derived from the SET Index, · adjusted for geometric returns by using logarithm neporiano to identify the behaviour of investors in this market. Data gathered from the SET includes both monthly and daily returns prices from January 1992 to December 2001.

This chapter is divided into four sections. Section 1 introduces the issue. Section 2 provides an overview of the anomalies in the stock market. Section 3 describes the nature of the methodology. Section 4 reports the empirical findings on the day of the week effect and the January effect. Section 5 discusses the anomaly issues in the Thai stock market. Finally, the conclusion of the chapter is provided in Section 6.

7.2 Anomalies in the Stock Market

Anomalies refer to regularities that appear in the trading of stocks. Many researchers have found certain empirical regularities that influence stock returns and which are not predicted by any of the traditional asset pricing models. Two most significant forms of regularities are the day of the week effect and the January effect.

Some empirical studies on the day of the week and weekend effects, include Cross (1973), Fama (1965), French (1980), Gibbons and Hess (1981), Keim and Stambaugh (1984), Jaffe and Westerfield (1985), Abraham and Ikenberry (1994), Aggarwal and Tandon (1994), Al-Loughani and Chappell (2001), and Cabello and Ortiz (2002). According to the EMH, the expected daily returns on stocks are the same for all days of the week, i.e. the expected returns of a selected stock is the same for Monday as it is for the rest of the week. However, French (1980) examined the average daily return on the NYSE-listed securities and found evidence that the average returns on Monday were negative, whereas the other days of the week had positive average returns.

The January effect could be viewed as a similar phenomenon to the weekend effect except that the stock prices appear to be higher during the early days of January. The studies of Henk (2001), Nassir and Mohammad (1987) and Roll (1983) found average monthly returns in January were higher than the average returns in any other months. According to Sharpe, Alexander and Bailey (1999), there is no certain explanation to what actually causes expected stock returns to be higher in certain months than in others. However, in some cases, investors sell stocks at the end of the year to accrue capital losses which can be offset against capital gains to reduce tax liability, producing the so-called tax loss selling effect (but only if the tax year ends in December and this is not the case in the U.S. or Australia). This could cause average returns in January to be higher than any other month. This anomaly has also been documented by Reiganum (1983), Chen and Singal (2001), and Cabello and Ortiz (2002).

7.3 Tests of Anomalies in the Thai Stock Market

7.3.1 The Day of the Week Effect

A standard methodology is initially employed to test for daily seasonality in stock market adjusted returns by estimating the following regression formula:

$$R_t = \beta_1 D_1 + \beta_2 D_2 + \beta_3 D_3 + \beta_4 D_4 + \beta_5 D_5 + \varepsilon_t \tag{7.1}$$

where $\beta_1, \beta_2, ..., \beta_5$ are parameters, ε_t is an error term and D_1, D_2, D_3, D_4 and D_5 are dummy variables for Monday, Tuesday, Wednesday, Thursday, and Friday (i.e. $D_1 = 1$, if t is Monday, 0 otherwise).

The closing stock market index was used in the analysis. The period examined is from January 1992 to December 2001. The comparisons between pre-crisis and post-crisis periods are also undertaken. The Thai stock exchange market is open from Monday to Friday, so Saturday and Sunday were excluded from this period and the review covered 2454 trading days. Tested results are given in Appendix 4.

Adjusted returns were used in testing seasonal daily anomalies, and is calculated as $R_t = \ln(I_t / I_{t-1}) \times 100$, which is the logarithmic neporiano difference. In the case of a day following a non-trading day, the return is calculated using the closing price indices of the latest trading day.

7.3.2 The January Effect

Many empirical studies have found evidence of high returns during the month of January. Ho (1990), using daily returns for the period between 1975 and 1987, found that six of the Asia Pacific stock markets (Hong Kong, Korea, Malaysia, Philippines, Singapore and Taiwan) had significantly higher returns during January. Henke (2001) found positive returns in the Polish Stock Market for the months of January and February. In addition, Cabello and Ortiz (2002) also found positive returns during January in the Mexican Stock Market.

A typical model that is quite similar to seasonal daily anomalies is employed to test the month of the year effect or the January effect on adjusted returns (see Chapter 3) for the Stock Exchange of Thailand by estimating the following regression formula:

$$R_t = \beta_1 M_1 + \beta_2 M_2 + \beta_3 M_3 +,...,+ \beta_{12} M_{12} + \varepsilon_t \qquad (7.2)$$

where $\beta_1, \beta_2, \beta_3,..., \beta_{12}$ are parameters, ε_t is an error term, and M_1, M_2, M_3,..., and M_{12} are dummy variables for January, February, March ,..., until December (where $M_1 = 1$, during January, 0 otherwise).

7.4 Empirical Results

7.4.1 The Day of the Week Effect

The results of the estimated model along with the degrees of freedom, t-test, p-value, and adjusted R^2 are shown in Appendix 4.

a) The Overall Period, 1992–2001

$$R_t = -0.42\ D_1 + 0.26 D_2 + 0.55 D_3 + 0.42 D_4 + 0.66 D_5 + \varepsilon_t \ .$$

The estimated ordinary least-squares (OLS) regression equation indicates that the SET returns R_t is inversely related to the Monday D_1 returns but directly related to the Tuesday D_2, Wednesday D_3, Thursday D_4 and Friday D_5 returns.

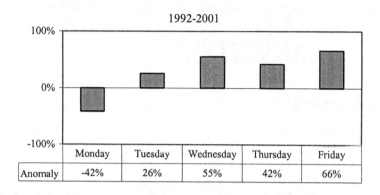

Fig. 7.1. The day of the week effect, 1992–2001, annualised

Tests for seasonality on daily returns during the pre-crisis and post-crisis periods are shown in Figures 7.2 and 7.3. The results, with some differences in the magnitude of average returns, are very similar to the overall period.

b) The Pre-Crisis Period, 1992–1996

$$R_t = -0.32\ D_1 + 25D_2 + 0.49D_3 + 0.40D_4 + 0.52D_5 + \varepsilon_t \ .$$

The estimated OLS regression equation indicates the SET returns is inversely related to Monday returns but directly related to the Tuesday, Wednesday, Thursday and Friday returns.

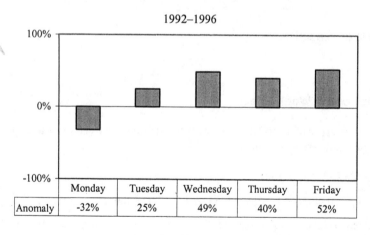

Fig. 7.2. The day of the week effect, pre-crisis, annualised

c) The Post-Crisis Period, 1997–2001

$$R_t = -0.51\,D_1 + 0.27D_2 + 0.61D_3 + 0.44D_4 + 0.79D_5 + \varepsilon_t\,.$$

Again, the estimated OLS regression equation indicates the SET returns is inversely related to Monday returns but directly related to the Tuesday, Wednesday, Thursday and Friday returns.

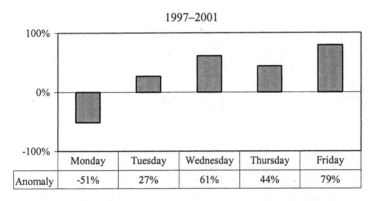

	Monday	Tuesday	Wednesday	Thursday	Friday
Anomaly	-51%	27%	61%	44%	79%

Fig. 7.3. The day of the week effect, post-crisis, annualised

In all three cases, Monday shows the lowest and negative returns and Tuesday produces a similar positive return compared to the pre-crisis period. It is interesting to see relatively high average stock returns on Wednesday and Friday compared to a low on Monday. During the post-crisis period, the differential between Monday and the best performing day is significantly large, reflecting the high volatility of the market after the crisis and the possibilities of obtaining extraordinary gains.

Examining the day of the week effect for particular years, between 1992–2001, we get the following results.

1) Year 1992

$$R_t = 0.21\ D_1 - 0.83D_2 - 0.16D_3 + 0.22D_4 + 0.15D_5 + \varepsilon_t\ .$$

The estimated OLS regression equation indicates the SET returns is inversely related to Tuesday and Wednesday returns but directly related to the Monday, Thursday and Friday returns. This result contradicts the other findings where average stock returns are usually negative on Monday but positive on other days of the week.

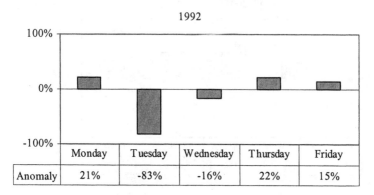

	Monday	Tuesday	Wednesday	Thursday	Friday
Anomaly	21%	-83%	-16%	22%	15%

Fig. 7.4. The day of the week effect, 1992, annualised

2) Year 1993

$$R_t = -0.28\ D_1 + 0.40D_2 + 0.91D_3 + 0.60D_4 + 0.73D_5 + \varepsilon_t\ .$$

The estimated OLS regression equation indicates the 1993 SET returns follows the usual pattern and is inversely related to Monday returns but directly related to the Tuesday, Wednesday, Thursday and Friday returns.

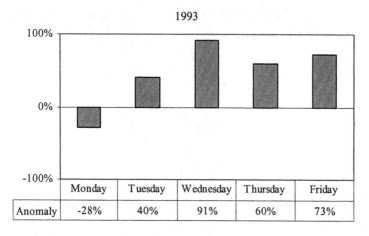

	Monday	Tuesday	Wednesday	Thursday	Friday
Anomaly	-28%	40%	91%	60%	73%

Fig. 7.5. The day of the week effect, 1993, annualised

3) Year 1994

$$R_t = -0.54 \, D_1 + 0.71D_2 + 0.54D_3 + 0.36D_4 + 0.61D_5 + \varepsilon_t \,.$$

The estimated OLS regression equation indicates the SET returns is inversely related to Monday returns but directly related to the Tuesday, Wednesday, Thursday and Friday returns.

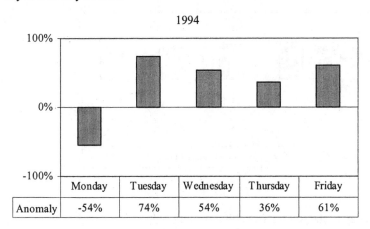

	Monday	Tuesday	Wednesday	Thursday	Friday
Anomaly	-54%	74%	54%	36%	61%

Fig. 7.6. The day of the week effect, 1994, annualised

4) Year 1995

$$R_t = -0.54 \, D_1 + 0.71D_2 + 0.54D_3 + 0.36D_4 + 0.61D_5 + \varepsilon_t \,.$$

The estimated OLS regression equation indicates the SET returns is inversely related to Monday returns but directly related to the Tuesday, Wednesday, Thursday and Friday returns.

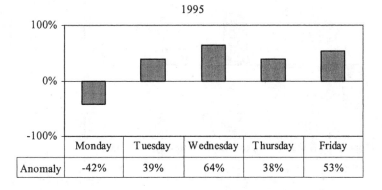

	Monday	Tuesday	Wednesday	Thursday	Friday
Anomaly	-42%	39%	64%	38%	53%

Fig. 7.7. The day of the week effect, 1995, annualised

5) Year 1996
$$R_t = -0.61\ D_1 + 0.55D_2 + 0.52D_3 + 0.46D_4 + 0.62D_5 + \varepsilon_t\ .$$

The estimated OLS regression equation indicates the SET returns is inversely related to Monday returns but directly related to the Tuesday, Wednesday, Thursday and Friday returns.

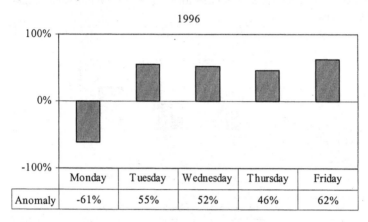

Fig. 7.8. The day of the week effect, 1996, annualised

6) Year 1997
$$R_t = -0.7\ D_1 - 0.04D_2 + 0.69D_3 + 0.22D_4 + 0.33D_5 + \varepsilon_t\ .$$

The estimated OLS regression equation indicates the SET returns is inversely related to Monday and Tuesday returns but directly related to the Wednesday, Thursday and Friday returns.

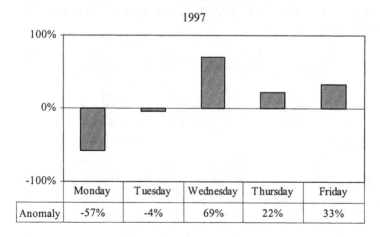

Fig. 7.9. The day of the week effect, 1997, annualised

7) Year 1998

$$R_t = -0.50D_1 - 0.02D_2 + 0.75D_3 + 0.78D_4 + 0.89D_5 + \varepsilon_t .$$

The estimated OLS regression equation indicates the SET returns is inversely related to Monday and Tuesday returns but directly related to the Wednesday, Thursday and Friday returns.

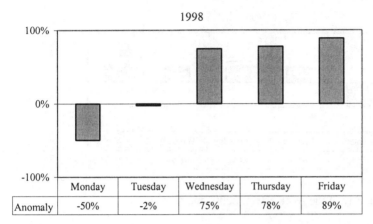

	Monday	Tuesday	Wednesday	Thursday	Friday
Anomaly	-50%	-2%	75%	78%	89%

Fig. 7.10. The day of the week effect, 1998, annualised

8) Year 1999

$$R_t = -0.18 D_1 + 0.38D_2 + 0.10D_3 + 0.32D_4 + 0.71D_5 + \varepsilon_t .$$

The estimated OLS regression equation indicates the SET returns is inversely related to Monday returns but directly related to the Tuesday, Wednesday, Thursday and Friday returns.

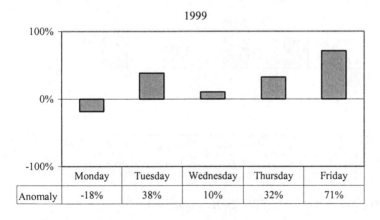

	Monday	Tuesday	Wednesday	Thursday	Friday
Anomaly	-18%	38%	10%	32%	71%

Fig. 7.11. The day of the week effect, 1999, annualised

9) Year 2000
$$R_t = -0.95D_1 + 0.64D_2 + 0.86D_3 + 0.61D_4 + 1.41D_5 + \varepsilon_t .$$

The estimated OLS regression equation indicates the SET returns is inversely related to Monday returns but directly related to the Tuesday, Wednesday, Thursday and Friday returns.

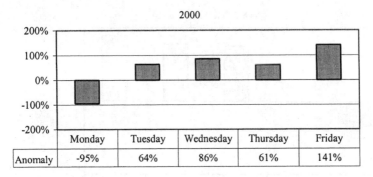

	Monday	Tuesday	Wednesday	Thursday	Friday
Anomaly	-95%	64%	86%	61%	141%

Fig. 7.12. The day of the week effect, 2000, annualised

10) Year 2001
$$R_t = -0.36D_1 + 0.40D_2 + 0.69D_3 + 0.30D_4 + 0.65D_5 + \varepsilon_t .$$

The estimated OLS regression equation indicates the SET returns is inversely related to Monday returns but directly related to the Tuesday, Wednesday, Thursday and Friday returns.

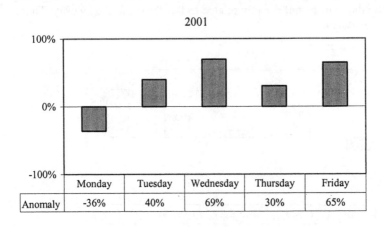

	Monday	Tuesday	Wednesday	Thursday	Friday
Anomaly	-36%	40%	69%	30%	65%

Fig. 7.13. The day of the week effect, 2001, annualised

To sum up, in most of the results, Monday shows the lowest negative returns. Tuesday generally reports positive returns, however, during 1997 and 1998, it shows negative return but at a much lower rate than Monday. Seasonality is also present in Wednesday, Thursday and Friday with positive returns. Friday records the highest percentage of anomalies in stock returns followed by Wednesday and Thursday respectively.

7.4.2 The January Effect

The month of the year anomaly (the January effect) results are illustrated as follows.

a) Overall period, 1975–2001

$$R_t = 3.01M_1 - 3.99M_2 - 3.75M_3 - 3.66M_4 - 1.16M_5 - 3.66M_6 - 2.79M_7 - 3.45M_8 - 3.67M_9 - 2.03M_{10} - 3.84M_{11} - 0.90M_{12} + \varepsilon_t \,.$$

The estimated OLS regression equation indicates that the SET returns R_t is inversely related to every month, i.e. February to December M_2 - M_{12} returns, except January.

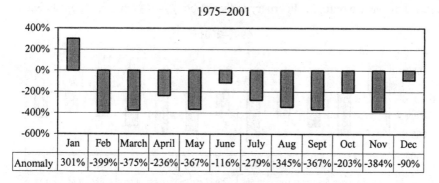

	Jan	Feb	March	April	May	June	July	Aug	Sept	Oct	Nov	Dec
Anomaly	301%	-399%	-375%	-236%	-367%	-116%	-279%	-345%	-367%	-203%	-384%	-90%

Fig. 7.14. The January effect, 1975–2001, annualised

b) Pre-crisis period, 1992–1996

$$R_t = -1.17\,M_1 - 0.95M_2 - 3.12M_3 - 0.52M_4 + 3.21M_5 + 1.88M_6 + 0.33M_7 + 3.70M_8 + 2.97M_9 + 4.92M_{10} - 2.90M_{11} + 6.00M_{12} + \varepsilon_t \,.$$

The estimated OLS regression equation indicates that the SET returns is inversely related to January, February, March, April and November returns but positively related to the May, June, July, August, September, October and December returns.

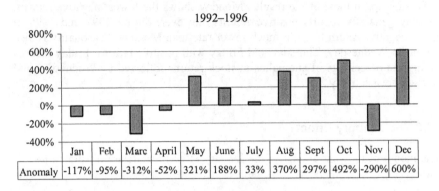

Fig. 7.15. The January effect, 1992–1996, annualised

c) Post-crisis period (1997–2001)

$$R_t = 12.68 - 19.57\beta_2 - 16.29\beta_3 - 10.72\beta_4 - 23.90\beta_5 - 10.84\beta_6 - 18.50\beta_7$$
$$-19.45\beta_8 - 16.07\beta_9 - 11.52\beta_{10} - 9.67\beta_{11} - 12.17\beta_{12} + \varepsilon_t .$$

The estimated OLS regression equation indicates the SET returns R_t is inversely related to every month, i.e. February to December $\beta_2 - \beta_{12}$ returns, except January.

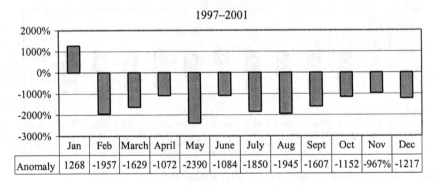

Fig. 7.16. The January effect, 1997–2001, annualised

Figures 7.14, 7.15, 7.16 and Table 7.2 summarize the findings on the month of the year effect or the January effect at the Stock Exchange of Thailand.

7.5 Anomalies in the Thai Stock Market

Traditionally, business and financial activities have a slow start on Mondays since all financial intermediaries, stock market, and other organizations are closed on Saturday and Sunday. This pause produces an inertia effect and slow start on Mondays as well as a quiet space where information such as bad news occurring during the weekend may have more effect on the Monday performance than it might, had it occurred during the busy work week.

Interestingly, the evidence of some negative returns on Tuesdays for the first two years of the post-crisis period is not in line with the traditional view of the day of the week effect. This may be caused by international factors which have considerable influence on emerging markets in most developing countries including Thailand. Movements in stock prices and the announcement of information from major international stock markets, i.e. Wall Street and Dow Jones, are observed by local investors after a delay. Thailand is in a different time zone than the United States and European countries, having a difference of about 13 hours with US central time and 7 hours with London. Therefore, stock price movement and any information announced in the US and UK on Monday would have an effect on the stock exchange of Thailand on Tuesday.

Friday generally records the highest anomalies in returns of the week and is most likely influenced by foreign portfolio investor behaviour. Table 7.1 sums up the empirical results of the day of the week effect.

Table 7.1. Empirical results, the day of the week effect

	Monday	Tuesday	Wednesday	Thursday	Friday
1992–2001	-0.42	0.26	0.55	0.42	0.66
1992–1996	-0.32	0.25	0.49	0.40	0.52
1997–2001	-0.51	0.27	0.61	0.44	0.79
1992	0.21	-0.83	-0.16	0.22	0.15
1993	-0.28	0.40	0.91	0.60	0.73
1994	-0.54	0.74	0.54	0.36	0.61
1995	-0.42	0.39	0.64	0.38	0.53
1996	-0.61	0.55	0.52	0.46	0.62
1997	-0.57	-0.04	0.69	0.22	0.33
1998	-0.50	-0.02	0.75	0.78	0.89
1999	-0.18	0.38	0.10	0.32	0.71
2000	-0.95	0.64	0.86	0.61	1.41
2001	-0.36	0.40	0.69	0.30	0.65

The 1992 result contradicts the classical view of seasonal daily anomalies where Monday and Friday appear to have undergone a certain reversal in roles. In this case, Monday (and Thursday) recorded the highest anomalies in returns while

Friday only posted a very moderate return compared to its usual high. Also, the volatility in stock returns on Thursday and Friday in 1992 dropped significantly to just around and below 20 per cent respectively. This compares to the pre-crisis period, which recorded positive returns of around 40–50 per cent. Continuing the contrary pattern for 1992, Tuesday exhibited the second largest negative return along with the only negative return on a Wednesday for the period 1992–2001.

In fact, speculative factors could come into play in this low-return Monday and high-return Tuesday and Friday. The differential between Monday and Tuesday is significantly large and creates a distinct possibility of obtaining extraordinary gains in this market through speculative activities. One scenario is that speculators could employ short-term trading to buy stocks on Monday and then sell on Tuesday. This would cause the stock return on Wednesday to be lower compared to Tuesday. Then speculators would buy again and sell on Friday. The result of such speculative behaviour and the effect from international portfolio markets is that stock market returns appear to be the lowest on Monday and the highest on Friday.

The typical seasonal monthly anomalies were clearly present in most of the periods, except during the pre-crisis period, when a positive the January effect was present. From the first day of trading on the Stock Exchange of Thailand in 1975, a positive the January effect was present throughout the whole period, 1975–2001. This behaviour is consistent with the null hypothesis advanced to explain the January effect in the U.S. stock market (Roseff and Kinney 1976; Ho 1990) where six Asian stock markets, Hong Kong, Korea, Malaysia, Philippines, Singapore, and Taiwan were investigated and higher returns were found during January. Table 7.2 summarizes the empirical results of the January effect.

Table 7.2. Empirical results, the January effect

Month	1975–2001	1992–2001	1992–1996	1997–2001
January	3.0143	4.5190	-1.1694	12.6812
February	-3.9920	-9.0208	-0.9485	-19.5670
March	-3.7461	-8.4667	-3.1205	-16.2867
April	-2.3641	-4.3848	-0.5188	-10.7247
May	-3.6661	-9.1060	3.2097	-23.8955
June	-1.1638	-3.2446	1.8774	-10.8404
July	-2.7919	-7.8525	0.3252	-18.5042
August	-3.4544	-6.6355	3.7021	-19.4471
September	-3.6694	-5.3155	2.9692	-16.0741
October	-2.0271	-2.0660	4.9156	-11.5216
November	-3.8384	-5.0485	-2.8992	-9.6718
December	-0.9024	-1.8478	5.9959	-12.1654
Degree of Freedom	317	118	58	58
Adjusted R Square	-0.0143	-0.0267	-0.0975	0.0090

A February and May effect were also found with extra low market returns. The presence of an overall "cycle" appears throughout the whole period, especially during the post-crisis period (but not the pre-crisis period) (see Figure 7.16). This cycle could be summarized as: January produces the highest return, followed by large negative returns on February and a general upturn in stock market performance to a high in June. There is a downward trend in July and August, followed by an upward trend through to December.

The most unusual stock market returns were found during the pre-crisis (1992–1996) period where the above cycle is not evident and January stock returns were low contrary to traditional the January effect views, where high stock returns are found. According to Sharpe, Alexander and Bailey (1995), there is no obvious reason to expect stock returns to be higher or lower in certain months than in others. However, for the case of Thailand, these unusual results could be explained by investors' rational speculative behaviour and asymmetric information problems, which dramatically increased during the peak of the Thai economy. Seven of the twelve months report positive returns which result in high May, June, August, September, October and December returns, with December the best performing month. As we have discussed in Chapter 2, the Thai economy during the boom period was characterised by foreign capital flows and a liberal financial policy. These factors combined with cheap labour to attract foreign investment in the Thai economy and in the stock market, which drove the stock market index from 800 points to around 1600 points within 5 years. In addition, speculative bubbles also contributed to the abnormally high rate of return in the Thai stock market during this pre-crisis period.

Comparing the results with other studies on the New York and Tokyo Stock Exchange, we found that our results are similar to the existing literature where the average return in January is clearly higher than the average monthly return in the remaining 11 months.

7.6 Anomalies and Investors Motives

It is suggested that investors could use these anomaly results to predict stock market movements on any particular days or months in order to generate extraordinary profit. For example, investors may buy a number of diversified stocks on Monday, and sell them on Friday to get an average return of approximately 130 per cent (see Figure 7.3), or buy them during December then sell them later during January (see Figure 7.16). By doing so, the primary motivation of the stock market investment can be violated where investors are assumed to secure their returns commensurate with risks for a particular stocks, and for a longer period of time. In fact, they could enjoy these extraordinary excess returns in a short-term, and this could became their dominant motive (Moosa 2003b).

7.7 Conclusions

Empirical evidence from the analysis in this chapter suggests the existence of the day of the week effect and the January effect. The returns differential between Monday and the best performing day is significantly large. This raises the issue of speculation, which we discussed in the previous chapter, where we have seen that there was an opportunity to obtain extraordinary gains in the Thai stock market especially during the pre-crisis period. However, the return volatility after the crisis was greater than before and contributed to the instability of the market immediately after the crisis.

The January effect was also present in most of the time periods except during the pre-crisis periods examined when an unusual negative return in January was identified, along with an unusual positive return in seven other months, December being the month with the highest return followed closely by October. Financial liberalization, massive foreign capital inflows and low labour costs were the major factors that contributed to the boom in the Thai economy as well as its stock market. In addition, a speculative factor also contributed to this "mostly every month" high return on the Thai stock market.

During the post-crisis period, the January effect was identified. The results showed a seasonal trend of returns where February and May were the poorest performing months followed by an overall upward trend until June. A downward trend was detected during July and August, with an improvement in stock return until November and slightly lower return in December.

To confirm the findings of the presence of anomalies in the Thai stock market and seasonal variability of stock prices and to establish the formal frameworks for such fluctuations, we will discuss in the next chapter various models to test further the volatility aspects of the Thai stock market. Various linear and non-linear Generalised Autoregressive Conditional Heteroscedasticity (GARCH) models will be used to identify the level of volatility in the market.

8 Volatility Models

8.1 Introduction

Following the Asian economic crisis and the devaluation of the Thai baht, most financial markets in South East Asian countries, particularly in Thailand, experienced a crash in capital markets and dramatic declines in exchange rates of major currencies (Titman and Wei 1999). The Thai currency lost half of its value against the US dollar within a few months after the announcement of its currency devaluation in 1997. As a result of the crisis, the Thai stock market crashed and stock prices suddenly fell by 70 per cent by the end of 1997, causing the market to be very volatile in subsequent years.

A controversial area of investigation in empirical finance has been the study of the relative volatility of financial time series such as stock prices and returns. The question whether the stock market is excessively volatile or not has produced conflicting and opposing empirical evidence. The choice of models for studying volatility has been controversial and the literature on volatility inconclusive.

Volatility modelling in the emerging financial markets, especially in the stock exchange market, has attracted growing attention by academics in recent years. Volatility modelling is used as a simple risk measure in asset pricing models and undoubtedly, it has been of enormous use in applications such as stocks and derivatives pricing. The study of volatility in the stock market is also crucial for portfolio and risk management. A good understanding of volatility is very useful for investors in the stock market, since high volatility could mean extraordinary gains or losses and hence greater uncertainty.

In fact, there are a large number of volatility models now used in the financial industry. These models and tests can broadly be grouped under three catagories: 1) variance bound tests pioneered by Shiller; 2) cointegration related VAR methods; and 3) ARCH and GARCH models based on a time varying risk premium (Mills 1999; Cuthbertson 1996). Due to the problems associated with tests mentioned in types 1 and 2 above and the inclusiveness of these test for detecting excessive volatility, the Autoregressive Conditional Heteroscedasticity (ARCH) and Generalized-ARCH (GARCH) type of models have been considered appropriate and been applied increasingly to test the presence of excessive volatility in recent years. Several are accepted and used: ARCH and GARCH models; ARMA and ARIMA models; and Stochastic Volatility (SV) models. Simple measures such as standard deviation are also used in applied empirical finance (Islam and Oh 2003).

Even though there is literature on forecasting volatility with various types of models, the choice of the best volatility model is not agreed upon among financial experts. Yu (2002) states that there is no single superior model for analysing and forecasting volatility. Therefore, different stock analysts, who have non-identical expectations and positions, could have different preferences and views of what constitutes volatility risk and the choice of which volatility models should be used.

In this study, ARCH and GARCH type models are adopted due to their advantages and appropriateness. The purpose of this study is not to test the models but to compare the results of five ARCH and GARCH type models, consisting of both linear and non-linear models, used for identifying and predicting volatility on the stock price and seasonal anomalies in Thailand.

This chapter is set out as follow. Section 8.2 reviews various volatility models such as ARCH, ARMA and SV; comments on their limitations are also provided. Section 8.3 shows the adopted GARCH type volatility models to be used in this empirical study to investigate the level of volatility in the Thai stock market. Section 8.4 reports the empirical results on the volatility of the Thai stock market. Section 8.5 discusses the volatility issues in the market. Finally, Section 8.6 concludes this chapter.

8.2 Models for Volatility

For a volatility model being considered to be reliable, it should provide accurate risk or volatility results across different assets, time horizons and risk levels within the same asset class (Danielsson 2002). Some good examples of evaluation and comparison between volatility models are the studies of Poon and Granger (2003), Barndorff-Nielsen, Nicalato and Shephard (2001), Hansen and Lunde (2001), Brooks et al. (2000), and Aydemir (1998).

8.2.1 Autoregressive Conditional Heteroscedasticity (ARCH) Models

Engle (1982) developed a model to describe time-varying variance. The methodology is called Autoregressive Conditional Heteroscedasticity (ARCH) (see Mills 1999). The concept of the ARCH model has led to the development of other related formulations in order to identify and explain the variance of time series. Engle introduced the linear ARCH(q) model where the time varying conditional variance is postulated to be a linear function of the past q squared innovations. The ARCH (q) model is defined by:

$$r_t = \mu + \sigma_t \varepsilon_t \qquad (8.1)$$

and:

$$\sigma_t^2 = \lambda + \alpha_1 (r_{t\text{-}1} - \mu)^2 +,...,+\alpha_q (r_{t\text{-}q} - \mu)^2 \tag{8.2}$$

where r_t is the SET returns, μ is the conditional mean of the return process and is constant, $\varepsilon_t \sim NID(0,1)$ is conditionally Gaussian (*NID* denotes normally and independently distributed), σ_t is the first alternative of the stochastic volatility models and is modelled by a stochastic process, λ_1 and α are real constants, and ε_t are zero mean, uncorrelated, random variables or white noise.

The model could also be represented as:

$$\sigma_t^2 = \lambda + \sum \alpha_1 r_{t-1}^2 + \varepsilon_t . \tag{8.3}$$

Hence the volatility σ_{t+1}^2 can be represented by:

$$\sigma_{t+1}^2 = E((r_{t+1} - \mu)^2 \mid \Phi_t) \tag{8.4}$$

$$\sigma_{t+1}^2 = \lambda + \alpha_1 (r_{t-1} - \mu)^2 +,...,+\alpha_q (r_{t-q} - \mu)^2$$

where Φ_t is the information set at the end of period t. This is an AR(q) model in terms of $(r_t - \mu)^2$. Therefore, the optimal one-day ahead forecast of period $t+1$ volatility can be obtained based on the returns on the most recent q days. In general, an h-day ahead step forecast can be formed as follows:

$$\hat{\sigma}_{t+h}^2 = \lambda + \alpha_1 (\hat{r}_{t+h-1} - \mu)^2 +,...,+\alpha_q (\hat{r}_{t+1-q} - \mu)^2 \tag{8.5}$$

where $\hat{r}_{t+h-1} = r_{t+h-j}$ if $1 \le h \le j$ and $(\hat{\sigma}_{t+h-j}^2 = (\hat{r}_{t+h-1} - \mu)^2$ if $h > j$.

The ARCH (1) Model

This simple ARCH model exhibits constant unconditional variance but non-constant conditional variance. Recall the equation (8.1):

$$r_t = \mu + \sigma_t \varepsilon_t$$

given that:

$$\varepsilon_t = u_t \sqrt{(\lambda + \alpha \varepsilon_{t-1}^2)} \tag{8.6}$$

where $u_t \sim IID(0,1)$ (IID, Independent and Identically Distributed, or strict white noise); and λ and $\alpha > 0$.

Note that $\sqrt{(\lambda + \alpha \varepsilon_{t-1}^2)}$ is the conditional standard deviation; and σ_t is defined as:

$$\sqrt{E(\varepsilon_t^2 \mid \varepsilon_{t-1}^2, \varepsilon_{t-2}^2, ..., \varepsilon_{t-i}^2)} .\tag{8.7}$$

The simplest form of ARCH (1) model for the:

a) *conditional expectation* of ε_t given that ε_t is equal to zero, is defined as:

$$E(\varepsilon_t \varepsilon_{t-1}) = E(u_t \mid \varepsilon_{t-1})\sqrt{\lambda + \alpha \varepsilon_{t-1}^2} = 0\tag{8.8}$$

note that $E(u_t \mid \varepsilon_{t-1}) = E(u_t) = 0$ since $u_t \sim IID(0,1)$;

b) *conditional variance* is defined as:

$$Var(\varepsilon_t \mid \varepsilon_{t-1}) = E(u_t^2 \mid \varepsilon_{t-1})(\lambda + \alpha \varepsilon_{t-1}^2)\tag{8.9}$$

note that $E(u_t^2 \mid \varepsilon_{t-1}) = E(u_t^2) = 1$ since $u_t \sim IID(0,1)$.

Thus, the conditional mean and variance of r_t are given by the following formulae:

$$E(r_t \mid r_{t-1}) = \mu\tag{8.10}$$

and:

$$Var(r_t \mid r_{t-1}) = (\lambda + \alpha \varepsilon_{t-1}^2).\tag{8.11}$$

Therefore, the conditional variance of r_t is time varying. However, it can be easily seen that the unconditional variance is time invariant given that ε_t^2 is stationary:

$$Var(r_t) = Var(\varepsilon_t) = \frac{\lambda}{(1-\alpha)}.\tag{8.12}$$

First Order Autoregressive Process with ARCH Effects

For more complicated models such as AR(1)-ARCH(1), we obtain similar results provided that the process for t is stationary given that the autoregressive parameter is smaller than one in absolute value.

Assume the following first order autoregressive process:

$$r_t = \theta r_{t-1} + \varepsilon_t \tag{8.13}$$

where $\varepsilon_t = u_t \sqrt{\lambda + \alpha \varepsilon_{t-1}^2}$, $u_t \sim \text{IIN}(0,1)$, and $\lambda > 0$, $\alpha = 0$.

a) The *conditional expectation* of ε_t given that ε_t is equal to zero is:

$$E(\varepsilon_t \varepsilon_{t-1}) = E(u_t^2 \mid \varepsilon_{t-1})(\lambda + \alpha \varepsilon_{t-1}^2) = 0 \tag{8.14}$$

note that $E(u_t \mid \varepsilon_{t-1}) = E(u_t) = 0$.

b) The *conditional variance* is given by the following formula:

$$Var(\varepsilon_t \mid \varepsilon_{t-1}) = E(u_t^2 \mid \varepsilon_{t-1})(\lambda + \alpha \varepsilon_{t-1}^2) = \lambda + \alpha \varepsilon_{t-1}^2 \tag{8.15}$$

note that $E(u_t^2 \mid \varepsilon_{t-1}) = E(u_t) = 1$ since $u_t \sim \text{IIN}(0,1)$.

Then the conditional mean and variance of r_t are given by the following formulae:

$$E(r_t \mid r_{t-1}) = \theta r_{t-1} \tag{8.16}$$

and:

$$Var(r_t \mid r_{t-1}) = (\lambda + \alpha \varepsilon_{t-1}^2). \tag{8.17}$$

To find the unconditional variance of r_t we recall the following property for the variance:

$$Var(r_t) = E(Var(r_t \mid r_{t-1})) + Var(E(r_t \mid r_{t-1})). \tag{8.18}$$

The left hand-side formula $E(Var(r_t \mid r_{t-1}))$ is equal to $E(\lambda + \alpha \varepsilon_{t-1}^2)$, $\lambda + \alpha E(\varepsilon_{t-1}^2)$ and $\lambda + \alpha Var(\varepsilon_{t-1})$. The right hand-side formula $Var(E(r_t \mid r_{t-1}))$ is equal to $\theta^2 Var(r_{t-1})$. Then if the process is covariance stationarity, we have:

$$Var(r_t) = \frac{\lambda + \alpha Var(\varepsilon_{t-1})}{1 - \theta^2} \tag{8.19}$$

or:

$$Var(r_t) = \frac{1}{(1-\alpha)(1-\theta^2)}$$

since:

$$Var(\varepsilon_{t-1}) = \frac{\lambda}{(1-\alpha)}.$$

According to Aydemir (1998), the important property of ARCH models is their ability to capture the tendency for volatility clustering in stock prices data, i.e. a tendency for large or small swings in prices to be followed by large or small swings in random direction. In addition, Barndorff-Nielsen, Nicolato and

Shephard (2001) and Aydemir (1998) also found that the ARCH/GARCH type models are significantly outperformed by other models including the ARMA and SV models.

8.2.2 Autoregressive Moving Average (ARMA) Models

Recalling the ARMA models in Chapter 3 where autoregressive in order p, [AR(p)] can be expressed as:

$$y_t = \gamma_1(y_{t-1}) + \gamma_2(y_{t-2}) +,...,+ \gamma_p(y_{t-p}) + \varepsilon_t \tag{8.20}$$

where y_t = the actual or data value at time t, γ = the constant value, and ϵ_t = the residual or error term.

Moving average of order q, [MA(q)] can be expressed as:

$$y_t = \varepsilon_t - \theta_1(\varepsilon_{t-1}) - \theta_2(\varepsilon_{t-2}) -,...,- \theta_q(\varepsilon_{t-q}). \tag{8.21}$$

The general presentation for ARMA models is:

$$y_t = \gamma_{0,1} + \sum_{j=1}^{p} \gamma_j y_{t-j} + \sum_{j=0}^{q} \theta_j \varepsilon_{t-j}. \tag{8.22}$$

These models are widely used in the finance literature especially during the last decade. Some studies such as Schwert (1990), French, Schwert and Stambaugh (1987) and Poterba and Summer (1986) use the ARMA process for modelling volatility of the stock market. According to Aydemir (1998), the advantages of these models include the following: 1) the theory of the Gaussian model is well understood, therefore, the ARMA models are well developed; 2) modelling data within an ARMA structure is considerably easy; and 3) these models are capable of data analysis, forecasting and control. However, several limitations of the ARMA models include: 1) these models have definite limitations in mimicking the properties where sudden bursts of the data at irregular time intervals, and periods of high and low volatility are detected, i.e. the data of the SET returns that covers the pre- and post-Asian economic crisis; and 2) the ARMA type models are based on the assumption of constant variance. Most financial data exhibit changes in volatility and this feature of the data cannot be captured due to this assumption.

8.2.3 Stochastic Volatility (SV) Models

There are several types of Stochastic Volatility (SV) models, one the most popular being the discrete-time SV model, the continuous-time SV model and the jump diffusion model with SV. The relevant type of SV model applicable to Thai stock data is the discrete-time SV model, where s_t denotes the stock price at time t and the detrended return process y_t is defined as (Jiang 1998):

$$y_t = \ln\left(\frac{s_t}{s_{t-1}}\right) - \mu_t. \tag{8.23}$$

The SV model of stock return may be written as:

$$y_t = \sigma_t \varepsilon_t \tag{8.24}$$

where $\varepsilon_t \sim IID$. The most popular SV specification assumes that h_t follows an AR(1) process as:

$$h_{t+1} = \phi h_t + \eta_t, \ |\phi| < 1 \tag{8.25}$$

where η_t is an innovation. This process is satisfied using the idea of Exponential GARCH (EGARCH) and this specification ensures that the conditional variance remains positive.

According to Barndorff-Nielsen, Nicolato and Shephard (2001) and Aydemir (1998), there are several advantages in using SV models. SV properties can be found and manipulated much easier than ARCH/GARCH type models and they can also mimic the fat tail property observed in the data. Finally, they also induce an incomplete market. However, Hansen and Lunde (2001) disagree that these SV models are superior to the ARCH/GARCH type model when using returns of stock indices or bonds. Furthermore, in SV models, the persistence in volatilities can be captured by specifying a random walk process. This specification is analogous to the IGARCH specification.

8.3 Adopted Volatility Models – GARCH Type Models

The use of univariate parametric models such as ARCH and GARCH type models in estimating and forecasting the financial market volatility has been growing in popularity, especially when dealing with incomplete or emerging financial markets such as in Thailand. A most commonly used modified ARCH model has been the Generalized ARCH (GARCH) model developed by Bollerslev (1986). Other ARCH-type models are characterized by Nelson (1991), who introduced the Exponential GARCH (EGARCH). Glosten, Jagannathan and Runkle (1993) have developed the GJR-GARCH(p,q) model to estimate the relationship between the expected value and the volatility of nominal excess return on stocks. Ding, Granger and Engle (1993) developed a model which extends the ARCH class of models to identify a wider class of power transformations, called Power Generalized ARCH or PGARCH.

These models consist of linear and non-linear types – non-linear models are EGARCH, GJR-GARCH and PGARCH. Franses and Dijk (2000) conclude that linear time series models do not yield reliable forecasts. However, this does not imply that linear models are not useful, and these models are used in comparing the results for the index price of the Stock Exchange of Thailand.

8.3.1 GARCH(p,q)

In empirical applications of the ARCH(q) model, it is often difficult to estimate models with a large number of parameters. This motivates Bollerslev (1986) to use the Generalized ARCH or GARCH(p,q) specification to circumvent this problem.

The GARCH(p,q) model is defined as:

$$r_t = \mu + \sigma_t \varepsilon_t \tag{8.26}$$

and:

$$\sigma_t^2 = \lambda + \sum_{i=1}^{q} \alpha_i (r_{t-i} - \mu)^2 + \sum_{i=1}^{p} \beta_i \sigma_{t-i}^2 . \tag{8.27}$$

The model could also be represented as:

$$\sigma_t^2 = \lambda + \sum_{i=1}^{q} \alpha_i \varepsilon_{t-i}^2 + \sum_{i=1}^{p} \beta_i \sigma_{t-i}^2 \tag{8.28}$$

or:

$$\sigma_t^2 = \lambda + \alpha(L)\varepsilon_{t-1}^2 + \beta(L)\sigma_{t-1}^2 .$$

A sufficient condition for conditional variance in the GARCH(p,q) model to be well defined is that all the coefficients in the infinite order linear ARCH model must be positive. Given that $\alpha(L)$ and $\beta(L)$ have no common roots and that the roots of the polynomial in L, $1 - \beta(L) = 0$ lie outside the unit circle, this positive constraint is satisfied, if and only if, the coefficients of the infinite power series expansion for $\dfrac{\alpha(L)}{1-\beta(L)}$ are non-negative.

Rearranging the GARCH(p,q) model by defining $v_t \equiv \varepsilon_t^2 - \sigma_t^2$, it follows that:

$$\varepsilon_t^2 = \lambda + (\alpha(L) + \beta(L))\varepsilon_{t-1}^2 - \beta(L)v_{t-1} + v_t \tag{8.29}$$

which defines an ARMA (Max(p,q),p) model for ε_t^2.

In addition, the model is covariance stationary if and only if all the roots of $(1 - \alpha(L) - \beta(L))$ lie outside the unit circle. If all the coefficients are non-negative, this is equivalent to the sum of the autoregressive coefficients being smaller than 1. The analogy to the ARMA class of models also allows for the use of standard time series techniques in the identification of the order of p and q. In most empirical applications with finitely sampled data, the simple GARCH(1,1) is found to provide a fair description of the data.

The GARCH(1,1) is used to construct multi-period forecasts of volatility. When $\alpha + \beta < 1$, the unconditional variance of ε_{t+1} is $\dfrac{\lambda}{1 - \alpha - \beta}$. If we rewrite the following GARCH(1,1) as:

$$\sigma_t^2 = \lambda + \alpha(\varepsilon_{t-1}^2) + \beta(\sigma_{t-1}^2) \tag{8.30}$$

$$= \lambda + \alpha(\varepsilon_{t-1}^2 - \sigma_{t-1}^2) + (\alpha + \beta)\sigma_{t-1}^2.$$

The coefficient measures the extent to which the impact of volatility will extend into the next period's volatility, while $(\alpha + \beta)$ measures the rate at which this effect reduces over time. Recursively substituting and using the law of iterated expectation, the conditional expectation of volatility j periods ahead is:

$$E_t[\sigma_{t+j}^2] = (\alpha + \beta)^j \left[\frac{\sigma_t^2 - \lambda}{1 - \alpha - \beta} \right] + \left[\frac{\sigma_t^2 - \lambda}{1 - \alpha - \beta} \right]. \tag{8.31}$$

Note that the multi-period volatility forecast reverts to its unconditional mean at rate $(\alpha + \beta)$.

8.3.2 EGARCH

Even though the GARCH model has the capability to capture thick tailed returns, volatility clusterings are not well suited to capture the leverage effect since the conditional variance is a function only of the magnitudes of the lagged residuals and not their signs. Nelson (1991) introduced the exponential GARCH (EGARCH) where σ_t^2 depends on both the sign and the size of lagged residuals.

The EGARCH(1,1) model is represented as follows:

$$\ln \sigma_t^2 = \lambda_1 + \beta_1 \ln \sigma_{t-1}^2 + \gamma_1 \left(\left[\left| \frac{\varepsilon_{t-1}}{\sigma_{t-1}} \right| - (2/\pi)^{1/2} \right] + \delta \left[\frac{\varepsilon_{t-1}}{\sigma_{t-1}} \right] \right). \tag{8.32}$$

In fact, the EGARCH model always produces a positive conditional variance σ_t^2 for any choice of λ_1, β_1, γ_1 so that no restrictions need to be placed on these coefficients (except $|\beta_1| < 1$). Because of the use of both $|\epsilon_t / \sigma_t|$ and $(\epsilon_t / \sigma_t), \sigma_t^2$, it will also be non-symmetric in ε_t and, for negative δ, it will exhibit higher volatility for large negative ε_t. In addition, the EGARCH model is capable of capturing any asymmetric impact of shocks on volatility. This model allows volatility to be affected differently by good and bad news.

8.3.3 GARCH-M

A number of theories in finance assume some kind of relationship between the mean of a return and its variance. A way to take this into account is to explicitly write the returns as a function of the conditional variance or, in other words, to include the conditional variance as another regressor. The GARCH in Mean Model (GARCH-M) allows for the conditional variance to have mean effects. Most of the time this conditional variance term will have the interpretation of time varying risk premium.

Recall the equation (8.28):

$$\sigma_t^2 = \lambda + \alpha(\varepsilon_{t-1}^2) + \beta(\sigma_{t-1}^2)$$
$$= \lambda + \alpha(\varepsilon_{t-1}^2 - \sigma_{t-1}^2) + (\alpha + \beta)\sigma_{t-1}^2$$

and ARCH-M:

$$r_t = \psi\sigma_t^2 + \varepsilon_t \tag{8.33}$$

where $\varepsilon_t = v_t\sigma_t$, and $v_t \sim N(0,1)$:

$$\sigma_t^2 = w + \lambda + \alpha\varepsilon_{t-1}^2. \tag{8.34}$$

Then r_t may be expressed as:

$$r_t = \psi(\lambda + \alpha\varepsilon_{t-1}^2) + \varepsilon_t. \tag{8.35}$$

Consider the following formula (extension form of the above equation):

$$r_t = \theta x_t + \psi\sigma_t^2 + \varepsilon_t. \tag{8.36}$$

Therefore, GARCH-M could be defined as:

$$\sigma_t^2 = \lambda + \alpha(L)\varepsilon_{t-1}^2 + \beta(L)\varepsilon_{t-1}^2. \tag{8.37}$$

Consistent estimation of θ and ψ is dependent on the correct specification of the entire model. The estimation of GARCH in mean type of models is numerically unstable and many empirical applications have used the ARCH-M type of models which are easier to estimate.

8.3.4 GJR-GARCH

Glosten, Jagannathan and Runkle (1993) have extended the GARCH(p,q) model to estimate the relationship between the expected value and the volatility of nominal excess return on stocks. Their GJR-GARCH is an alternative model capturing asymmetries in financial data. A univariate regression GJR-GARCH(p,q) process, with q coefficients α_i, ..., q, p coefficients, β_i, for i=1, ..., p and k linear regression coefficients b_i, for i=1,..., k, can be represented by:

$$r_t = \mu + x_t^T b_i + \varepsilon_t \tag{8.38}$$

and:

$$\sigma_t^2 = \lambda + \sum_{i=1}^{q} \alpha_i + (\gamma S_{t-1}) \varepsilon_{t-1}^2 + \sum_{i=1}^{p} \beta_i \sigma_{t-1} . \tag{3.39}$$

This model allows the impact of the squared residual on conditional volatility to be different when the residuals are negative (first lagged) than when the residuals (first lagged) are positive. For $\gamma > 0$, all negative residuals are weighted and thus generate a different volatility in subsequent periods than do positive residuals of equal magnitude. In other words, negative shocks increase volatility more than positive shocks. Thus, the leverage of firm increases with negative return, inducing a higher volatility.

8.3.5 PGARCH

Ding, Granger and Engle (1993) suggest a model which extends the ARCH class of models to identify a wider class of power transformations than simply taking the absolute value or squaring the data as in the conventional models. This class of models is called Power ARCH (PARCH) and Power Generalized ARCH (PGARCH).

PGARCH is defined as:

$$\sigma_t^2 = \lambda + \sum_{i=1}^{p} \beta_i \sigma_{t-i}^2 + \sum_{i=1}^{q} \alpha (|\varepsilon_{t-i}| + \lambda \varepsilon_{t-i})^2 . \tag{3.40}$$

It has been found that the sample autocorrelation function for absolute returns and squared returns remains significantly positive for very long lags. The pattern of the sample autocorrelation for various speculative returns is quite different from that of the theoretical autocorrelation functions given by the GARCH(p,q) or EGARCH(p,q) process. Ding and Granger (1996) propose a two-component GARCH model which gives a much better description of the real data:

$$\sigma_t^2 = \frac{\lambda}{(1 - \beta_1)(1 - \beta_2)} + \sum_{i=1}^{p} \alpha_1 \beta_1^{i-1} \varepsilon_{t-i}^2 + \sum_{j=1}^{q} \alpha_2 \beta_2^{j-1} \varepsilon_{t-j}^2 . \tag{3.41}$$

The intuition behind this two-component model is that one can use two different variance components, each of them having an exponentially decreasing autocorrelation pattern, to model the long-term and short-term movements in volatility.

8.4 Data and Estimation Results

In GARCH model estimates, we have used daily adjusted return data of the Thai stock market closing index from 2nd January 1992 to 28th December 2001. The adjusted return is calculated as $R_t = \ln(I_t / I_{t-1}) \times 100$. Monthly data is used only for the estimate of standard deviation.

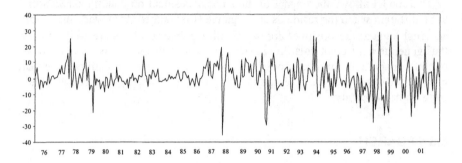

Fig. 8.1. Monthly returns series for the SET, 1975–2001

Yu and Bluhm (2001), use the historical return information to compute the volatility of the stock market. As anticipated, volatility of the Thai stock market index during 1992–2000, measured by standard deviation, is considerably high. The average monthly volatility during the overall period in Table 3.2 is around 11 per cent. A visual perspective on the volatility of returns can be gained from the plots of monthly and daily returns for each series in Figures 8.1. Here, the findings are in accordance with the recent international analysis of equity returns and volatility by Worthington and Higgs (2001) where high volatility was present immediately after the crisis.

In comparing the five models, we use only the first order and the first lag for all five models for consistency, i.e. GARCH(1,1), EGARCH(1,1), GARCH-M(1,1), GJR-GARCH(1,1) and PGARCH(1,1).

The following GARCH models are developed to examine the volatility relating to the daily rate of return and seasonal factors (see Chapter 7) for the Thai stock market index from 1992 to 2001. We focus the test on two time-frame periods, which are pre-crisis (1992–1996) and post-crisis (1997–2001). The comparison is made to estimate the level of volatility during these periods.

The seasonal factors include seasonal daily anomalies $(d_1,...,d_5)$, seasonal monthly anomalies $(m_1,...,m_{12})$ and the yearly series effect $(y_1,..y_{10})$. Overall, there are a total of 27 variables. The results for the coefficient, standard error, α, and β are found using an *iterative procedure*. Under this iterative procedure, we assume the given value of λ and estimated parameters α and β, we then use the estimate of λ to re-estimate α and β. Tables 8.1 to 8.10 present the results of these estimates.

Table 8.1. Estimation results of the GARCH(1,1), 1992–1996

Explanatory variables	Model coefficient [β]	Standard error
$$\sigma_t^2 = \lambda + \sum_{i=1}^{q}\alpha_i\varepsilon_{t-i}^2 + \sum_{i=1}^{p}\beta_i\sigma_{t-i}^2$$		
d_1	-0.5360	0.1426
d_2	*0.2694	0.1070
d_3	*0.5888	0.0970
d_4	*0.3220	0.1022
d_5	*0.4986	0.1014
m_1	*0.3000	0.1723
m_2	-0.0767	0.1723
m_3	-0.1172	0.1534
m_5	0.1877	0.1412
m_6	0.0043	0.1807
m_7	0.0599	0.1548
m_8	0.1039	0.1595
m_9	0.0419	0.1609
m_{10}	0.1628	0.1705
m_{11}	-0.2826	0.0153
m_{12}	*0.2266	0.1814
y_1	*0.3256	0.1162
y_2	*0.3045	0.1116
y_3	0.1765	0.1197
y_4	0.1200	0.1128

Iteration = 15   Log-Likelihood = -2045   Wald Chi-Square Test = 82.76
Note: The variables m_4 and y_5 have been dropped due to multi-colinearity problems. The figures with asterisks indicate significant results. According to the result for our

GARCH(1,1) model $\sigma_t^2 = \lambda + \sum_{i=1}^{q}\alpha_i\varepsilon_{t-i}^2 + \sum_{i=1}^{p}\beta_i\sigma_{t-i}^2$, the estimates are $\lambda = 0.0812$, and α

= 0.8258.

Table 8.2. Estimation results of the EGARCH(1,1), 1992–1996

Explanatory variables	Model coefficient [β]	Standard error
$\ln \sigma_t^2 = \lambda_1 + \beta_1 \ln \sigma_{t-1}^2 + \gamma_1 \left(\left[\left| \dfrac{\varepsilon_{t-1}}{\sigma_{t-1}} \right| - (2/\pi)^{1/2} \right] + \delta \left[\dfrac{\varepsilon_{t-1}}{\sigma_{t-1}} \right] \right)$		
d_1	-0.5484	0.1428
d_2	*0.2807	0.1039
d_3	*0.5994	0.1100
d_4	*0.3265	0.1022
d_5	*0.4950	0.1021
m_1	*0.2986	0.1671
m_2	-0.0816	0.1775
m_3	-0.1573	0.1624
m_5	0.1330	0.1378
m_6	-0.0317	0.1748
m_7	0.0455	0.1421
m_8	0.0892	0.1477
m_9	-0.2297	0.1529
m_{10}	0.1339	0.1628
m_{11}	-0.2297	0.1529
m_{12}	0.1798	0.1646
y_1	*0.3057	0.1121
y_2	*0.2856	0.1079
y_3	*0.2034	0.1123
y_4	0.1115	0.1081

Iteration = 40   Log-Likelihood = -2039   Wald Chi-Square Test = 82.89
Note: The variables m_4 and y_5 have been dropped due to multi-colinearity problems. The figures with asterisks indicate significant results of the EGARCH(1,1) model,

$\ln \sigma_t^2 = \lambda_1 + \beta_1 \ln \sigma_{t-1}^2 + \gamma_1 \left(\left[\left| \dfrac{\varepsilon_{t-1}}{\sigma_{t-1}} \right| - (2/\pi)^{1/2} \right] + \delta \left[\dfrac{\varepsilon_{t-1}}{\sigma_{t-1}} \right] \right)$, the estimates are $\lambda =$

0.0322, and $\alpha = 0.9580$.

Table 8.3. Estimation results of the GARCH-M(1,1), 1992–1996

Explanatory variables	Model coefficient [β]	Standard error
$\sigma_t^2 = \lambda + \alpha(L)\varepsilon_{t-1}^2 + \beta(L)\varepsilon_{t-1}^2$		
d_1	-0.5789	0.1494
d_2	*0.2660	0.1070
d_3	*0.5872	0.0969
d_4	*0.3174	0.1023
d_5	*0.4944	0.1012
m_1	*0.2999	0.1722
m_2	-0.0726	0.1727
m_3	-0.1196	-0.1196
m_5	0.1841	0.1413
m_6	0.0070	0.1798
m_7	0.0671	0.1544
m_8	0.1166	0.1593
m_9	0.0532	0.1608
m_{10}	0.1654	0.1702
m_{11}	-0.2947	0.1552
m_{12}	*0.2110	0.1800
y_1	*0.3262	0.1158
y_2	*0.3081	0.1145
y_3	0.1685	0.1197
y_4	0.1222	0.1123

Iteration = 22   Log-Likelihood = -2045   Wald Chi-Square Test = 83.59
Note: The variables m_4 and y_5 have been dropped due to multi-colinearity problems. The figures with asterisks indicate significant results. According to the result for the GARCH-M(1,1) model $\sigma_t^2 = \lambda + \alpha(L)\varepsilon_{t-1}^2 + \beta(L)\varepsilon_{t-1}^2$, our estimates are $\lambda = 0.0848$, and $\alpha = 0.0285$.

Table 8.4. Estimation results of the GJR-GARCH(1,1), 1992–1996

Explanatory variables	Model coefficient [β]	Standard error
$$\sigma_t^2 = \lambda + \sum_{i=1}^{q}\alpha_i + (\gamma S_{t-1})\varepsilon_{t-1}^2 + \sum_{i=1}^{p}\beta_i\sigma_{t-1}$$		
d_1	-0.5216	0.1377
d_2	*0.2573	0.1070
d_3	*0.5813	0.0971
d_4	*0.3155	0.1044
d_5	*0.4936	0.1053
m_1	*0.2765	0.1639
m_2	-0.1062	0.1694
m_3	-0.1609	0.1537
m_5	0.1650	0.1447
m_6	-0.0362	0.1758
m_7	0.0250	0.1494
m_8	0.0623	0.1559
m_9	0.0602	0.1508
m_{10}	0.1424	0.1636
m_{11}	-0.2865	0.1469
m_{12}	*0.2102	0.1686
y_1	*0.3175	0.1116
y_2	*0.3014	0.1052
y_3	0.1679	0.1160
y_4	0.1206	0.1084

Iteration = 22   Log-Likelihood = -2041   Wald Chi-Square Test = 83.82
Note: The variables m_4 and y_5 have been dropped due to multi-colinearity problems. The figures with asterisks indicate significant results. The GJR-GARCH(1,1) model

$$\sigma_t^2 = \lambda + \sum_{i=1}^{q}\alpha_i + (\gamma S_{t-1})\varepsilon_{t-1}^2 + \sum_{i=1}^{p}\beta_i\sigma_{t-1}$$, gives the results of λ = 0.0853, and α = -0.0836.

Table 8.5. Estimation results of the PGARCH(1,1), 1992–1996

Explanatory variables	Model coefficient [β]	Standard error
$\sigma_t^2 = \lambda + \sum_{i=1}^{p} \beta_i \sigma_{t-1}^2 + \sum_{i=1}^{q} \alpha(|\varepsilon_{t-i}| + \lambda \varepsilon_{t-i})^2$		
d_1	-0.5494	0.0439
d_2	-0.1809	0.0578
d_3	0.1369	0.0690
d_4	-0.1717	0.0547
d_5	*0.3261	0.0641
m_1	*0.3781	0.0647
m_2	0.0286	0.1357
m_3	-0.0376	0.0750
m_5	0.1091	0.0675
m_6	-0.0134	0.0215
m_7	0.1010	0.0817
m_8	0.1581	0.0612
m_9	0.0884	0.0732
m_{10}	0.1949	0.1088
m_{11}	-0.1200	0.0982
m_{12}	0.1801	0.1082
y_1	*0.3110	0.4328
y_2	*0.2849	0.0614
y_3	*0.2553	0.0541
y_4	0.1131	0.0520

Iteration = 78   Log-Likelihood = -2041   Wald Chi-Square Test = 141.46
Note: The variables m_4 and y_5 have been dropped due to multi-colinearity problems. The figures with asterisks indicate significant results. According to the result for the

PGARCH(1,1) model $\sigma_t^2 = \lambda + \sum_{i=1}^{p} \beta_i \sigma_{t-1}^2 + \sum_{i=1}^{q} \alpha(|\varepsilon_{t-i}| + \lambda \varepsilon_{t-i})^2$, our estimates are $\lambda =$

0.0382, and $\alpha = 0.8596$.

Table 8.6. Estimation results of the GARCH(1,1), 1997–2001

Explanatory variables	Model coefficient [β]	Standard error
$$\sigma_t^2 = \lambda + \sum_{i=1}^{q}\alpha_i\varepsilon_{t-i}^2 + \sum_{i=1}^{p}\beta_i\sigma_{t-i}^2$$		
d_1	-0.4435	0.2540
d_3	*0.2486	0.1756
d_4	*0.4418	0.1692
d_5	*0.2427	0.1731
m_1	*0.6923	0.1740
m_2	*0.2924	0.2769
m_3	-0.0412	0.2459
m_4	-0.1877	0.2862
m_5	-0.0872	0.2872
m_6	-0.5993	0.2792
m_7	-0.0909	0.2927
m_8	-0.3927	0.2982
m_9	-0.1281	0.2767
m_{10}	-0.0811	0.2798
m_{11}	-0.0555	0.2891
m_{12}	0.0621	0.2999
y_6	-0.1904	0.1743
y_8	*0.3329	0.1636
y_9	-0.0316	0.1777
y_{10}	*0.3235	0.1770

Iteration = 11   Log-Likelihood = -2622   Wald Chi-Square Test = 63.29
Note: The variables d_2 and y_7 have been dropped due to multi-colinearity problems. The figures with asterisks indicate significant results. According to the result for the

GARCH(1,1) model $\sigma_t^2 = \lambda + \sum_{i=1}^{q}\alpha_i\varepsilon_{t-i}^2 + \sum_{i=1}^{p}\beta_i\sigma_{t-i}^2$, our estimates are $\lambda = 0.4427$, and α

= 0.7323.

Table 8.7. Estimation results of the EGARCH(1,1), 1997–2001

Explanatory variables	Model coefficient [β]	Standard error
$\ln \sigma_t^2 = \lambda_1 + \beta_1 \ln \sigma_{t-1}^2 + \gamma_1\left(\left[\left\|\frac{\varepsilon_{t-1}}{\sigma_{t-1}}\right\| - (2/\pi)^{1/2}\right] + \delta\left[\frac{\varepsilon_{t-1}}{\sigma_{t-1}}\right]\right)$		
d_1	-0.4702	0.2356
d_3	*0.2976	0.1636
d_4	*0.5158	0.1602
d_5	*0.2963	0.1623
m_1	*0.7656	0.1715
m_2	*0.2966	0.2623
m_3	-0.0684	0.2211
m_4	-0.2053	0.2587
m_5	-0.0354	0.2676
m_6	-0.5745	0.2618
m_7	-0.0813	0.2653
m_8	-0.4934	0.2244
m_9	-0.1540	0.2580
m_{10}	-0.0633	0.2579
m_{11}	-0.1739	0.2940
m_{12}	0.0502	0.2940
y_6	-0.2876	0.1771
y_8	*0.3799	0.1600
y_9	-0.0589	0.1756
y_{10}	*0.3023	0.1706

Iteration = 44   Log-Likelihood = -2620   Wald Chi-Square Test = 74.62
Note: The variables d_2 and y_7 have been dropped due to multi-colinearity problems. The figures with asterisks indicate significant results of EGARCH(1,1),

$\ln \sigma_t^2 = \lambda_1 + \beta_1 \ln \sigma_{t-1}^2 + \gamma_1\left(\left[\left\|\frac{\varepsilon_{t-1}}{\sigma_{t-1}}\right\| - (2/\pi)^{1/2}\right] + \delta\left[\frac{\varepsilon_{t-1}}{\sigma_{t-1}}\right]\right)$. Our estimates are λ = 0.1729, and α = 0.8919.

Table 8.8. Estimation results of the GARCH-M(1,1), 1997–2001

Explanatory variables	Model coefficient [β]	Standard error
$$\sigma_t^2 = \lambda + \alpha(L)\varepsilon_{t-1}^2 + \beta(L)\varepsilon_{t-1}^2$$		
d_1	-0.6846	0.2842
d_3	*0.2482	0.1752
d_4	*0.4521	0.1700
d_5	*0.2191	0.1721
m_1	*0.6865	0.1734
m_2	*0.2090	0.2730
m_3	-0.1133	0.2434
m_4	-0.2049	0.2860
m_5	-0.0821	0.2838
m_6	-0.6256	0.2744
m_7	-0.1262	0.2899
m_8	-0.4299	0.2689
m_9	-0.1479	0.2689
m_{10}	-0.1995	0.2793
m_{11}	-0.1012	0.2852
m_{12}	0.0080	0.3013
y_6	-0.1189	0.1700
y_8	*0.4013	0.1620
y_9	0.0880	0.1786
y_{10}	*0.4462	0.1818

Iteration = 12   Log-Likelihood = -2620   Wald Chi-Square Test = 70.34
Note: The variables d_2 and y_7 have been dropped due to multi-colinearity problems. The figures with asterisks indicate significant results. According to the result for the GARCH-M(1,1) model $\sigma_t^2 = \lambda + \alpha(L)\varepsilon_{t-1}^2 + \beta(L)\varepsilon_{t-1}^2$, our estimates are $\lambda = 0.4139$, and $\alpha = 0.0503$.

Table 8.9. Estimation results of the GJR-GARCH(1,1), 1997–2001

Explanatory variables	Model coefficient [β]	Standard error
$\sigma_t^2 = \lambda + \sum_{i=1}^{q} \alpha_i + (\gamma S_{t-1})\varepsilon_{t-1}^2 + \sum_{i=1}^{p} \beta_i \sigma_{t-1}$		
d_1	-0.4376	0.2540
d_3	*0.2398	0.1747
d_4	*0.4273	0.1674
d_5	*0.2289	0.1719
m_1	*0.6809	0.1735
m_2	*0.2982	0.2755
m_3	-0.0410	0.2488
m_4	-0.1968	0.2832
m_5	-0.0899	0.2832
m_6	-0.5910	0.2775
m_7	-0.0842	0.2950
m_8	-0.3946	0.2950
m_9	-0.1080	0.2740
m_{10}	-0.0902	0.2810
m_{11}	-0.0532	0.2868
m_{12}	0.0583	0.2990
y_6	-0.1908	0.1746
y_8	*0.3319	0.1617
y_9	-0.0465	0.1775
y_{10}	*0.3106	0.1766

Iteration = 13   Log-Likelihood = -2621   Wald Chi-Square Test = 62.51
Note: The variables d_2 and y_7 have been dropped due to multi-colinearity problems. The figures with asterisks indicate significant results. According to the result for the GJR-

GARCH(1,1) model, where $\sigma_t^2 = \lambda + \sum_{i=1}^{q} \alpha_i + (\gamma S_{t-1})\varepsilon_{t-1}^2 + \sum_{i=1}^{p} \beta_i \sigma_{t-1}$, our estimates are

$\lambda = 0.3964$, and $\alpha = -0.0311$.

Table 8.10. Estimation results of the PGARCH(1,1), 1997–2001

Explanatory variables	Model coefficient [β]	Standard error
$\sigma_t^2 = \lambda + \sum_{i=1}^{p}\beta_i\sigma_{t-1}^2 + \sum_{i=1}^{q}\alpha\left(\left|\varepsilon_{t-i}\right| + \lambda\varepsilon_{t-i}\right)^2$		
d_1	-0.4530	0.2492
d_3	*0.2649	0.1736
d_4	*0.4664	0.1684
d_5	*0.2559	0.1759
m_1	0.0708	0.1751
m_2	*0.2982	0.2756
m_3	-0.0445	0.2393
m_4	-0.1849	0.2803
m_5	-0.0728	0.2829
m_6	-0.5868	0.2762
m_7	-0.0848	0.2888
m_8	-0.4003	0.2904
m_9	-0.1078	0.2738
m_{10}	-0.0713	0.2742
m_{11}	-0.0821	0.2832
m_{12}	0.0682	0.2998
y_6	-0.2097	0.1748
y_8	*0.3369	0.1637
y_9	-0.0461	0.1785
y_{10}	*0.3101	0.1768

Iteration = 14   Log-Likelihood = -2621   Wald Chi-Square Test = 63.94
Note: The variables d_2 and y_7 have been dropped due to multi-colinearity problems. The figures with asterisks indicate significant results. According to the result for the

PGARCH(1,1) model $\sigma_t^2 = \lambda + \sum_{i=1}^{p}\beta_i\sigma_{t-1}^2 + \sum_{i=1}^{q}\alpha\left(\left|\varepsilon_{t-i}\right| + \lambda\varepsilon_{t-i}\right)^2$, our estimates are λ= 0.3174, and α = 0.7502.

The Thai stock market has been the most volatile during the post-crisis period. The performance of the volatility models is dependent on how much historical data has been used to specify the model. The estimation horizon used in the study covers the SET returns data during the pre- and post-crisis periods separately in order to ensure the accuracy of the estimation.

8.5 Volatility in the Thai Stock Market

According to the GARCH(1,1) model, six seasonal variables exhibit significant volatility of the stock returns. These variables are Tuesday, Wednesday, Thursday, Friday, January and December, years 1992 and 1993. GARCH-M(1,1) also exhibits similar results. Interestingly, non-linear exponential GARCH models such as EGARCH(1,1), GJR-GARCH(1,1) and PGARCH(1,1) produce very similar results but with less significant variables. PGARCH exhibits the least number of significant variables, where only Friday, January and years 1992, 1993 and 1994 are significant. EGARCH adds four seasonal daily variables which are Tuesday, Wednesday, Thursday, and Friday. GJR-GARCH gives one additional significant variable which is December. The results of volatility on stock return for the post-crisis period are reported in Tables 8.6 to 8.10.

We can summarize the finding as follows:

   a) During the pre-crisis period, Wednesday and Friday exhibit the highest volatility among all tested models except PGARCH. This finding is consistent with the day of the week effect discussed in Chapter 7 (see Figures 7.4 to 7.8 for comparison).
   b) Return volatility is present during January and years 1992 and 1993 on all models. During the pre-crisis, the unusual rate of return on January opposes the traditional view of the January effect, as negative returns were reported. Looking at the stock prices during 1992 and 1993, the closing index on 2nd January 1992 recorded 712.02 points, and 2 years later it jumped to 1682.85 points on 30 December 1993. The issues of speculative and arbitrage opportunity on stock return explain this high volatility.
   c) The average return volatility throughout the pre-crisis period records between 0.03 to 0.08 which is not considered significant. During this period there was an upward trend on the Thai stock market index price and return. Average monthly volatility β is considered low at between -0.2 and 0.2.

For the post-crisis analysis, the degree of volatility between stock market index return and seasonal anomalies could be seen as follows:

a) There are commonalities between all GARCH-type models, where Wednesday, Thursday, Friday, January, February, years 1999 and 2001 exhibit significant volatility.
b) Stock returns during January are very volatile compared to other variables with results of around 0.6–0.7. The January effect plays a major role in this high fluctuation in stock price.
c) For the day of the week effect, Thursday exhibits the highest volatility. According to the daily seasonal anomalies results in figures 7.8 to 7.12, high volatility in return is present on Thursday where the return was 22% in 1997, 78% in 1998, 32% in 1999, 61% in 2000 and 30% in 2001.
d) The return volatility for the post–crisis period is much higher than the pre-crisis period at around 0.16 to 0.44 compared to pre-crisis volatility of only 0.02.

8.6 Conclusions

The purpose of this chapter has been to compare models and identify stock market volatility by examining the determinants of movements in the volatility of stock returns such as time varying risk prima with seasonal factors such as the day of the week effect, the month of the year effect, and the year effect. The Stock Exchange of Thailand market index return serves as an interesting example for analysis of the presence of such volatility.

Empirical analyses reveal that distributions of the stock market index deviate from normality with volatility changing over time and being serially correlated, which was described in Chapter 4. The results of the volatility tests show that the Thai stock market was quite volatile during the sample period. The results show that Monday is the least volatile, while other working days exhibit significant volatility. January, February and December are among the most fluctuating months in stock returns. During the economic boom in 1992 and 1993, there was high speculative and arbitrage opportunity as well as in 1999 and 2001. These results correspond with results from the previous chapters pertaining to the tests for rational speculative bubbles and anomalies, which are partially responsible for the experienced volatility. The comparison between the pre- and post-crisis periods provides evidence that following the crisis, the volatility in stock market returns was much higher than in the pre-crisis period.

The presence of high volatility, shown by the volatility tests, in the Thai stock market are due to a number of financial and institutional characteristics of a developing economy such as: 1) the level of transactions costs of trading; 2) the effectiveness of reporting standards and disclosure requirements; 3) availability of professional processing of new information; and 4) financial market imperfection such as asymmetric information, adverse selection and moral hazard (see Chapter 2).

9 Summary and Conclusions

9.1 Introduction

Financial econometrics can be effectively applied to investigate the characteristics of the financial systems, in general, and the stock markets in particular, of developing countries. This book presents such an application of financial econometrics to the emerging stock market of Thailand.

The Stock Exchange of Thailand was established in 1975, its growth as the center of the capital market was very slow until the late 1980s. However, during and after the financial and economic liberalization in Thailand, the growth rate was considered to be one of the highest in the region. Prior to the crisis, the market had a different institutional structure and investor constituency compared to that of developed markets along with different levels of efficiency, stability, information and information processing mechanisms available to the average investor. Given that the SET sets its benchmark against other developed markets, such as the New York Stock Exchange, the issue is whether the SET serves as a capital market that transmits information and allocates resources efficiently. If it does not so, what are the implications to investors and policy planners in terms of issues such as stock valuation, speculative bubbles, anomalies, volatility and market efficiency?

This situation is also aggravated by the conditions of the financial system in Thailand where the system and the relevant public policies were not well developed before recent changes in the global and Thai financial systems such as globalisation and financial liberalisation. According to the results found in previous chapters, it is suggested that existing problems such as asymmetric information, adverse selection and moral hazard have worsened the emerging financial and monetary concerns in the developing economies, including the Thai economy.

An understanding of the empirical characteristics of the financial system from an exploratory study like the present one is crucial especially for policy makers who design and develop appropriate policies for the country's financial system and stock market. The applications of financial econometric methods to emerging financial markets in developing countries provide detailed insights into the Thai financial system and the stock market, which are useful for financial and policy planning in Thailand and other similar countries.

9.2 Major Empirical Finance Findings

It was stated in Chapter 1 that, for empirical finance research, the characteristics of the stock market can be investigated under three broad groups of issues: (1) the specific characteristics of the stock market; (2) the general characteristics of the financial market and system; and (3) the general characteristics of the market system of an economy. The major findings of the present study, in terms of the specific characteristics of the stock market in developing countries like Thailand, are summarised below in this section. The findings of this study in terms of the other two groups of issues are discussed in the next section. It should be emphasised that although the empirical evidence generated in this study is specific to the Thai stock market, similar evidence is expected to exist in economies with similar socio-economic, financial and economic structures as those of Thailand, especially other Asian developing economies and emerging stock markets.

Experience in applying a comprehensive set of financial econometric techniques to the emerging stock markets is also summarized to comment on the applicability to, and usefulness of, these techniques in such markets.

9.3 The Empirical Characteristics of the Stock Market

9.3.1 Efficiency

The empirical results provide the evidence against EMH in the Thai financial system and the stock market, which can be explained by such characteristics as the existence of market failure, absence of developed systems and policies, unavailability of information, inside information, asymmetric information, moral hazard, and an incomplete market. The results from the run test and ACF test of stock returns confirm the evidence against EMH. Moreover, the evidence of high volatility and predictability and the presence of daily and monthly seasonal anomalies is opposed to the EMH theory. In the real world, markets cannot be absolutely efficient. The Thai stock market is essentially a typical example of the real world, and daily decisions and events cannot always be reflected immediately into a market.

The above stated tests and evidence do not support possible martingale, random walk, white noise and fair game properties of the Thai stock prices and returns.

9.3.2 Valuation

The Thai stock market is considered as a part of the whole financial system, which also includes the financial market, foreign exchange market, money and capital markets, and goods, gold and commodities markets. They are interdependent, if the conditions of one market change, there will be a change in the stock market index price and return. According to the TSMM model, we conclude that the interest rate, bond price, P/E ratio, market capitalization, foreign exchange rate, and consumer price index have a long-run relationship with the stock price and hence determine its value.

9.3.3 Rational Speculative Bubbles

The empirical evidence concerning speculative behaviour in the Thai stock market is also consistent with that of the financial markets in many developing counties. Rational speculative bubbles were present in the Thai stock market especially during the pre-crisis period, while there was none present immediately after the post-crisis period but were observed after a few years of the crisis. Both the Duration Dependence Test and Weibull Hazard model confirm this finding. The presence of a high degree of speculative risks and a detection of collapsible bubbles in the stock market enables investors to avoid their speculative investment decisions since their decisions are unlikely to provide a stable and growing rate of return for long-term investment.

9.3.4 Anomalies

Empirical evidence from the analysis proves the existence of the day of the week effect and January effect. This raises the issue of speculative behaviour where investors see the opportunity for extraordinary gains. Mondays always exhibit negative returns, and this is consistent with the findings of other researchers. The January effect is also present in most time periods except during the pre-crisis. The unusual positive returns during the pre-crisis period were shown to be caused by speculation and massive foreign capital inflow.

9.3.5 Volatility

The volatility of stock returns in the Thai market appears to be consistent in terms of the standard deviation and volatility modelling. Comparing both linear and non-linear GARCH models we conclude that there is evidence of high volatility in the Thai stock market especially in 1992, 1993 and after the crisis period. January, February and December exhibit high volatility and so do most of the working days except Monday.

9.3.6 Other Characteristics

The econometric tests in this study also provide implications for other issues of the financial market such as predictability, fair game, persistence and mean reversion, and the random walk, white noise and martingale properties of the financial time series. Generally, if stock prices and returns are not predictable then these time series have the properties of martingale, fair game, random walk and white noise implying the validity of EMH. Since the empirical tests in Chapter 5 show the possibility of predictability of stock prices and returns, it can be argued that the time series of stock prices and returns in Thailand during the study period did not show the above properties of time series – evidence against EMH.

9.4 Welfare Economics of the Financial System: Institutions and Policies

Welfare economics, especially new[3] welfare economies (Islam 2001), provides a framework for evaluating alternative states of the financial sector and the economy, as well as suggests the appropriate policies and institutions to achieve the social welfare maximizing state of the financial sector and the economy.

Fry (1995) notes four major differences in the characteristics of a financial system of developed and developing countries (see Chapter 1). In addition, there are also some other problems in the financial market operation and in the development of the financial implications such as banking institutions, money and capital market including stock exchanges, and governments. These problems include market failures, asymmetric information, moral hazard, adverse selection, insider trading, etc. Because of these characteristics of the financial market institutions and systems of developing countries, especially Thailand, these countries experienced such instability and high volatility of their financial market throughout the last decade.

Fry (1995) and Stiglitz (1993) argue that there is an important role for government intervention to ensure that the long-term stability, functionality and performance of the financial market are achieved. The findings of this research regarding different financial sector issues such as an inefficient financial market, speculative bubbles, anomalies and volatility in the stock market, are due to these characteristics of the Thai financial market, institutions and system. The evidence of inefficient markets in Chapter 4 and 7, implies that historical data can be used to predict the movement of future stock prices, and violates an essential function of the efficient financial market in terms of an appropriate use of information, a situation caused by market failures, externalities and other characteristics of the Thai stock market discussed above and in Chapter 2. The evidence of inefficient markets implies that such markets are unlikely to be fully competitive.

For example, the stock market failure arises from costly information which is accentuated because of asymmetric information, adverse selection and moral hazard. Rational speculative behaviour often occurs due to the lack of the required information available in the market, as discussed in Chapter 6. In this situation, if one individual obtains valuable information or conducts research to determine the profitability of particular stocks and then trades upon that information, others can benefit from following this action. On the other hand, if the reaction is opposite when one withdraws or sells stock according to the negative information or noise, the stock market may experience institutional and information failure and also produces greater volatility. The evidence of stock market volatility found in Chapter 8 has been, therefore, characteristic of the Thai stock market. This is also often the case in the most developing countries.

According to Hunter and Terry (2002), Fry (1995) and Drake (1980), a successful stock market should have at least two main features. First, the stock prices and returns should not fluctuate much from real prices and returns. Second, the stock market should grow at a rapid, but steady pace. While the fluctuation of prices and returns is the focus of volatility and anomalies theories, the determination of stable real prices and returns is the concern of stabilisation policies. The financial market should perform a good allocative and payment function, and foster economic development. Implicit in financial system and stock market theories are questions about the role of relevant financial policies in the stabilisation and growth of the stock market making the financial system more efficient and suitable for economic development.

According to Hossain and Chowdhury (1996), the role of economic, monetary and financial policies for developed countries is associated with the taming of business cycles. Whereas, in developing countries, the role of economic, monetary and financial policies is linked with the promotion of economic growth and development. Such disparity in the role of policy reflects the differences in economic issues and priorities of policies-makers in developed and developing countries. The principles for appropriate government intervention in the financial and stock market have been stressed by leading economists such as Stiglitz (1993) (see also, Stiglitz and Greenwald 2003).

Stiglitz (1993) argues that there is an important role for government intervention in the financial market due to pervasive market failure, especially, when the market is not efficient in a functional sense, and thus more regulation and policies should be considered to control the behaviour of stock market operation in order to reduce volatility and anomalies, and ultimately to reduce the opportunity for speculation and arbitrage. The outcome of the EMH test and the characteristics of institutions and markets in the Thai financial system can be used in "public policy assessment of the desirability of mergers and acquisitions, short-termism and regulation of financial institutions" (Islam and Oh 2001, p. 233) which are all relevant and contemporary issues relating to the improvement of the Thai stock market.

A set of financial and other related policies need to be formulated which can help develop the Thai financial system to produce efficient transmission of information, efficient allocation of financial and real resources, macroeconomic stability, and social welfare enhancing economic development. Stigliz (1993) and Fry (1995) suggest a number of policy options to improve the stock market as well as the overall financial system of developing countries. Most developing countries, however, should focus on creating macroeconomic stability, the development of an efficient legal, social and institutional set up, and regulatory supervision in order to develop a sound financial system. Macroeconomic stability also necessitates consistent macroeconomic policies, particularly in fiscal and monetary areas.

Adequate financial supervision in financial and stock market sectors should be undertaken to strengthen the financial system. This involves: (a) providing incentives for agents and institutions to conduct effective information processing and monitoring functions and to strengthen disclosure, accounting and auditing requirements; and (b) encouraging financial and stock market development.

In terms of financial sector policies, there are some key policies where the findings from the present study can be useful for policy decisions. These policies include the appropriate development and regulation of the stock market, determining appropriate priorities to the allocation of public resources and policies to different sub-sectors in the financial sector such as the bond, stock and money markets. The development of a well functioning future market is another issue for concern. Policies for financial innovation, institution development, financial engineering, corporate financial management and governance are also essential.

A detailed discussion the functions and roles of the government may be seen in Fry (1995). It may, however, be stressed that the choice of a set of financial and stock market policies should be based on a consideration of the economic development and social welfare implications.

9.5 Financial Econometrics: Modelling and Applications

The application of suitable and accurate financial econometric methods and models in analysing emerging financial markets is controversial. A general conclusion which can be drawn from all the applications of a wide range of financial econometric techniques is that it is possible to select a set of suitable financial econometric techniques which can be adopted to investigate the emerging and enduring issues in finance.

Regarding the uses of different specific methods, the following conclusions can be drawn. Descriptive statistics and univariate time series methods are useful in revealing the empirical characteristics of the financial system of developing countries. For testing different financial issues, different specific financial econometric methods and models are found useful. These specific models are listed in Section 1.9.1 in Chapter 1 and discussed in previous Chapters 3 to 8.

9.6 Future Research

In the present study, most financial econometric issues have been addressed. However, some issues need more in-depth investigation such as the choice of the techniques used to study volatility. Different order levels and lag times have been employed to compare these results, which could have been found by applying more in-depth investigations with the current findings. Future studies may also focus on modelling a stochastic process for asset pricing with economic variables. The use of GARCH models with macroeconomic variables could be an interesting area to investigate. The usefulness of assuming a normal distribution in economic analysis and finding alternatives to normal distributions could also be tested.

A study of a more qualitative nature, perhaps on investor behaviour could also be useful to gain an inside understanding of speculative issues. Other areas of possible future study on stock price and return are the identification of systematic and unsystematic risk, vector cointegration, and the effects of insider information.

Although Thai stock prices and returns have shown a high degree of volatility and anomalies, formal non-linear complex dynamic chaos models need to be developed to understand further the non-linear and chaotic behaviour of the stock market.

9.7 Conclusions

Empirical development finance needs to be treated as a separate discipline in finance since financial markets and systems of developing countries have some distinct characteristic different from developed countries. This study provides a financial econometric analysis of the emerging Thai stock market, during the pre- and post-crisis periods to provide evidence in support of this view. The results of these studies show that the Thai financial system and market do not show the characteristics of a developed or sound financial system and they are generally consistent with the characteristics of the financial system of a developing economy as stated in Mishkin (1997), Fry (1995), McKinnon (1976, 1973) and Shaw (1973), among others.

All the characteristics of the SET from the point of view of its market index prices and returns reveal the prevalence of an inefficient financial market. Substantial empirical evidence throughout these chapters supports the rejection of the hypothesis of the process being white noise in either the short-term or long-term analysis. Run tests and autocorrelation function tests also confirm the existence of an inefficient market. The notion of existing market inefficiency is supported by the evidence of rational bubbles, anomalies and volatility.

Although further research is necessary, the findings appear to be consistent with the view that significant market imperfections and failures exist in the financial system of a developing economy (Stiglitz 1993), especially in the Thai financial system. However, the explanations and implications of these market imperfections can be only be properly understood within the context of the characteristics and institutional foundations of the economy and society of a developing economy, rather than in terms of the emerging information paradigm in finance and economics.

Appropriate policies are necessary for the development of an efficient and appropriate financial system which has the characteristics required for efficient information management, efficient allocation of resources, stability of the macro-economy and economic development that provides optimum social welfare (Stiglitz 1993; Clarke and Islam 2004). This is an exercise in normative social choice (Islam 2001; Clarke and Islam 2004).

Appendix 1 Structure of Financial Institutions in Thailand

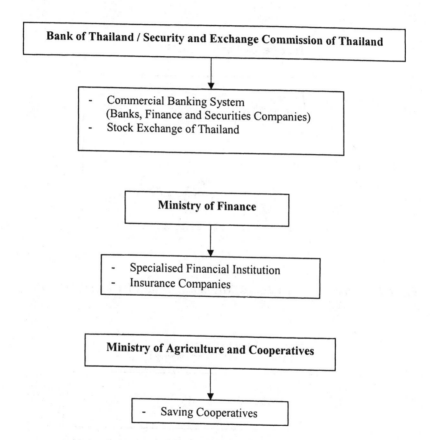

Source: Bank of Thailand 2002.

Fig. A1.1 Structure of financial institutions in Thailand

Appendix 2 Market Efficiency and ARIMA Test Results

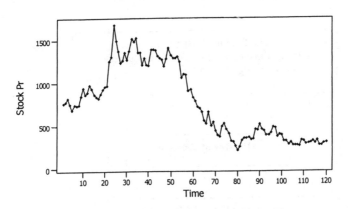

Fig. A2.1. Time series plot for ARIMA model on the SET Index, 1992–2001

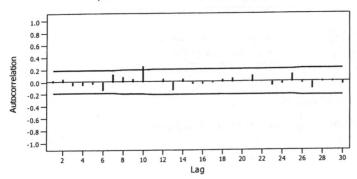

Fig. A2.2. Correlogram of autocorrelation function, 1992–2001

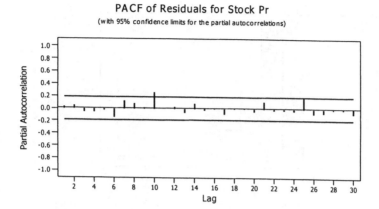

Fig. A2.3. Correlogram of partial autocorrelation function, 1992–2001

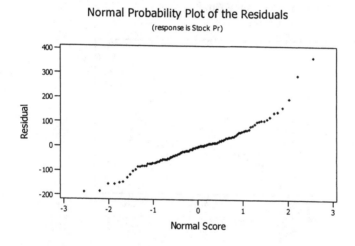

Fig. A2.4. Normal probability plot of the residuals, 1992–2001

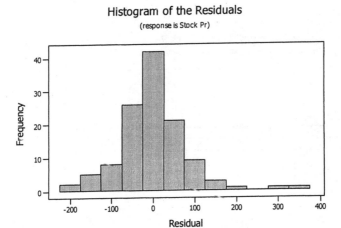

Fig. A2.5. Histogram of the residuals, 1992–2001

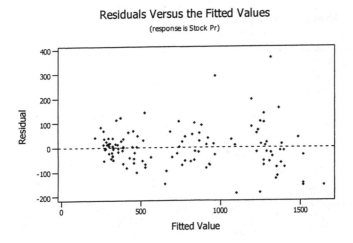

Fig. A2.6. Residual versus the fitted values, 1992–2001

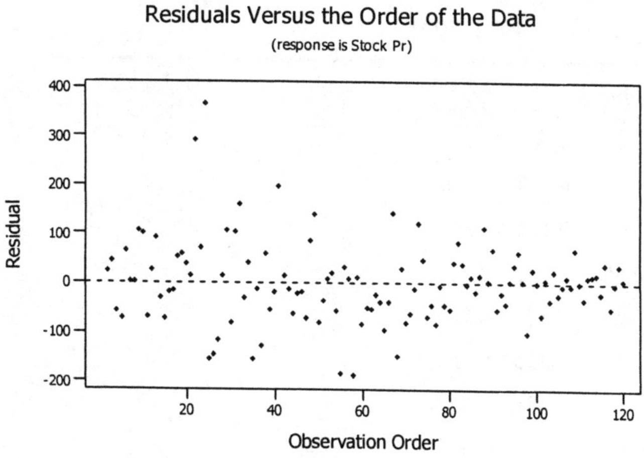

Fig. A2.7. Residual versus the order of the data, 1992–2001

Table A2.1. ARIMA results, 1992–2001

Estimates at each iteration

Iteration	SSE	Parameters		
0	807012	0.100	0.100	-3.386
1	805962	0.082	0.118	-3.545
2	805256	-0.068	-0.032	-4.123
3	804382	-0.218	-0.181	-4.702
4	803416	-0.368	-0.331	-5.280
5	802487	-0.518	-0.481	-5.859
6	801489	-0.668	-0.626	-6.440
7	800657	-0.691	-0.627	-6.534
8	800655	-0.692	-0.628	-6.541
9	800655	-0.692	-0.628	-6.542

Relative change in each estimate less than 0.0010

Final estimates of parameters

Type	Coef	StDev	T
AR 1	-0.6925	0.6093	-1.14
MA 1	-0.6282	0.6564	-0.96
Constant	6.54	12.40	-0.53

Differencing: 1 regular difference

Number of observations: Original series 120, after differencing 119

Residuals: SS = 800655 (backforecasts excluded)

MS = 6902 DF = 116

Modified Box-Pierce (Ljung-Box) Chi-Square statistic

Lag	12	24	36	48
Chi-Square	16.1(DF=10)	22.5(DF=22)	36.5(DF=34)	51.0(DF=46)

Appendix 3 Regression Test Results

Table A3.1. Percentages of correlation coefficients, 1992–2001

	SMI	PE	DY	MC	BD	BL	IR	MMI	BND	FX	EX	IM	GLD	GDP	CPI	GE
SMI	100															
PE	93	100														
DY	4	-7	100													
MC	85	73	-19	100												
BD	-64	-65	-57	-21	100											
BL	22	12	24	51	-4	100										
IR	39	42	59	14	-75	45	100									
MMI	-76	-64	-26	-54	62	8	-13	100								
BND	-64	-67	-31	-16	86	38	-43	72	100							
FX	-84	-80	-21	-59	80	-16	-50	79	77	100						
EX	-75	-76	-31	-37	90	-1	-62	69	89	93	100					
IM	-55	-65	-25	-13	85	11	-65	41	84	75	91	100				
GLD	86	78	37	69	-76	42	61	-71	-61	-88	-80	-61	100			
GDP	-19	-21	-11	-6	25	3	-22	13	26	22	29	29	-20	100		
CPI	-77	-76	-35	-33	91	18	-51	79	97	87	93	83	-75	27	100	
GE	-51	-59	-15	-12	68	36	-33	53	81	59	71	70	-43	29	78	100

Table A3.2. Percentages of correlation coefficients, 1992–1996

	SMI	PE	DY	MC	BD	BL	IR	MMI	BND	FX	EX	IM	GLD	GDP	CPI	GE
SMI	100															
PE	91	100														
DY	-95	-91	100													
MC	88	65	-83	100												
BD	68	40	-61	91	100											
BL	51	20	-46	86	93	100										
IR	-65	-67	62	-39	-20	-3	100									
MMI	49	26	-52	77	74	85	-21	100								
BND	52	20	-46	86	91	99	-6	87	100							
FX	-47	-41	50	-48	-31	-31	22	-28	-32	100						
EX	56	26	-51	86	89	95	-11	84	96	-41	100					
IM	52	22	-47	84	91	96	-1	80	96	-38	96	100				
GLD	62	55	-68	75	67	68	-24	74	65	-30	64	63	100			
GDP	36	8	-31	65	77	80	-6	70	78	-18	72	76	50	100		
CPI	46	14	-40	82	91	98	-4	85	98	-22	92	93	64	81	100	
GE	35	6	-28	64	73	79	-9	67	79	-11	79	73	44	68	83	100

Table A3.3. Percentages of correlation coefficients, 1997–2001

	SMI	PE	DY	MC	BD	BL	IR	MMI	BND	FX	EX	IM	GLD	GDP	CPI	GE
SMI	100															
PE	48	100														
DY	40	-13	100													
MC	79	41	-7	100												
BD	-66	-40	-74	-9	100											
BL	72	41	71	17	-97	100										
IR	36	36	60	-24	-85	85	100									
MMI	-34	25	-25	-50	-6	6	44	100								
BND	-75	-26	-60	-35	78	-86	-57	13	100							
FX	-73	-42	-18	-53	55	-64	-31	28	72	100						
EX	-70	-49	-30	-34	69	-81	-63	-7	80	83	100					
IM	-45	-58	-10	-10	60	-69	-69	-49	60	58	85	100				
GLD	78	29	69	37	-83	88	60	-22	-87	-74	-75	-52	100			
GDP	-14	-11	-6	-9	9	-14	-15	-8	12	8	17	16	-12	100		
CPI	-88	-35	-68	-45	88	-92	-60	27	91	76	78	53	-92	11	100	
GE	-14	-30	6	-12	8	-12	-11	-14	6	5	15	21	3	19	7	100

Table A3.4. Results of residual estimation, $\mu_y = y_t - \alpha_0 - \alpha x_t$

e-PE	e-DY	e-MC	e-BD	e-BL	e-IR	e-MMI	e-BND	e-FX	e-GLD	e-GDP	e-CPI	e-GE
-147.03	-23.86	430.66	-383.55	124.69	-116.21	-284.15	-515.46	-298.32	-222.19	-43.91	-525.65	-383.55
-121.82	-6.30	397.57	-369.83	144.75	-96.81	-264.75	-491.27	-274.55	-202.79	-24.00	-498.36	-375.74
-143.33	38.93	402.91	-301.15	184.25	-56.94	-224.88	-432.89	-230.30	-162.92	18.60	-464.75	-326.94
-154.68	-25.67	375.49	-370.93	122.31	-118.69	-286.63	-499.23	-290.74	-224.67	-47.75	-518.85	-408.38
-125.36	-104.34	342.86	-446.13	48.30	-190.82	-358.76	-556.77	-369.43	-296.80	-118.66	-561.54	-453.72
-136.42	-37.03	366.45	-405.96	109.29	-128.21	-296.15	-489.86	-315.13	-234.19	-57.06	-489.65	-298.10
-104.67	-41.05	322.53	-391.45	102.14	-135.24	-303.18	-489.83	-321.28	-241.22	-63.01	-492.05	-340.45
-107.75	-38.79	323.24	-380.72	101.93	-133.15	-301.09	-482.23	-327.06	-239.13	-61.21	-473.03	-343.71
-119.05	67.90	361.23	-272.80	200.41	-32.66	-200.60	-377.44	-228.32	-138.64	39.28	-370.92	-132.62
-69.64	164.43	392.63	-197.63	293.08	60.69	-107.25	-276.41	-123.61	-45.29	132.85	-280.81	-86.73
-50.44	85.27	354.50	-270.20	219.93	-14.45	-182.39	-351.35	-191.75	-120.43	61.30	-366.62	-142.97
-40.32	115.15	360.54	-240.31	244.78	13.76	-154.18	-336.92	-163.10	129.68	93.83	-346.29	-132.13
31.69	198.23	382.49	-157.69	324.58	94.82	-73.12	-248.27	-83.35	210.74	175.68	-258.51	-152.50
45.91	158.38	358.29	-176.54	286.46	57.99	-109.95	-275.63	-122.81	173.91	140.29	-278.64	-191.88
12.90	80.10	328.62	-271.41	213.71	-14.43	-182.37	-311.85	-198.29	101.49	68.01	-351.06	-214.85
36.90	57.31	316.43	-283.98	187.85	-34.37	-202.31	-337.15	-225.22	81.55	45.70	-354.54	-196.27
8.92	35.22	303.65	-287.61	162.49	-1.05	-221.89	-322.95	-248.30	61.97	24.82	-368.56	-236.64
27.13	90.38	311.73	-240.81	203.08	50.76	-170.08	-272.74	-190.81	113.78	83.94	-309.56	-58.25
47.44	143.23	323.05	-138.61	251.94	101.44	-119.40	-224.76	-138.38	164.46	133.86	-245.90	-83.34
22.97	181.06	328.88	-78.88	282.25	136.42	-84.42	-170.31	-108.65	199.44	173.15	-205.58	-56.71
33.82	189.49	323.44	-53.15	285.69	197.58	-76.16	-161.23	-99.07	207.70	175.08	-179.01	111.96
68.70	489.01	399.47	276.15	575.29	487.05	213.31	142.84	196.52	497.17	463.83	108.61	308.58
68.63	538.22	414.62	348.65	622.13	536.09	262.35	183.28	249.06	546.21	514.53	152.32	503.88
115.85	919.66	428.49	716.54	989.27	908.99	635.25	591.07	627.20	498.66	891.38	536.11	715.30
-114.90	738.30	368.48	525.57	787.29	719.59	463.01	392.10	435.18	309.26	702.05	352.28	493.48
-15.72	612.09	308.54	388.23	657.01	599.07	344.50	297.15	306.35	188.74	581.60	250.07	341.96
-120.88	476.30	248.73	242.75	514.22	466.13	215.37	181.41	170.79	55.80	448.31	135.45	296.74
-130.38	503.65	231.23	287.81	533.15	492.81	243.22	219.35	194.41	82.48	475.06	162.13	208.81
-21.44	597.03	205.20	370.36	616.06	583.01	338.25	314.96	286.36	172.68	565.33	270.65	326.34
-17.74	511.66	187.03	285.69	520.35	499.48	252.49	253.86	193.64	89.15	484.75	205.44	367.67
-38.27	617.88	170.85	386.62	617.10	603.02	352.38	367.16	298.93	192.69	589.01	308.98	391.53
32.14	769.01	119.27	616.36	755.76	750.97	507.47	537.97	446.45	340.64	737.67	475.47	616.73
35.03	729.06	135.03	554.93	709.53	685.40	462.15	527.03	405.14	301.52	699.70	454.67	897.63
39.37	773.01	149.66	587.36	750.01	728.52	508.61	573.38	446.07	344.64	743.54	497.79	473.66
152.13	602.77	127.65	422.69	578.16	562.13	351.62	415.65	285.37	178.25	577.87	313.08	490.14
218.28	599.42	115.39	424.59	559.10	559.78	343.66	408.12	284.77	234.30	577.82	310.73	525.57
217.44	452.04	107.34	297.42	407.68	417.43	191.77	286.41	139.36	91.95	436.26	186.70	316.18
190.60	524.28	87.38	351.21	476.13	488.16	259.25	375.07	207.03	162.68	508.43	266.47	321.22
98.78	447.80	25.61	293.05	392.69	363.47	197.56	344.41	126.05	90.89	437.00	203.96	368.23

Table A3.4. (cont.)

91.43	438.97	15.73	258.73	374.45	355.48	185.87	330.86	111.07	82.90	429.73	214.28	248.86
96.71	627.95	-7.02	499.06	542.88	539.10	367.36	560.63	296.87	266.52	614.07	423.64	502.98
73.97	631.41	-13.17	549.84	533.94	541.56	361.92	603.06	300.65	268.98	617.32	440.71	593.63
76.51	619.24	-30.83	531.46	520.38	529.89	352.37	591.58	292.91	257.31	606.37	438.08	497.55
110.41	549.70	-53.08	471.57	447.76	461.69	302.55	549.92	239.58	189.11	538.89	390.28	565.27
125.28	527.86	-57.98	441.98	414.88	441.02	289.40	538.24	218.03	168.44	511.53	393.26	685.23
123.13	503.72	-64.36	399.94	393.79	417.55	257.79	534.92	197.62	144.97	489.28	388.11	266.23
125.89	427.07	-53.28	348.24	311.60	343.41	194.92	476.49	124.36	70.83	415.86	313.97	279.99
123.49	513.60	-67.31	486.22	385.81	427.60	262.25	570.92	209.86	108.30	503.50	398.16	427.40
130.24	646.64	-96.65	635.99	517.20	557.12	390.06	627.42	346.37	237.82	633.74	543.21	559.56
130.95	556.50	-103.13	564.49	425.43	468.66	290.93	524.17	250.48	149.36	546.72	465.65	541.75
142.75	521.85	-97.83	550.65	390.77	436.52	266.17	518.85	220.53	117.22	517.96	442.32	705.58
141.10	524.90	-101.42	568.23	384.80	439.40	269.28	529.12	223.41	120.10	521.56	456.33	496.77
180.44	544.87	-104.64	609.54	398.57	458.70	287.79	553.89	247.52	139.40	541.58	484.21	582.22
175.70	478.20	-115.08	499.30	339.38	393.87	221.41	496.16	183.56	74.57	478.90	421.70	515.18
150.33	288.12	-132.02	305.87	158.15	210.83	53.79	310.37	-3.41	-108.47	353.74	243.06	313.44
141.44	328.08	-144.00	291.48	200.26	249.11	94.74	363.53	35.74	-70.19	392.38	305.46	498.57
144.59	324.60	-146.59	237.07	194.60	245.80	78.26	385.25	38.12	-73.50	327.24	306.55	725.21
135.55	126.87	-116.31	-10.80	6.55	57.12	-97.77	184.49	-147.50	-262.18	139.28	130.86	165.04
183.49	143.68	-135.10	-2.43	20.00	72.76	-76.64	247.74	-130.99	-246.54	155.64	157.63	275.58
176.97	43.42	-122.57	-88.44	-79.38	-21.64	-166.89	153.58	-221.02	-197.87	61.45	63.23	353.70
172.86	-2.62	-112.76	-86.30	-125.98	-65.17	-207.18	123.92	-253.18	-241.40	18.07	26.19	165.42
167.95	-67.29	-101.01	-162.79	-191.02	-125.65	-271.21	64.60	-312.78	-301.88	-42.05	-23.39	58.42
140.01	-86.91	-97.53	-210.68	-222.67	-147.78	-187.78	65.09	-331.42	-324.01	-63.75	-32.31	178.81
127.53	-132.89	-86.85	-288.46	-263.35	-191.92	-172.09	19.01	-369.87	-368.15	-107.82	-72.04	-78.42
92.08	-238.34	-66.04	-373.72	-365.18	-286.82	-376.04	-78.45	-477.89	-463.05	-202.15	-156.05	-62.06
92.38	-282.31	-56.52	-357.08	-405.08	-325.93	-379.50	-102.96	-517.44	-502.16	-238.38	-190.75	-41.56
71.12	-127.22	-87.63	-248.28	-259.39	-293.39	116.20	32.43	-104.52	-363.82	-99.32	-34.79	103.15
78.97	-308.03	-58.78	-307.48	-385.25	-456.78	-108.19	-108.59	-169.10	-527.21	-261.99	-130.24	-44.45
34.04	-256.34	-69.18	-325.16	-337.04	-414.47	44.18	-72.08	-31.03	-484.90	-222.49	-77.04	116.24
41.39	-368.41	-50.18	-474.85	-438.41	-511.80	134.09	-166.46	11.55	-582.23	-321.33	-152.57	-270.02
75.59	-431.21	-38.55	-423.68	-473.49	-563.54	-60.61	-202.83	-21.83	-633.97	-372.35	-182.29	-277.73
65.74	-458.01	-22.32	-459.44	-485.60	-586.32	-105.91	-229.38	266.26	-69.88	-401.02	-205.07	-277.43
36.43	-305.65	-61.17	-287.49	-355.21	-463.78	181.38	-62.23	724.16	52.66	-278.34	-51.92	-285.65
69.62	-263.92	-84.63	-281.61	-320.22	-430.59	255.06	17.40	232.67	85.85	-244.43	0.98	-218.80
-282.07	-306.42	-70.44	-362.81	-381.91	-499.90	240.34	-59.21	-16.77	16.54	-315.03	-37.50	-220.45
-469.92	-346.70	-66.93	-402.27	-424.81	-546.88	266.48	-94.68	-67.69	-31.32	-361.94	-64.77	-464.83
-373.59	-438.77	-64.67	-437.16	-505.89	-633.42	143.36	-210.94	-88.21	-117.86	-446.18	-136.00	-451.38
-371.98	-446.87	-64.26	-408.35	-503.75	-640.85	147.77	-200.93	-4.26	-124.41	-450.73	-128.13	-183.43
-292.89	-504.68	-49.48	-393.08	-548.57	-692.29	115.58	-288.90	-120.41	-176.73	-501.82	-177.49	-450.02
-185.47	-557.87	-33.91	-427.74	-593.80	-744.48	142.18	-351.53	-123.19	-228.92	-553.65	-218.55	-326.19
-243.11	-510.37	-49.15	-386.53	-547.19	-705.19	137.64	-296.44	-199.77	-188.75	-516.73	-183.66	52.75

Table A3.4. (cont.)

-220.56	-425.03	-84.81	-266.54	-476.95	-627.72	200.77	-213.46	-233.35	-111.28	-439.19	-110.60	-309.82
-148.97	-388.47	-95.94	-248.23	-431.49	-596.19	278.25	-170.04	-230.68	-80.63	-407.58	-87.88	-369.44
-174.07	-396.15	-92.07	-264.87	-432.58	-603.20	240.56	-165.65	-212.33	-81.51	-419.56	-105.78	-215.91
-173.99	-388.80	-93.62	-167.59	-421.25	-596.01	153.76	-174.60	-197.71	-74.32	-412.01	-87.70	-505.78
176.15	-410.35	-126.17	-124.25	-438.59	-327.12	120.79	-214.64	-194.41	-96.38	-433.35	-107.44	-451.55
228.57	-395.77	-137.08	-98.63	-421.16	-316.05	74.42	-220.29	-174.59	-85.31	-419.83	-100.77	-283.46
278.40	-282.90	-195.63	7.40	-301.78	-208.71	221.09	-109.18	-84.74	22.03	-311.77	-6.65	-110.07
-303.09	-288.48	-236.56	57.97	-304.55	-214.46	239.40	-86.32	-98.36	16.28	-316.80	-23.30	-291.73
-351.23	-218.47	-323.01	78.42	-231.96	-66.94	208.01	-38.69	-39.81	84.45	-245.11	42.55	-84.78
-369.02	-284.93	-282.51	-15.71	-287.65	-52.55	137.39	-106.31	-93.84	19.49	-311.01	-18.00	-326.33
-82.51	-302.14	-264.04	-48.92	-300.17	-69.09	99.59	-142.23	-57.48	2.95	-326.47	-23.64	-263.75
-51.22	-354.93	-224.69	-73.11	-345.67	-119.87	34.04	-176.53	8.92	-47.83	-377.03	-70.02	-2.31
-45.16	-346.36	-234.13	-69.40	-333.92	-113.81	-25.49	-155.77	-84.71	-41.77	-370.90	-59.55	-388.89
-162.04	-319.29	-272.22	-10.64	-305.17	-87.24	-177.98	-90.11	-44.15	-15.20	-342.10	-28.58	52.85
-349.08	-257.81	-328.53	-1.73	-245.00	-27.44	-268.09	-15.03	-52.12	24.45	-286.76	40.03	-158.94
-330.82	-262.33	-322.96	71.17	-248.96	-31.79	-141.10	-16.73	-55.59	20.10	-291.40	42.18	-309.65
-257.01	-373.29	-230.66	-19.98	-343.25	-135.04	-297.64	-135.44	-138.73	-83.15	-394.57	-50.18	-415.52
-66.24	-349.13	-257.42	-25.17	-314.77	-109.04	-257.68	-119.69	-118.85	61.69	-366.78	-21.86	-180.60
-54.83	-359.39	-243.22	-90.29	-321.42	-118.96	-238.92	-146.28	-119.59	136.15	-377.42	-42.68	-124.97
-34.06	-430.52	-209.71	-123.22	-391.92	-186.07	-324.71	-219.04	-139.04	80.72	-388.45	-105.38	-371.56
-11.63	-427.95	-215.64	-99.79	-386.11	-183.67	-342.71	-189.15	-136.20	-26.66	-436.23	-98.81	-311.05
-30.04	-472.49	-184.60	-166.29	-421.10	-224.69	-389.00	-236.69	-75.35	11.15	-478.83	-135.42	-480.17
-58.57	-446.98	-206.25	-135.15	-396.65	-201.53	-314.23	-216.43	-77.11	32.56	-454.95	-94.64	-362.60
-9.63	-480.20	-183.27	-169.13	-422.94	-232.07	-346.37	-223.14	-49.50	25.08	337.89	-116.37	-151.60
-5.39	-485.82	-178.98	-181.80	-422.08	-237.52	-307.87	-217.67	21.13	82.99	-491.45	-135.04	-354.99
30.42	-478.90	-187.44	-169.86	-414.34	-231.44	-278.75	-208.11	24.15	57.25	-486.09	-124.55	-208.63
31.38	-490.14	-183.01	-134.83	-419.86	-240.17	-403.36	-225.01	-11.25	23.99	-494.96	-135.37	-377.97
27.11	-420.70	-248.72	10.03	-356.16	-176.59	-327.04	-141.32	20.85	143.63	-430.73	-65.30	-351.68
15.02	-432.96	-242.23	9.36	-363.16	-184.16	-332.36	-158.13	26.83	120.88	-437.58	-57.56	-404.94
72.22	-475.27	-211.06	-26.25	-395.77	-217.42	-401.23	-204.92	77.08	150.10	-472.21	-90.82	-313.89
76.39	-465.57	-219.76	-9.63	-383.49	-208.73	-402.11	-206.52	119.44	121.12	-463.38	-60.11	-212.00
90.41	-454.40	-232.06	22.25	-374.35	-199.23	-391.08	-191.90	118.01	100.55	-457.69	-39.71	-388.38
82.80	-440.97	-241.85	21.00	-361.50	-186.81	-375.46	-161.07	126.93	65.38	-445.99	-36.10	-288.48
83.79	-468.68	-217.40	-5.74	-381.05	-211.67	-387.98	-201.97	123.05	56.29	-467.97	-60.96	-377.73
100.99	-427.62	-252.46	-2.41	-339.86	-173.79	-363.30	-173.18	91.42	43.95	-432.03	-27.48	-335.93
167.17	-493.35	-201.42	-54.22	-399.70	-232.32	-396.52	-207.49	45.13	-156.78	-492.21	-77.20	-102.74
166.51	-494.97	-204.17	-104.36	-397.13	-234.27	-382.98	-183.78	53.67	-104.42	-494.16	-92.37	42.38
110.04	-464.09	-233.26	-69.50	-369.39	-206.74	-313.79	-172.20	53.66	-53.53	-461.60	-71.33	-189.65

Table A3.5. Regression results

Summary output				

Regression statistics				
Multiple R	0.994			
R square	0.988			
Adjusted R square	0.987			
Standard error	47.251			
Observations	119.000			

ANOVA

	df	SS	MS	F
Regression	6.000	20,449,926.954		1,526.583
Residual	112.000	250,056.402		
Total	118.000	20,699,983.356		

	Coefficients	Standard error	t-stat	P-value
Intercept	760.179	257.468		0.004
PE	7.548	2.034		0.000
MC	0.0003	0.000		0.000
IR	8.576	2.203		0.000
BND	- 2.237	0.709	- 3.156	0.002
FX	6.493	1.510		0.000
CPI	- 7.109	3.167	- 2.245	0.027

Appendix 4 Day of the Week and January Effect Test Results

Table A4.1. The day of the week effect, 1992–2001

Summary output				

Regression statistics				
Multiple R	0.121507			
R square	0.014764			
Adjusted R square	0.013155			
Standard error	1.874231			
Observations	2454			

ANOVA				
	df	SS	MS	F
Regression	4	128.9129	32.22823	9.174662
Residual	2449	8602.707	3.512743	
Total	2453	8731.62		

	Coefficients	Standard error	t-stat	P-value
Monday	-0.41671	0.086636	-4.80991	1.6E-06
Tuesday	0.256609	0.120899	2.122496	0.033896
Wednesday	0.550528	0.120663	4.562528	5.3E-06
Thursday	0.421704	0.120604	3.496588	0.00048
Friday	0.658788	0.12084	5.451733	5.49E-08

Table A4.2. The day of the week effect, 1992–1996

Summary Output				

Regression statistics

Multiple R	0.130298			
R square	0.016978			
Adjusted R square	0.013757			
Standard error	1.439502			
Observations	1226			

ANOVA

	df	SS	MS	F
Regression	4	43.69736	10.92434	5.271943
Residual	1221	2530.114	2.072166	
Total	1225	2573.812		

	Coefficients	Standard error	t-stat	P-value
Monday	-0.32334	0.094305	-3.42862	0.000627
Tuesday	0.246798	0.131464	1.87731	0.060714
Wednesday	0.486297	0.131207	3.706326	0.00022
Thursday	0.401996	0.13108	3.066786	0.002211
Friday	0.523824	0.131464	3.984549	7.16E-05

Table A4.3. The day of the week effect, 1997–2001

Summary output				

Regression statistics

Multiple R	0.12176			
R square	0.014825			
Adjusted R square	0.011603			
Standard error	2.226192			
Observations	1228			

ANOVA

	df	SS	MS	F
Regression	4	91.21048	22.80262	4.601078
Residual	1223	6061.102	4.95593	
Total	1227	6152.313		

	Coefficients	Standard error	t-stat	P-value
Monday	-0.5093	0.145221	-3.50705	0.00047
Tuesday	0.265624	0.202863	1.309374	0.190653
Wednesday	0.613965	0.202466	3.032437	0.002477
Thursday	0.440322	0.202466	2.174795	0.029837
Friday	0.792788	0.202664	3.911838	9.66E-05

Table A4.4. The day of the week effect, 1992

Summary output				

Regression statistics				
Multiple R	0.231804			
R square	0.053733			
Adjusted R square	0.038093			
Standard error	1.585358			
Observations	247			

ANOVA

	df	SS	MS	F
Regression	4	34.53823	8.634557	3.435462
Residual	242	608.2334	2.513361	
Total	246	642.7716		

	Coefficients	Standard error	t-stat	P-value
Monday	0.195829	0.22648	0.864664	0.388079
Tuesday	-0.80814	0.320291	-2.52314	0.012273
Wednesday	-0.14607	0.320291	-0.45604	0.64877
Thursday	0.243184	0.318685	0.763084	0.446156
Friday	0.164402	0.318685	0.515874	0.606413

Table A4.5. The day of the week effect, 1993

Summary output

Regression statistics

Multiple R	0.240625
R square	0.057901
Adjusted R square	0.042199
Standard error	1.26391
Observations	245

ANOVA

	df	SS	MS	F
Regression	4	23.56296	5.890739	3.687548
Residual	240	383.3922	1.597468	
Total	244	406.9552		

	Coefficients	Standard error	t-stat	P-value
Monday	-0.27766	0.18436	-1.50605	0.13337
Tuesday	0.402784	0.25805	1.560873	0.119871
Wednesday	0.913021	0.256784	3.555598	0.000454
Thursday	0.602974	0.256784	2.348174	0.019678
Friday	0.730777	0.25805	2.831916	0.00502

Table A4.6. The day of the week effect, 1994

Summary output				

Regression statistics				
Multiple R	0.152869			
R square	0.023369			
Adjusted R square	0.007092			
Standard error	1.645427			
Observations	245			

ANOVA

	df	SS	MS	F
Regression	4	15.54811	3.887026	1.435688
Residual	240	649.7832	2.70743	
Total	244	665.3313		

	Coefficients	Standard error	t-stat	P-value
Monday	-0.5436	0.242605	-2.24069	0.025961
Tuesday	0.737864	0.336163	2.194958	0.029125
Wednesday	0.541704	0.336163	1.61143	0.1084
Thursday	0.359432	0.336163	1.069217	0.286046
Friday	0.611002	0.337803	1.808753	0.071741

Table A4.7. The day of the week effect, 1995

Summary output

Regression statistics
Multiple R	0.170744
R square	0.029154
Adjusted R square	0.01304
Standard error	1.240937
Observations	246

ANOVA

	df	SS	MS	F
Regression	4	11.14441	2.786102	1.809246
Residual	241	371.1217	1.539924	
Total	245	382.2661		

	Coefficients	Standard error	t-stat	P-value
Monday	-0.41957	0.182966	-2.29315	0.022701
Tuesday	0.389524	0.253525	1.536431	0.125744
Wednesday	0.641742	0.253525	2.531274	0.012002
Thursday	0.382685	0.253525	1.509453	0.132493
Friday	0.530211	0.253525	2.091353	0.037544

Table A4.8. The day of the week effect, 1996

Summary output				

Regression statistics				
Multiple R	0.160099			
R square	0.025632			
Adjusted R square	0.009324			
Standard error	1.35328			
Observations	244			

ANOVA

	df	SS	MS	F
Regression	4	11.51396	2.878489	1.571771
Residual	239	437.6966	1.831367	
Total	243	449.2106		

	Coefficients	Standard error	t-stat	P-value
Monday	-0.61476	0.19953	-3.08106	0.002304
Tuesday	0.548565	0.277826	1.974493	0.049477
Wednesday	0.521905	0.276477	1.887695	0.060278
Thursday	0.464789	0.276477	1.68111	0.094048
Friday	0.624387	0.277826	2.247404	0.025527

Table A4.9. The day of the week effect, 1997

Summary output				

Regression statistics				
Multiple R	0.116937			
R square	0.013674			
Adjusted R square	-0.00263			
Standard error	2.285579			
Observations	247			

ANOVA

	df	SS	MS	F
Regression	4	17.52648	4.38162	0.838769
Residual	242	1264.177	5.22387	
Total	246	1281.703		

	Coefficients	Standard error	t-stat	P-value
Monday	-0.57081	0.329895	-1.73029	0.084854
Tuesday	-0.04408	0.466542	-0.09448	0.924808
Wednesday	0.693376	0.45963	1.508554	0.132717
Thursday	0.220842	0.461853	0.478164	0.632965
Friday	0.328907	0.461853	0.712148	0.477059

Table A4.10. The day of the week effect, 1998

Summary output				

Regression statistics				
Multiple R	0.137986			
R square	0.01904			
Adjusted R square	0.002622			
Standard error	2.926769			
Observations	244			

ANOVA

	df	SS	MS	F
Regression	4	39.73664	9.934159	1.159723
Residual	239	2047.269	8.565979	
Total	243	2087.006		

	Coefficients	Standard error	t-stat	P-value
Monday	-0.49542	0.422443	-1.17276	0.24206
Tuesday	-0.02481	0.59142	-0.04196	0.96657
Wednesday	0.746516	0.597424	1.249557	0.212684
Thursday	0.777732	0.594368	1.308501	0.19196
Friday	0.888724	0.594368	1.495241	0.136171

Table A4.11. The day of the week effect, 1999

Summary output

Regression statistics

Multiple R	0.112098
R square	0.012566
Adjusted R square	-0.00389
Standard error	2.206302
Observations	245

ANOVA

	df	SS	MS	F
Regression	4	14.86706	3.716765	0.763546
Residual	240	1168.265	4.867769	
Total	244	1183.132		

	Coefficients	Standard error	t-stat	P-value
Monday	-0.18327	0.321822	-0.56946	0.569574
Tuesday	0.37972	0.448247	0.847124	0.39777
Wednesday	0.10263	0.450457	0.227835	0.819969
Thursday	0.32098	0.450457	0.712565	0.476807
Friday	0.709909	0.448247	1.583746	0.114568

Table A4.12. The day of the week effect, 2000

Summary output				

Regression statistics				
Multiple R	0.234758			
R square	0.055111			
Adjusted R square	0.039493			
Standard error	1.862411			
Observations	247			

ANOVA

	df	SS	MS	F
Regression	4	48.95812	12.23953	3.528692
Residual	242	839.395	3.468575	
Total	246	888.3532		

	Coefficients	Standard error	t-stat	P-value
Monday	-0.95305	0.277632	-3.4328	0.000703
Tuesday	0.637039	0.380908	1.672423	0.095733
Wednesday	0.856388	0.380908	2.248282	0.025459
Thursday	0.611037	0.382689	1.596694	0.111639
Friday	1.409037	0.382689	3.681937	0.000285

Table A4.13. The day of the week effect, 2001

Summary output				

Regression statistics
Multiple R	0.150633			
R square	0.02269			
Adjusted R square	0.006402			
Standard error	1.659292			
Observations	245			

ANOVA
	df	SS	MS	F
Regression	4	15.3414	3.835349	1.393025
Residual	240	660.7804	2.753251	
Total	244	676.1218		

	Coefficients	Standard error	t-stat	P-value
Monday	-0.36179	0.242033	-1.49482	0.136276
Tuesday	0.395828	0.340498	1.162496	0.246189
Wednesday	0.694603	0.337113	2.060449	0.040434
Thursday	0.299904	0.335507	0.893883	0.37228
Friday	0.647474	0.338775	1.911221	0.057167

Table A4.14. The January effect, 1975-2001

Summary output				

Regression statistics				
Multiple R	0.1449			
R square	0.020996			
Adjusted R square	-0.01408			
Standard error	8.940274			
Observations	319			

ANOVA

	df	SS	MS	F
Regression	11	526.2466	47.8406	0.598542
Residual	307	24538.05	79.9285	
Total	318	25064.3		

	Coefficients	Standard error	t-stat	P-value
January	3.01433	1.753332	1.719201	0.086586
February	-3.99204	2.479586	-1.60996	0.108434
March	-3.74605	2.479586	-1.51076	0.131879
April	-2.36412	2.479586	-0.95343	0.341122
May	-3.66613	2.479586	-1.47853	0.140292
June	-1.16459	2.456519	-0.47408	0.635779
July	-2.79186	2.456519	-1.13651	0.256629
August	-3.45443	2.456519	-1.40623	0.160667
September	-3.66939	2.456519	-1.49374	0.136271
October	-2.02708	2.456519	-0.82518	0.409909
November	-3.83843	2.456519	-1.56255	0.119189
December	-0.90235	2.456519	-0.36733	0.713626

Table A4.15. The January effect, 1992-1996

Summary output				

Regression statistics				
Multiple R	0.328296			
R square	0.107779			
Adjusted R square	-0.09669			
Standard error	9.006464			
Observations	60			

ANOVA

	df	SS	MS	F
Regression	11	470.3373	42.75794	0.527118
Residual	48	3893.587	81.11639	
Total	59	4363.924		

	Coefficients	Standard error	t-stat	P-value
January	0.477863	4.027813	0.118641	0.906055
February	-2.59572	5.696188	-0.45569	0.650664
March	-4.76775	5.696188	-0.83701	0.406736
April	-2.16602	5.696188	-0.38026	0.705432
May	1.562455	5.696188	0.274298	0.785032
June	0.230149	5.696188	0.040404	0.967939
July	-1.32204	5.696188	-0.23209	0.817453
August	2.054875	5.696188	0.360746	0.719872
September	1.321912	5.696188	0.23207	0.817471
October	3.268382	5.696188	0.573784	0.568793
November	-4.54646	5.696188	-0.79816	0.42871
December	4.348606	5.696188	0.763424	0.448947

Table A4.16. The January effect, 1997-2001

Summary output				

Regression statistics				
Multiple R	0.414652			
R square	0.171936			
Adjusted R square	-0.01783			
Standard error	13.13164			
Observations	60			

ANOVA

	df	SS	MS	F
Regression	11	1718.632	156.2393	0.90605
Residual	48	8277.12	172.44	
Total	59	9995.752		

	Coefficients	Standard error	t-stat	P-value
January	9.069628	5.872648	1.544385	0.129063
February	-15.9554	8.305179	-1.92114	0.060663
March	-12.6752	8.305179	-1.52617	0.133529
April	-7.1131	8.305179	-0.85647	0.395996
May	-20.284	8.305179	-2.44233	0.018326
June	-7.22886	8.305179	-0.8704	0.388412
July	-14.8926	8.305179	-1.79317	0.079248
August	-15.8355	8.305179	-1.90671	0.062554
September	-12.4625	8.305179	-1.50057	0.140017
October	-7.91001	8.305179	-0.95242	0.345656
November	-6.06021	8.305179	-0.72969	0.469126
December	-8.55381	8.305179	-1.02994	0.308202

List of Figures

List of Tables

List of Appendices

Bibliography

Abdullah DA, Hayworth SC (1993) Macroeconometrics of stock price fluctuations. Quarterly Journal of Business and Economics 32:49–63

Abelson P, Joyeux R (2000) Economic forecasting. Allen and Unwin, Sydney

Abraham A, Ikenberry DL (1994) The individual investor and the weekend effect. Journal of Financial and Quantitative Analysis 29:263–277

Aggrawal A, Tandon K (1994) Anomalies or illusions? evidence from stock markets in eighteen countries. Journal of International Money and Finance 13:83–106

Akdenis L, Salih A, Caner M (2002) Time varying betas help in asset pricing: the threshold CAPM. Working Paper, University of Pittsburgh, Pittsburgh

Akrasanee N, Jansen K, Pongpisanupichit J (1993) International capital flows and economic adjustment in Thailand. Thailand Development Research Institute, Bangkok

Allen F, Gale D (1990) Incomplete markets and incentives to set up an options exchange. Geneva Papers on Risk and Insurance 15:17–46

Allen F, Gale D (2000) Bubble and crises. The Economic Journal 110:236–255

Al-Loughani N, Chappell D (2001) Modelling the day of the week effect in the Kuwait stock exchange: a nonlinear GARCH representation. Journal of Applied Financial Economics 11:353–359

Asia Week (2000) Thailand: struggling out of a deep hole.
http://www.asiaweek.com/asiaweek/features/financial500.2000

Aydemir AB (1998) Volatility modelling in finance. In: J Knight, S Satchell (eds) Forecasting volatility in the financial markets. Reed Educational and Professional Publishing, Oxford

Baillie R, McMahon P (1989) The foreign exchange market. Cambridge University Press, Cambridge

Ball R (1978) Anomalies in relationships between securities yields and yield-surrogates. Journal of Financial Economics. 6:103–126

Balvers RJ, Cosimano TF, McDonald B (1990) Predicting stock returns in an efficient market. Journal of Finance 45:1109–1135

Bank of Thailand (2000a) Economic conditions. Monetary Policy Group, Bangkok

Bank of Thailand (2000b) Financial institutions and markets in Thailand.
http://www.bot.or.th

Bank of Thailand (2002) Roles of the bank of Thailand. http://www.bot.or.th

Banz RW (1981) The relationship between return and market value of common stocks. Journal of Financial Economics 9:3–18

Barndorff-Nielson OE, Nicalato E, Shephard N (2001) Some recent developments in stochastic volatility modelling. Working Paper, University of Aarhus, Denmark

Berry M, Burmeister E, McElroy M (1988) Sorting out risks using known APT factors. Financial Analysts Journal 44:9–42

Berument H, Kayimaz H (2001) The day of the week effect on stock market volatility. Journal of Economics and Finance 25:181–193

Binswanger M (1999) Stock markets, speculative bubbles and economic growth. Edward Elgar Publishing, London

Black F (1986) Noise. Journal of Finance 41:529–543

Black F, Jensen MC, Scholes M (1972) The capital asset pricing model: some empirical tests. In: M Jensen (eds) Studies in the theory of capital markets. Praeger, New York, pp 79–121

Black K, Eldredge D (2002) Business and economic statistics: using Microsoft EXCEL. South Western, Ohio

Bodie Z, Kane A, Marcus A (1993) Investment. Irwin, Cambridge, Massachusetts

Bollerslev T (1986) Generalized autoregressive conditional heteroscedasticity. Journal of Econometrics 31:307–327

Bond SR (2001) The behavior of stock prices: lesson from current research on company investment. Institute for Fiscal Studies and Nuffield College, Oxford

Box GEP, Jenkins GM (1976) Time series analysis: forecasting and control. Holden Day, San Francisco

Brigham EF, Gapenski LC (1994) Financial management: theory and practice. 7th edn, Dryden Press, New York

Brooks R et al. (2000) A multi-country study of power ARCH models and national stock market returns. Journal of International Money and Finance 19:377–397

Brown SJ, Otsuki T (1990) Macroeconomic factors and the Japanese equity markets: the CAPMD project. In: E Elton and M Gruber (eds) Japanese capital markets. Ballinger, New York

Butler KC, Malaikah SJ (1992) Efficiency and inefficiency in thinly traded stock markets: Kuwait and Saudi Arabia. Journal of Banking and Finance 16:97–201

Cabello A, Ortiz E (2002) Day of the week and month of the year anomalies at the Mexican stock market. Paper presented to International Trade and Finance Association, Ramkhumhang University, May, Bangkok

Campbell JY, Shiller RJ (1987) Cointegration and tests of present value models. Journal of Political Economy 95:1062–1088

Campbell JY, Lo AW, MacKinlay AC (1997) The econometrics of financial markets. Princeton University Press, New Jersey

Charemza W, Deadman DF (1995) Speculative bubbles with stochastic explosive roots: the failure of unit root testing. Journal of Empirical Finance 2:153–163

Charest G (1978) Split information, stock returns and market efficiency. Journal of Financial Economics 6:265–330

Chen H, Singal V (2001) What drives the January effect? Working Paper, Merrick School of Business, University of Baltimore, Baltimore

Chen NF (1983) Some empirical tests of the theory of arbitrage pricing. Journal of Finance 38:1393–1414

Chen NF, Roll R, Ross S (1986) Economic forces and the stock market. Journal of Business 59:83–403

Cheng ACS (1995) The UK stock market and economic factors: a new approach. Journal of Business Finance and Accounting 22:129–142

Chew DH (1997) Introduction: financial innovation in the 1980s and 1990s. Irwin Mc Graw-Hill, New York

Chia SY, Pacini M (1997) ASEAN in the new Asia: issues and trends. Working Paper, Institute of Southeast Asia Studies, Singapore

Chiat HS, Finn FJ (1983) Random walks on the stock exchange of Singapore. Accounting and Finance 23:81–87

Clarke M, Islam SMN (2004) Economic growth and social welfare: operationalising social choice theory. North Holland, Amsterdam

Cooper JCB (1982) World stock markets: some random walk tests. Applied Economics 14:515–531

Cowles A (1933) Can stock market forecasters forecast? Econometrica 1:309–324

Cross F (1973) The behaviour of stock prices on Friday and Monday. Financial Analyst Studies 29:67–69

CSES (Center for Strategic Economic Studies) (1998) Crisis in East Asia: global watershed or passing storm? Conference Report, Victoria University, Melbourne

Cuthbertson K (1996) Quantitative financial economics: stocks, bonds, foreign exchange. John Wiley and Sons, London

Dabek RA (1999) Valuation of a technology. Intellectual Property Licensing Seminar, University of Dayton School of Law, Dayton, Ohio, http://www.udayton.edu/~lawtech/cle99lic-dabek

Danielsson J (2002) Why risk models can't be trusted. ERisk, March, http://www.Erisk.com

Dhakal D, Kandil M, Sharma SC (1993) Causality between the money supply and share prices: a VAR investigation. Quarterly Journal of Business and Economics 32:52–74

Diba B, Grossman H (1988) Explosive rational bubbles in stock prices. American Economic Review 78:520–530

Ding Z, Granger CWJ (1996) Modeling volatility persistence of speculative returns: a new approach. Journal of Econometrics 73:185–215

Ding Z, Granger CWJ, Engle RF (1993) A long memory property of stock market returns and a new model. Journal of Empirical Finance 1:83–106

Dixon C (1999) The development implications of the Pacific Asian crises: the Thai experience. Third World Quarterly 20:439–452

Eatwell J, Milgate M, Newman P (1990) Time series and statistics. Macmillan, London

Eatwell J, Milgate M, Newman P (1987) Finance. Macmillan, London

EMEAP (2002) Financial markets and payment systems in EMEAP economies. http://www.emeap.org:8084/RedBook/

Engle RF (1982) Autoregressive conditional heteroscedasticity with estimates of the variance of United Kingdom Inflation. Econometrica 50:987–1007

Fama EF (1990) Stock returns, expected returns, real activity. Journal of Finance 45:1089–1108

Fama EF (1965) The behaviour of stock market prices. Journal of Business 38:34–105

Fama EF (1970) Efficient capital markets: a review of theory and empirical work. Journal of Finance 25:383–417

Fama EF (1976) Foundations of finance. Basic Books, New York

Fama EF (1981) Stock returns, real activity, inflation, money. American Economic Review 71:545–565

Fama EF (1991) Efficient capital markets: II. Journal of Finance 96:1575–1617

Fama EF, French K (1988) Dividend yields and expected stock returns. Journal of Financial Economics 22:3–25

Fama EF, French KR (1989) Business conditions and expected returns to stocks and bonds. Journal of Financial Economics 25:23–50

Fama EF, French KR (1992) The cross-section of expected stock returns. Journal of Finance 50:131–155

Fama EF, French K, Booth D, Sinquefield R (1993) Differences in the risks and returns of NYSE and NASD stocks. Financial Analysts Journal 49:37–41

Fifield S, Power D, Sinclair C (2002) The role of economic and fundamental factors in emerging market share return. Paper presented to International Trade and Finance Association, Ramkhumhang University, May, Bangkok

FitzHerbert R (1998) Blueprint for investment: a long term contrarian approach. 2nd edn, Wrightbooks, Victoria

Fox J (2001) When bubbles burst. Fortune, 29 May

Franses PH, Dijk D (2000) Non-linear time series models in empirical finance. Cambridge University Press, London

French KR (1980) Stock returns and the weekend effect. Journal of Financial Economics 8: 55–70

French KR, Schwert GW, Stambaugh RF (1987) Expected stock returns and volatility. Journal of Financial Econometrics 19:3–30

Friend I, Blume M, Crockett J (1970) Mutual funds and other institutional investors: a new perspective. McGraw-Hill, New York

Fry MJ (1995) Money, interest, banking in economic development. 2nd edn, The Johns Hopkins University Press, Baltimore

Fung HG, Lie CJ (1990) Stock market and economic activities: a causal analysis. In: SG Rhee and RP Chang (eds) Pacific-basin capital markets research. Elsevier Science, Amsterdam

Fung L (2001) Time series analysis of rational speculative bubble: a simulation experiment. Working Paper, Department of Management, Birkbeck College, London

Gay GD, Kolb RW (1984) International finance: concepts and issues. Prentice Hall, Virginia

Gibbons MR, Hess P (1981) Day of the week effects and asset returns. Journal of Business 54:579–596

Glosten L, Jagannathan R, Runkle D (1993) Relationship between the expected value and the volatility of nominal excess return on stocks. Journal of Finance 48:1779–1801

Gourieroux C, Jasiak J (2001) Financial econometrics: problems, models, methods. Princeton University Press, New Jersey

Grabbe JO (1996) International financial markets. Prentice Hall, New Jersey

Gujarati DN (2003) Basic econometrics. McGraw-Hill, New York

Hansen PR, Lunde A (2001) A comparison of volatility models: does anything beat a GARCH(1,1). Working Paper, Centre for Analytical Finance, University of Aarhus, Denmark

Harman YS, Zuehlke TW (2001) Testing for rational bubbles with a generalized Weibull Hazard. Working Paper, Department of Finance, Miami University, Oxford

Harvey CR (1991) The world price of covariance risk. Journal of Finance 46:111–157

Harvey CR (1995a) Predictable risk and returns in emerging markets. Review of Financial Studies 8:773–816

Harvey CR (1995b) The risk exposure of emerging equity markets. The World Bank Economic Review 12:19–50

Henke H (2001) Tax-selling and window dressing: an investigation of the January effect on the Polish stock market. Working Paper, Department of Economics, Europa University, Viadrana, Germany

Ho YK (1990) Stock return seasonalities in Asia Pacific markets. Journal of International Financial Management and Accounting 2:44–77

Ho YK (1991) The Hong Kong financial system. Oxford University Press, New York

Hossain A, Chowdhury A (1996) Monetary and financial policies in developing countries: growth and stabilization. Routlege, London

Hunt B, Terry C (2002) Financial institutions and markets. 3rd edn, Nelson, Melbourne

Ikenberry D, Rankine G, Stice EK (1996) What do stock splits really signal? Journal of Finance 48:65–91

IMF (International Monetary Fund) (2002) International financial statistics. CD-Rom, Washington DC

International Financial Risk Institute (2001) Background to the financial and economic turbulence of 1997–1998. http://newrisk.ifci.ch/145900.htm

Islam S (2001) Applied welfare economics: measurement and analysis of social welfare by econometric consumption models. Research Monograph 1/2001, CSES, Victoria University, Melbourne

Islam S, Oh KB (2000) Econometric analyses of e-commerce stocks: valuation, volatility and predictability. Seminar paper, CSES, Victoria University, Melbourne

Islam S, Oh KB (2003) Applied financial econometrics in e-commerce. Contributions to Economic Analysis, North Holland Publishing, Amsterdam

Islam S, Watanapalachaikul S (2002a) Financial issues in the developing economy: an empirical investigation of the Thai telecommunications sector. Paper presented to International Trade and Finance Association, Ramkhumhang University, May, Bangkok

Islam S, Watanapalachaikul S (2002b) Financial market and reform strategy in developing countries: a case study of the Thai telecommunication sector. Paper presented to Economic Recovery and Reform, Thammasart University, October, Bangkok

Islam S, Watanapalachaikul S (2002c) Stock valuation in a developing economy: a case study of Thai telecommunications stocks. Paper presented to Asia Pacific Economics and Business Conference, October, Sarawak

Islam S, Watanapalachaikul S (2002d) Time series financial econometrics of Thai stock valuation. Seminar paper, September, Victoria University, Melbourne

Islam S, Watanapalachaikul S (2003) Time series financial econometrics of the Thai stock market: a multivariate error correction and valuation model. Paper presented to Global Business and Economic Development, Asian Institute of Technology, January, Bangkok

Islam S, Oh KB, Watanapalachaikul S (2001) Empirical characterization and financial issues of the Thai telecommunication industry. Seminar paper, November, Victoria University, Melbourne

Islam S, Oh KB, Watanapalachaikul S (2001a) Stock valuation: a case study of the Thai telecommunication industry. Seminar paper, July, Victoria University, Melbourne

Jaffe JR (1974) Special information and insider trading. Journal of Business 47:410–428

Jaffe JR, Westerfield R (1985) The weekend effect in common stock returns: the international evidence. Journal of Finance 40:433–454

Jegadeesh N, Titman S (1993) Returns to buying winners and selling loosers: implications for stock market efficiency. Journal of Finance 48:65–91

Jensen M (1978) Some anomalous evidence regarding market efficiency. Journal of Financial Economics 12:33–56

Jensen M, Ruback RS (1983) The market for corporate control: the scientific evidence. Journal of Financial Economics 11:5–50

Jiang GJ (1998) Stochastic volatility and option pricing. In: J Knight, S Satchell, Forecasting volatility in the financial markets. Reed Educational and Professional Publishing, Oxford

Juttner DJ, Hawtrey KM (1997) Financial markets: money and risk. 4th edn, Addison Wesley Longman, Melbourne

Keane S (1983) Stock market efficiency. Phillip Allan Publishers, Oxford

Keim DB, Staumbaugh RF (1984) A further investigation of the weekend effect in stock returns. Journal of Finance 39:818–835

Kendall MJ (1953) The analysis of economic time series, part 1: prices. Journal of the Royal Statistical Society 96:11–25

Kiranand S (1999) An investigation of Asian stock markets integration. Dissertation, Chulalongkorn University, Bangkok

Ko KS, Lee SB (1991) A comparative analysis of the daily behavior of stock returns: Japan, the US and the Asian NICs. Journal of Business Finance and Accounting 18:219–234

Koehler AB, Snyder RD (1999) Forecasting models and prediction intervals for the multiplicative Holt-Winters method. Working Paper, Monash University, Melbourne

Kwon CS, Shin TS, Bacon FW (1997) The effect of macroeconomic variables on stock market returns in developing markets. Multinational Business Review 5:63–70

Leightner JE (1999) Globalization and Thailand's financial crisis. Journal of Economic Issues 33:367–373

Lewis S (1998) Banking system and capital market development: the case of Thailand. Malaysian Journal of Economic Studies 35:95–111

Lie F, Brooks R, Faff R (2000) Modelling the equity beta risk of Australian financial sector companies. Australian Economic Papers 39:301–311

Lintner J (1965) The valuation of risky assets and the selection of risky investments in stock portfolios and capital budgeting. Review of Economics and Statistics 47:13–37

Lo A (1996) Market efficiency: stock market behaviour in theory and practice. Edward Elgar Publishing, London

Madala GS (2001) Introduction to econometrics. 3rd edn, John Wiley and Son, West Sussex

Masuyama S, Vandenbrink D, Yue CS (1999) East Asia's financial systems: evolution and crisis. Institute of Southeast Asian Studies, Singapore

McConnell JJ, Muscarella CJ (1985) Corporate capital expenditure decisions and the market value of the firm. Journal of Financial Economics 14:399–422

McKinnon R (1973) Money and capital in economic development. Brookings Institution, Washington

McKinnon R (1976) Money and finance in economic growth development, Marcel Dekker, New York

McQueen G, Thorley S (1994) Bubbles, stock returns, duration dependence. Journal of Financial and Quantitative Analysis 29:196–197

Mctaggart D, Findlay C, Parkin M (1996) Macroeconomics. Addison-Wesley Publishing Company, Melbourne

Michaely R, Thaler R, Womack K (1995) Price reactions to dividend initiations and omissions: overreaction or drift? Journal of Finance 50:573–608

Mills TC (1999) The econometric modelling of financial time series. Cambridge University Press, Cambridge

Mishkin FS (1997) Understanding financial crises: a developing country perspective. The International Bank for Reconstruction and Development, World Bank, Washington DC

Mishkin FS (1999) Lessons from the Thai Asian crisis. Journal of International Money and Finance 18:709–723

Moosa IA (2003a) International finance: an analytical approach. 2nd edn, McGraw Hill, Sydney

Moosa IA (2003b) International financial operations: arbitrage, hedging, speculation. Palgrave, London

Mudholkar G et al.(1996) A generalization of the Weibull distribution with application to the analysis of survival data. Journal of the American Statistical Association 91:1575–1583

Myrdal G (1981) Asian drama: an inquiry into the poverty of nations. In: MP Todaro (ed.) Economic development in the third world. 2nd edn, Longman, New York

Nasseh A, Strauss J (2000) Stock prices and domestic and international macroeconomic activity: a cointegration approach. The Quarterly Review of Economics and Finance 40:229–245

Nassir A, Mohammad S (1987) The January effect of stocks traded at the Kuala Lumpur stock exchange: an empirical analysis. Hong Kong Journal of Business Management 5:35–50

Nelson DB (1991) Conditional heteroskedasticity in asset returns: a new approach. Econometrica 59:347–370

Nikolova S (2002) Lecture notes on debt and money market. University of Florida, Gainesville

Nuntajindawat N (1995) The efficiency of the stock market in Thailand. Dissertation, Asian Institute of Technology, Bangkok

Oh KB (2001) An empirical analysis of financial issues in the Australian electronic commerce sector. Dissertation, Victoria University, Melbourne

Palepu K, Healy P, Bernard V (2000) Business analysis and valuation: using financial statements. 2nd edn, South Western College, Ohio

Peirson G et al. (1995) Business finance. 6th edn, McGraw-Hill, Sydney

Piero A (1996) Stock prices, production and interest rates: comparison of three European countries with the USA. Empirical Economics 2:221–234

Poon S, Granger C (2003) Forecasting volatility in financial markets: a review. Working Paper, Strathclyde University, Glasgow

Poterba J, Summers L (1986) The persistence of volatility and stock market fluctuations. American Economic Review 76:1141–1151

Pratt SP et al. (1996) Valuing a business: the analysis and appraisal of closely held companies. 3rd edn, McGraw-Hill, New York

Rappoport P, White E (1993) Was there a bubble in the 1929 stock market? Journal of Economic History 53:549–574

Reinganum MR (1983) The anomalous stock market behavior of small firms in January: empirical tests for tax-loss selling effects. Journal of Financial Economics 12:89–104

Rodan G, Hewison K, Robison R (2001) The political economy of South-East Asia: conflicts, crises and change. Oxford University Press, Melbourne

Roll R (1983) The turn of the year effect and the return premia of small firms. Journal of Portfolio Management 3:379–402

Rosiff MS, Kenney WR (1976) Capital market seasonality: the case of stock returns. Journal of Financial Economics 3:379–402

Samuelson PA (1965a) Proof that properly anticipated prices fluctuate randomly. Industrial Management Review 6:41–50

Samuelson PA (1965b) Rational theory of warrant pricing. Industrial Management Review, Spring

Schwert GW (1983) Size and stock returns, other empirical regularities. Journal of Financial Economics 12:3–12

Schwert GW (1987) Effects of model specification on tests for unit roots in macroeconomic data. Journal of Monetary Economics 20:73–103

Schwert GW (1990) Stock volatility and the crash of 87. Review of Financial Studies 3:77–102

Seyhun N (1986) Insiders' profits, costs of trading, market efficiency. Journal of Financial Economics 16:189–212

Sharma JL, Kennedy RE (1977) A comparative analysis of stock price behaviour on the Bombay, London and New York stock exchanges. Journal of Financial and Quantitative Analysis 12:391–413

Sharpe RF (1964) Capital asset prices: a theory of market equilibrium under conditions of risk. Journal of Finance 19:425–442

Sharpe WF (1966) Mutual fund performance. Journal of Business, January

Sharpe WF, Cooper, GM (1972) Risk-return classes of New York stock exchange common stocks. Financial Analysts Journal 28:46–54

Sharpe WF, Alexander G, Bailey J (1995) Investments. 5th edn, Prentice-Hall, New York

Sharpe WF, Alexander G, Bailey J (1999) Investments. 6th edn, Prentice-Hall, New York

Shaw E (1973) Financial deepening in economic development. Oxford University Press, New York

Shiller R (1989) Market volatility, MIT Press, Massachusetts

Shiller R (1984) Stock prices and social dynamics. Brooking Papers on Economic Activity 2:457–498

Siamwalla A, Vajragupta Y, Vichyanond P (1999) Foreign capital flows to Thailand: determinants and impact. Thailand Development Research Institute, Bangkok

Statman M (1988) Investor psychology and market inefficiencies. Equity Market and Valuation Methods, The Institute of Chartered Financial Analysts, California

Stiglitz JE (1993) The role of the state in financial markets. In Proceedings of the World Bank Annual Conference on Development Economics, The World Bank, Washington DC

Stock Exchange of Thailand (2002a) Listed company info 1975–2001

Stock Exchange of Thailand (2002b) http://www.set.or.th

Sukhamongkhon S (1994) A test of microeconomic factors on the stock exchange of Thailand using the APT model. Dissertation, University of Birmingham, Birmingham

Takagi S (2002) Fostering capital markets in a bank-based financial system: a review of major conceptual issues. Asian Development Review 19:67–97

Tan A, Kapur B (1986) Pacific growth and financial interdependence. Allen and Urwin, Sydney

Temby C (1998) Technical analysis for trading index warrants. Wrightbooks, Victoria

Thomas S (1995) An empirical characterisation of the Bombay stock exchange. Center for Monitoring Indian Economy, University of Southern California, California

Tirle J (1982) On the possibility of speculation under rational expectation. Econometrica 50:1163–1181

Titman S, Wei K (1999) Understanding stock market volatility: the case of Korea and Taiwan. Pacific-Basin Finance Journal 7:41–66

Tongzon J (1998) The economies of South East Asia: the growth and development of ASEAN Economies. Edward Elgar, Massachusetts

Warr P (1996) Thailand's macroeconomic miracle: stable adjustment and sustained growth. Oxford University Press, Kuala Lumpur

Watanapalachaikul S, Islam S (2004) Are emerging stock markets excessively volatile? A study of the Thai stock market. Mimeo, Center for Strategic Studies, Victoria University, Melbourne

Watanapalachaikul S, Islam S (2004) Speculative bubbles in the Thai stock market: econometric tests and implications. Mimeo, Center for Strategic Studies, Victoria University, Melbourne

Watanapalachaikul S, Islam S (2004) The behaviour of an emerging financial market: a time series financial econometric analysis and implications. Mimeo, Center for Strategic Studies, Victoria University, Melbourne

Watsham TJ, Parramore K (1997) Quantitative methods in finance. Thomson Learning, London

West KD (1987) A specification test for speculative bubbles. Quarterly Journal of Economics 102:553–580

Williamson J (1972) Measuring mutual fund performance. Financial Analysts Journal, November/December

Williamson J, Mahar M (1998) A survey of financial liberalization. Essays in International Finance, no 211, Princeton University, New Jersey

Winter PR (1960) Forecasting sales by exponentially weighted moving averages. Management Science 6:324–342

Wong KA, Kwong KS (1984) The behaviour of Hong Kong stock prices. Applied Economics 16:905–917

Wongbangpo P, Sharma S (2002) Stock market and macroeconomic fundamental dynamic interactions: ASEAN-5 countries. Journal of Asia Economics 13:27–51

Working H (1934) A random-difference series for use in the analysis of time series. Journal of the American Statistical Association 29:11–24

World Bank (1996) The World Bank Economic Review 10

Worthington A, Higgs H (2001) A multivariate GARCH analysis of equity returns and volatility in Asian equity markets. Discussion papers in economics, Finance, International Competitiveness, University of Queensland, Brisbane

Wu G, Xiao Z (2002) Are there speculative bubbles in stock markets? evidence from an alternative approach. Working Paper, University of Michigan Business School, Michigan

Wu Y (1997) Rational bubbles in the stock market: accounting for the US stock price volatility. Economic Inquiry 35:309–319

Yalawar YB (1988) Bombay stock exchange: rates of return and efficiency. Indian Economic Journal 35:68–121

Yu J (2002) Forecasting volatility in the New Zealand stock market. Applied Financial Economics 12:193–202

Yu J, Bluhm HW (2001) Forecasting volatility: evidence from the German stock market. Working Paper, Department of Economics, University of Auckland, Auckland

Index

About the Authors

Dr. Sardar M. N. Islam is a director, Sustainable Growth Program, Victoria University, Australia. He is also associated with the Financial Modelling Program and the Law and Economics Program there. He has published 11 books and monographs and more than 150 technical papers on Corporate Governance, Mathematical Finance, E-Commerce and Economics.

Dr. Sethapong Watanapalachaikul is a research officer at Victoria University, Australia. He has published several articles in empirical finance in the emerging financial markets.

Printing and Binding: Strauss GmbH, Mörlenbach